95 Theses on
Humanism

95 Theses on
Humanism
Christianity and Enlightenment, Secularism and Freethinking

Ignace Demaerel

Translated by Esther Hoop

RESOURCE *Publications* · Eugene, Oregon

95 THESES ON HUMANISM
Christianity and Enlightenment, Secularism and Freethinking

Copyright © 2018 Ignace Demaerel. All rights reserved. Except for brief quotations in critical publications or reviews, no part of this book may be reproduced in any manner without prior written permission from the publisher. Write: Permissions, Wipf and Stock Publishers, 199 W. 8th Ave., Suite 3, Eugene, OR 97401.

Resource Publications
An Imprint of Wipf and Stock Publishers
199 W. 8th Ave., Suite 3
Eugene, OR 97401

www.wipfandstock.com

PAPERBACK ISBN: 978-1-5326-5536-4
HARDCOVER ISBN: 978-1-5326-5537-1
EBOOK ISBN: 978-1-5326-5538-8

Manufactured in the U.S.A.   07/12/18

Original edition: '95 stellingen over het humanisme—Christendom en Verlichting, secularisme en vrijzinnigheid', 2017, published by Boekscout, Soest (The Netherlands), 232 p. (ISBN 978 940 2239157)

Translated by Esther Hoop

Cover picture by Sem Brys

Contents

Acknowledgements | ix

Preface | xi

Introductory remarks | xv

1. Humanism: A Bit of History | 1
   1.1 What is 'humanism'? | 1
   1.2 Humanism in the 14th and 16th century. | 3
   1.3 The 'Prince of the Humanists': Erasmus | 4
   1.4 The 'Enlightenment' | 7
   1.5 The search for a 'reasonable religion' | 12
   1.6 The French Revolution | 13
   1.7 How 'Christian' were the Middle Ages actually? | 15
   1.8 Abuses in the Church at that time | 18
   1.9 How 'dark' actually were the Middle Ages? | 20
   1.10 How 'light' was the Enlightenment? | 24

2. The Humanistic Vision | 29
   2.1 'Modern' Humanism | 29
   2.2 Humanism as ideology. | 32
   2.3 'Believing in man' | 35
     2.3.1 What does 'I believe in man' mean? | 35
     2.3.2 Man as 'measure of all things' | 38
     2.3.3 Man: champion of unreliability | 41
   2.4 The humanistic and Christian image of man | 44
     2.4.1 The 'value' of man | 44
     2.4.2 Images of God | 45

2.4.3 Afterlife or here-and-now | 46
2.4.4 The view on good and evil | 48
2.4.5 Man: naked monkey or 'god'? | 50
2.5 Materialism versus idealism | 51
   2.5.1 What is the 'spirit' and spiritual poverty? | 52
   2.5.2 Philosophical materialism and 'flat' materialism | 53
   2.5.3 The spiritual world: castle in the air or 'the' reality? | 55
2.6 Science, philosophy, and reason | 57
   2.6.1 Science versus religion: real or false contradiction? | 57
   2.6.2 Scientism: must science save the world? | 60
   2.6.3 Miracles vs laws of nature | 61
   2.6.4 Should philosophy save the world? | 63
   2.6.5 Rational, rationalistic, reasonable or wise? | 65
   2.6.6 A higher rationality | 67
   2.6.7 What is 'believing' then? | 69
2.7 The main principles of humanism | 72
   2.7.1 Humanism as a framework for meaning: life questions, goals, and transcendence | 72
   2.7.2 Separation between Church and State | 74
   2.7.3 Critical sense and rationality | 76
   2.7.4 Active pluralism | 77
   2.7.5 Free research | 80
2.8 The (moral) values of humanism | 81
   2.8.1 Autonomy and self-determination | 82
   2.8.2 Self-realization | 85
   2.8.3 Freedom | 87
   2.8.4 Tolerance | 89
   2.8.5 Openness and broad-mindedness | 92
   2.8.6 Human dignity | 93
   2.8.7 Brotherhood / solidarity | 95
   2.8.8 Conclusion: humanism and morality? | 96
     2.8.8.1 The 'humanistic' values? | 96
     2.8.8.2 Do absolute moral standards exist? | 97
     2.8.8.3 Humane or humanistic? | 99
2.9 Atheism | 100
   2.9.1 Religion: abuse, violence, and wars | 100
   2.9.2 Atheism, science, and (un)belief | 102
2.10 Secularity and neutrality | 104

Contents

    2.10.1 Secularization and secularism | 104
    2.10.2 Neutrality: politically, morally, and ideologically? | 107

3 Humanism in Practice | 110
  3.1 The battle for worldviews | 111
    3.1.1 Organized freethinking | 111
    3.1.2 Freemasonry and free thinking | 114
    3.1.3 The war for power and perception | 117
    3.1.4 Excesses of humanism | 122
  3.2 The 'fruit' of humanism | 124
    3.2.1 Medical ethics | 124
    3.2.2 Marriage, family, and relationships | 125
    3.2.3 Sexuality, pornography, prostitution | 127
    3.2.4 Postmodernism, relativism, and nihilism | 129
    3.2.5 Spiritual emptiness and new idols | 130
  3.3 Christian humanism and humanist Christianity | 133
    3.3.1 A reasonable, modern, adjusted belief? | 133
    3.3.2 Academic theology | 134
    3.3.3 Humanism in the churches | 136
    3.3.4 A clash of god images! | 141
    3.3.5 Water or wine? | 143

4 Conclusion: humanism vs. Christianity | 146
  4.1 Historically: history falsification | 146
  4.2 Theoretically: inconsistent | 148
  4.3 Spiritually: meagerness | 150
  4.4 Morally: 'long live anarchy'! | 155
  4.5 Practically: derailment | 157
  4.6 Subconsciously: irrational allergies and fears | 159
  4.7 And the future? A dreadful vision | 162
  4.8 And nine more comparisons | 163
    4.8.1 The Titanic | 163
    4.8.2 The banking crisis | 164
    4.8.3 The sorcerer's apprentice | 165
    4.8.4 The torch opposite the sun | 165
    4.8.5 The sun and planets | 167
    4.8.6 Conductor and orchestra | 168
    4.8.7 Diagnosis and medicine | 169
    4.8.8 Genetically modified food | 169

Contents

4.8.9 The sustainability of the planet | 170
4.9 Finally: anthropocentrism or theocentrism? | 172

Previous publications by Ignace Demaerel | *177*

Bibliography | *179*

Index | *181*

Acknowledgements

It is with a thankful heart that I see this English translation of my book being published. This is the fruit of almost twenty years of thinking and observing, analyzing and getting new insights, picking up interesting thoughts or quotes from the media (magazines, books . . .) or even just from random conversations. So, a lot of people contributed to this book, many of them probably not even aware of it. I thank all of these friends or coworkers for sharing their thoughts with me; their wise insights or one-liners are somewhere in these pages.

I especially thank Esther Hoop for the translation; she has been a great encouragement to me with her willingness and enthusiasm to bring this message to the broader world. And also a big thanks to Renée Bennett, Brigid Alty, and Richard Atkinson for proofreading the manuscript; the many hours of faithful work are greatly appreciated. Very special thanks goes to my wife Miet, who supported me all the time, allowing me to withdraw over several years for many hours and days to focus on this project, which burned so strongly in my heart. I know she also has sacrificed much, already by standing at my side for thirty-two years. I owe her more than I can express.

Preface

At regular intervals, our western world is thoroughly shaken up by crises: political crisis, economic crisis, banking crisis, crisis of confidence . . . But underlying these, at a deeper level and therefore often unnoticed, our culture has been in an existential and foundational crisis for centuries. The European continent has been considered 'thoroughly Christian' for about fifteen hundred years. Since the French Revolution, the Church has been driven out of its leadership role as a moral and spiritual authority. In the last century, and especially the last decades, religion and the Church have lost social influence at an incredibly high pace—the well-known process of secularization. Nowadays, people often talk about the 'post-Christian' era. But if Christianity is 'passé', what has replaced it? Some say, jokingly, that humanism has become the new 'state religion'. Is this correct, and if so, what does this mean?

By all means, since this crisis, a spiritual war rages over who and what will take the empty 'moral throne'. As with any revolution, we see that once the old king has been expelled, the 'opposition' falls apart in countless splinter groups. Some say, "No, we deliberately leave the seat empty." But it is not that simple, because with each power vacuum there are several candidates ready to grab the throne. More recently other players want to also participate in the game. Due to migration, Muslims enter Europe and some—although small groups—are already dreaming aloud of sharia in Europe. Whether we want it or not, whether we like it or not, this invisible war is taking place around us.

But then what is this humanism? Is it a worthier, better belief system than Christianity? What are actually humanist beliefs? What does it mean exactly when someone says, 'I believe in man'? As one starts to ask more questions, it does not seem that easy to explain, and a hundred people may

Preface

give a hundred different answers. Is this new mindset as consistent, rational and humane as it represents itself? If it claims to be 'critical', then it should also stand critical examination?

Christianity itself has also changed significantly since the Enlightenment and the rise of humanism. Modernity has invaded it, and this brings strong opponents and proponents. Some sigh with relief, "Ah, finally, the Church has become modern and has adapted to all scientific insights." The other camp sighs bitterly, "The Church has renounced her core message, betrayed her Master again and has added so much water to the wine that it has become completely tasteless." Emotions between 'liberals' and 'conservatives', 'the orthodox' and 'the modern' can escalate intensely. This we see in numerous concrete debates. The question is whether this modern Christianity is 'humanist Christianity' or rather 'Christian humanism'.

> "The kind of thinking that will solve the world's problems will be of a different order to the kind of thinking that created them in the first place."
> —Albert Einstein

In the midst of these animated discussions between belief systems, the question arises again and again: when people reject the message of Christianity or of the Bible, did they ever really understand it to start with? What exactly is it that people reject? God, the Church, certain church leaders, an institution (or its dominant character), certain practices, certain dogma's . . .? It is generally known that people, who reject God, reject a certain image of God. But how do they get this image of God? Of course, they get it from certain believers who proclaim or demonstrate it, but did these Christians themselves understand it correctly? Part of this book, therefore, seeks to clean up this image of the Christian faith, to straighten it, and to sharpen the focus. A rediscovery of Jesus' message from the source texts is always more surprising than one would think!

On the 31st of October 1517, Martin Luther nailed his famous '95 Theses against Indulgences'[1] to the door of the Church in Wittenberg. Martin Luther's '95 Theses' were well-thought-out and substantiated arguments against this practice, which in his time had got completely out of hand. Luther had no idea at that time that this piece of paper would unleash a total revolution and rewrite the spiritual map of Europe thoroughly and forever.

---

1. Indulgences were/are a practice of the Roman Catholic Church whereby people could buy forgiveness of sins for money, or in any case penalty reduction in purgatory. An indulgence was the paper certificate for this.

Preface

These theses originated with him from an honest indignation—say, a holy anger—against blatantly wrong practices, which conflicted with the Bible as well as with plain common sense. He was a whistle-blower avant-la-lettre, and it could be called a miracle he did not have to pay for this with his life.

These '95 Theses on Humanism' are born out of the same kind of indignation as Luther's, from observing how in our time, dozens of ideas and practices are propagated and become widely accepted without serious examination. They are steadily repeated and reinforced in the media and in popular speech, as if everyone agrees on them, but can they stand a more thorough investigation? Is there no-one who can see that the modern spirit of this age has derailed into superficiality? That this has gone way too far and is in conflict with common sense and human dignity? Despite a measure of indignation about this, these propositions are not just emotional slogans, but well-founded on arguments which anyone is welcome to evaluate. And, as was the case with Luther, they are an invitation to a solid debate on this subject.

These 95 theses are about humanism, not about humanists. Among humanists there are many people of goodwill and sincerity. This book has no intention of attacking or hurting people. It focuses on the belief system, the approach to life itself and aims to critically analyze and hold up to the light the ideas and values behind it, according to its own principles.

Introductory remarks

Though no war has been fought in Europe for seventy years now, the 'war for souls' rages no less fiercely. A spiritual war should be fought with spiritual weapons; words are fought with words and ideas with ideas, not by force, weapons or oppression. Actually, whoever seizes earthly weapons is already losing. Unfortunately, as in most wars, a dirty war is also waged here with improper means (just as the Church used torture and stakes, (communist) atheism used mass executions and concentration camps). But even without physical weapons, this war can be 'dirty'. Words can kill and surely wound through scorn, mocking, caricatures, intimidation, generalizations, silencing the other, denying access to the media and so forth . . . An open debate in terms of content between Christianity and secular humanism was or is rarely conducted. Honest questions and empathy, an open attitude that wants to learn and listen respectfully to the others . . . we must admit that there are very few who can muster this. The most beautiful scenario would be if there were not even a fight, but that all parties would come together and seek the truth together. When all would say, "We all put our 'being right' in the middle. And in my heart, I determine that, if you convince me with better arguments, I will turn to your view." Even stronger, "convince me please when I see it wrong because I do not want to run the risk of continuing in error the rest of my life." Are not hunger for truth and lifelong learning invaluable qualities? The reality, however, usually shows a very different picture, often a trench war in which one automatically (!) stands up for

> "I have always been convinced, and still am, that if this God exists, then He is the only thing that matters—the rest on earth is of secondary importance, is actually of no importance, compared to that."
> —Prof. Etienne Vermeersch, Belgian moral philosopher and atheïst

Introductory Remarks

'their own' group. The question whether this 'own group' is more right than the other is totally irrelevant, pardon me, the question may not even be asked. We then defend 'our own' at any price and the truth has become subordinate to group interests.

This book has the intention of laying the cards on the table. That is, insofar at least as a person can know oneself. Those criticizing another must be prepared to apply the same sharp standards for themselves, and not use double standards. Condemning our 'enemy' for mistakes we make ourselves does not really help the world. It is intellectually incorrect to 'shoot down' people of another belief on the basis of a caricature and without a thorough investigation. There is a fundamental right to defense in both directions.

> "If you were to look into the heart of your enemy, what do you think you would find that is different from what is in your own heart?"

I want to be very honest and transparent in my expositions: many others are intellectually better placed than I am to write this book, with more knowledge of history or of the present social realities. I do not pretend to know everything, but I just want to give a few incentives in the right direction. I also do not pretend to be original. Almost all thoughts I have read somewhere else, picked up, noted and collected, and maybe connected them in a new way or supplemented them with my own observations. The ultimate goal is that this debate can be fairer and conducted with 'more light'; how can an 'enlightened person' be against this?

Humanists and freethinkers pride themselves on their open mindedness, so I trust that they—or some among them—will have the courage to read this book to the end. Surely, we can expect non-believing readers to make the mental effort to move themselves into the other point of view, just as the believer must do. This is just a matter of intellectual sincerity. Whoever never seriously considers the possibility 'What if I should be wrong'? can hardly call him or herself a sincerely searching and broad-minded person. I realize that many statements in this book will certainly not be easy for humanists to hear. It is challenging for anyone to listen to criticism, especially if it touches on the deepest of beliefs, but I hope that the willingness to apply self-criticism foils the natural tendency to self-defense.

I want to be open, kind and loving, but on the other hand I will not beat around the bush either. Far too often in such dialogues we see that people, reacting against an old hostility, now want to be 'so sweet' to each other. It is then easy to say, "In fact, we have more similarities than

Introductory Remarks

differences, it amounts to the same thing, we basically mean the same thing." This is obviously well-meaning and preferable over aggression and conflict, and yet it violates the facts. For fear of hurting one another, we denounce the truth and water down the wine of our convictions. Ultimately this also does not help anyone, and we do not even respect ourselves. Naming things openly, though risky (you just have to hope the other can handle it), is often much more liberating.

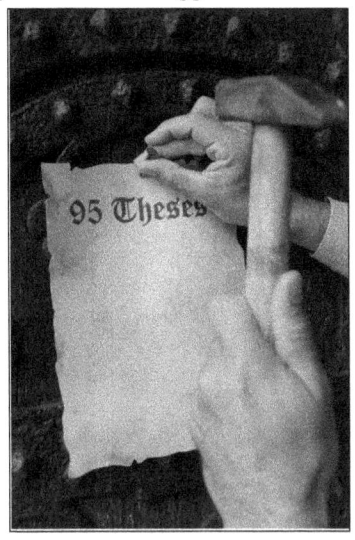

This book has been written from suffering this world; from earnest compassion with the dramatic situation of mankind. From deep grief over how people are destroying the planet, and over the countless unnecessary miseries people inflict on themselves and others... Then, soft or superficial love does not help anymore. A surgeon who does not cut deep enough allows the patient to die. I cannot keep myself busy with amusing and entertaining people while the Titanic is sinking. There are already enough cookbooks being written...

> "All I want to know are the thoughts of God; the rest are details."
> —Albert Einstein

What is personally irritating me is when in a debate (in the media) the truth is violated or (deliberately) distorted, when caricatures are created, improper arguments mixed together, or stereotypes unceasingly repeated without verifying them. In case personal emotions rise between the lines, this is the reason.

For when the truth is twisted, one cannot remain silent; we have to be outraged about this. We are going against a mindset here, a way of thinking, against a 'spirit' that is all around in this age, and so I cannot and will not soften my words. I experience this so strongly in my spirit and I do not want to make things sweeter or more acceptable—our society is already far too 'sugary'. I feel comforted by Jesus in this. He too was not always 'nice' and used unusually sharp words against the Pharisees—probably because otherwise they would not hit their mark. I do not want to apologize myself here for the sharpness of my words. If someone must undergo surgery, he also prefers the surgeon to use a sharp knife and does not ask him, 'Please,

Introductory remarks

do not hurt me'. He knows that this needs to happen to save his life. If this is so for our physical health, then does it not apply even more to our spiritual well-being when it comes to the great questions of life or the higher values?

Certain pieces of text will undoubtedly generalize when I talk about 'a humanist', and this may perhaps seem unfair to some. I genuinely try to weigh my words and be subtle, but generalizations are inevitable. There are also many types of humanists (in a strict and broader sense) and not every criticism applies in the same way to every type. May everyone please put on the shoe that fits.

I do not mince my words in this book, but I speak freely. I will not allow myself to be bound by what is regarded as politically or theologically correct in a certain period. The old prophets held to this too. A prophet looks at the same reality as other people, but he climbs to a higher lookout from which to view everything from above, with a higher standard. He cannot resign himself to the world 'as it is'; he refuses to get accustomed to 'what everyone does' and is easily annoyed by what others find 'normal'. He uses hard and sharp words which the people of this world do not understand and do not like. Thus, sometimes he makes himself very unpopular by rubbing the wrong way. But he knows he must do this because it burns in his heart like a fire. And if he does not bring it out, it destroys him.

In my line of argument, I want to accommodate the non-believing readers as much as possible, and so I use particularly philosophical, rational, 'horizontal' arguments. When I compare humanism with Christianity and use, for example, Bible quotes, I do not ask them to blindly believe these as 'revelation from above'. But I also ask them to not blindly reject them from an overly critical or suspicious attitude. The Bible also deserves to be approached with an open mind. When I quote Jesus here, I will merely consider him as a moral teacher, and as such, he also deserves to be fully listened to. When I make faith statements about faith in this book, I do not want to state them as dogma. I always explain them as best possible to enable the discovery of their 'alternative logic'. Finally, I want to ask every non-believing reader, when judging Christianity, to always distinguish between what the Church teaches and does, and what Jesus says and does. This can sometimes be a sky-wide difference, which I will elaborate in later chapters as well as the reasons why. We cannot emphasize enough that churches and Christians in history have shown a very weakened and skinny image of what Jesus meant, sometimes even the opposite.

Introductory remarks

I also want to make it very clear that it is not my aim to set out my own vision. I regard it as completely irrelevant to add yet another vision to the billions already on this globe. This only increases the confusion and the number of books, and the number of felled trees. My aim is to uncover the vision of Jesus, to unwrap it. His opinion puts weight on the scale—not mine. But explaining his perspective to contemporaries nowadays is a 'heathenish' work. You almost do not know where to begin in order to remove the countless prejudices, skewed images and misinterpretations around his person.

This book is not meant to be an academic work. This may be a weakness, but at the same time perhaps also a strength. It wants to be readable to an 'intelligent sixteen-year-old' who is not afraid of mental effort, and it also wants to stay close to everyday reality. For example, I do not apply a systematic source listing as is expected in a scientific work. One of the reasons for this is that for fifteen years now I have been collecting quotes and ideas from an endless number of sources: statements of TV programs or movies, quotes from emails or the internet, magazines and newspapers, or just from private conversations. Many are 'taken out of life', and do not come from academic literature which sometimes 'stands far from our bed' and can be more theoretically correct and nuanced, but is also drier and non-committal.

A large part of this book will also be devoted to explaining the Christian faith itself. As humanism directly derives from it and clearly opposes it, we need to investigate whether the criticisms are valid, and whether the Christian faith has been well understood. Therefore, the surgeon's knife must also be used to dissect what the core of Jesus' message is from the later additions, mixtures, and the dead weight. For when we put humanism and Christianity next to each other, we must be able to compare the core of one with the core of the other.

In this book, I absolutely do not have the pretense to speak on behalf of 'Christianity'. I realize well enough that there are many churches and streams, many angles and positions, and that many Christians may not agree with some of my analyses. I do not even claim that I am right, and they are wrong. But what I do try is to base myself on the words of Jesus themselves, not on what was made of it later (popular traditions, cultural interpretations, institutions . . .). There is no other type of Christianity than what Jesus preached. Even though his infinitely high standard cannot be fully realized by anyone, we should not change his norm itself.

Introductory Remarks

This book is quite polemical, not because this is my preference or my style, but the polemic was started by those attacking the Church. Christians already tend to not defend themselves but to turn the other cheek and be kind to the enemy . . . This gives the impression that Christians do not have an intellectual response. The debate in the media is already distorted because the 'alternatives' are given much more room. One seems to think as it were, "We already know more than enough about Christianity, so now others must be heard"—as if all that is new is, by definition, more interesting and better.

While writing this book, the number of pages grew out of proportion. Therefore, I decided to split my thought material into two books. In this book, I will discuss the 95 theses and the surrounding themes rather briefly ('staccato'). I plan a later book for a deeper and more complete elaboration, the philosophical backgrounds, the underlying concepts of man and God. Therefore, if certain statements seem premature or 'sloganesque', I can refer the reader, who wishes to know the full argument, to the sequel.

Since the original book was written in Dutch and in the context of Brussels, Belgium, many quotes and examples are taken from this culture and environment. This might be a handicap, and it would have been an option to 'translate' these parts to other nations and their specific spiritual context. But on the other hand, I'm sure many of these situations or developments are very similar in the western countries, and I trust the readers will be able to make this jump themselves.

> *"See, this only have I found: that God made man upright, but they have sought out many schemes."*
> —Ecclesiastes 7:29

1

Humanism

A Bit of History

1.1 What is 'humanism'?

This question at the beginning of this book is likely to be the most important of all. The flag of 'humanism' can cover, after all, very different meanings in daily language, resulting in many misunderstandings and confusion. This creates fog, smoke screens and blurred debates, whereby the same

1. For many people the word 'humanism' is synonymous with 'humane'. Humanism however has developed itself into a veritable ideology, which, just like the religions it contests, has become an institution, a system, a power structure and can be equally militant, imperialistic, and intolerant.

concept can sometimes be used to mean the opposite. 'Humane' and 'humanistic' have the same root but differ as much from each other as 'social' and 'socialist'. A person can be very social, and at the same time distance him or herself totally from the socialist ideology and party. Sometimes 'humanism' is used as a synonym for 'being humane' (hence a moral quality), but usually it refers to a real belief system or an ideology.

In this book, we want to very strictly 'think straight'. 'Humanism' comes from the Latin word *humanus* meaning 'human'. The ending 'ism' always indicates that this one concept is regarded as a central and dominant principle (think for instance of rationalism, voluntarism, materialism, socialism . . .). In this sense, humanism is a stream of thought or philosophy of life that makes 'man' the highest principle. Nowadays, the term 'humanism' is mostly used in the sense of a non-confessional view on life meaning that everything has its starting point in man and in reason, and thereby opposes any supernatural explanation or appeal to a god. It is true that others define 'humanism' more broadly, as a general concept of 'a people-oriented attitude to life'. For them, humanism can be both secular and Christian, and 'secular humanism' then indicates the non-confessional version. In this book, we deal more with 'secular humanism' for the sake of the etymological meaning (man as the highest principle). From this point of view, the expression 'Christian humanism' or 'humanist Christianity' is, in our opinion, not consistent (we explain this later in chapter 3.3). Therefore, concepts such as 'humanism', 'freethinking', 'secularism' or 'atheism' will sometimes be used interchangeably. This can appear confusing, and 'humanism' can thus seem to be a container concept. In practice, however, these four words also blend together and are not strictly separated; people do mix them up in daily language. By all means, 'man at the center of everything', this they certainly have in common.

2. 'Humane' and 'humanistic' have the same root but differ as much from each other as 'social' and 'socialist'. Every '-ism' is a disproportionate extrapolation of one principle (or a part thereof). To suggest that only socialists are social is an insult to all other people, and sometimes certain socialist individuals or regimes can exhibit highly antisocial behavior.

First of all, it is helpful to explain the origin of the concept of 'humanism' itself. In the 14th and 16th century, this meant something totally different from the secular version of today. Let history refresh our memory and bring some clarification. In the next chapter, we want (1) to place humanism in its proper historical context, (2) appreciate it for its good intentions and accomplishments, (3) critically investigate whether its criticisms of the Church[1] were correct and (4) critically research if what it replaces it with is a valid alternative, of the same value or better than what it attacks.

---

1. In this book, humanism usually stands opposite 'the Church'. It must be clarified that I do not mean with this the Church institution (in this case the Roman Catholic Church) but the whole of all Christian churches. In practice, of course and especially when we talk about the Middle Ages, the Catholic institution stands often in the foreground as the representative of Christendom, but I always mean 'Church' also in the broader sense.

1.2 Humanism in the 14th and 16th century.

The oldest origin of humanism must be sought in Italy in the 1300's. This new movement was then a purely Italian phenomenon. A number of intellectuals and artists (such as Dante, Boccaccio, Petrarca) looked with sadness at the political and cultural decline of Italy. At the same time, they exalted the illustrious past of Rome, ancient antiquity. They sought to restore pure literary Latin and introduced *studia humanitatis*, which means the study of *litterae humaniores*, comprising mainly subjects such as grammar, rhetoric, poetry, and moral philosophy. The word *humanitas*[2] referred to the pursuit of the fine arts (especially the ancient classics), in contrast to the sacred arts, and thus was not in the least directed against God. This trend was primarily a cultural phenomenon and did not have any ideological intentions! It was esthetically inspired, and its primary interest was form, not content. In fact, the Italian humanists were pronounced Christians (also Bruni, Ficino, Pico della Mirandola). Petrarca for example began to direct himself much more toward God by the end of his life by pulling back in solitude toward prayer because he discovered that worldly literature could not give him the happiness he was looking for. From 1450 this movement also began to permeate the rest of Europe. People were tired of the strict scholastic culture with its abstract thought systems, and were attracted to the beauty of classical antiquity, which paid more attention to the beauty of men and the earth.

Although the beginning of humanism as a stream of thought is situated in the 16th century, some believe we find traces hereof with the ancient Greek sophists (a philosophy around the 5th century BC). Protagoras (± 490–420 BC) made the following statement gladly quoted by humanists, "Man is the measure of all things, of the things that are what they are, and of the things that are not what they are not." But we need to make two

---

2. The word *humanitas* was derived by the Renaissance humanists from the Roman philosopher Cicero, who identified with it the ideal of the educated, developed, morally high-ranking man who mastered the art of living, in short, someone who had achieved 'true humanity'. Again, we do not find any ideological (anti-religious) meaning in this word.

side notes here. First, what Protagoras meant exactly is actually not clear, but he probably did not mean that man should be the center of the universe, but rather that a statement is only true or not true in respect to the person who says it, because he can only view it from his own perspective. He said this in the context of epistemology which emphasized the inevitable subjectivity of our judgments. Secondly, this statement was not at all targeted against religion or godliness; the ancient Greek culture was also religious to the core. This statement did not give rise to the emergence of a 'humanist' or atheist stream, and that was also not at all the intention.

Finally, 16th century humanism originated after the Middle Ages and had a completely different focus. It was mainly a reaction against the inhumane things that were done in the name of God: the inquisition with its bloody persecution of heretics, dissidents, witches, the intolerance, fanatical religious wars, and ruthless stakes. This response was very understandable and was also needed. It was even very Christian and inspired by the idea that a loving God would never want such things! The first humanists were invariably deeply religious people who reacted against the excesses of the Church institution and wanted to return to the original simplicity of the gospel. No one turned away from God, from the Bible, not even from the Church. The protest was directed against abuses, against the repression and dominance of the Church institution, and the lack of freedom in the area of art and science. In short, 'humanism' did not have the meaning in that time that it now tends to have (a secular, atheistic, sometimes anti-church view of life)[3].

1.3 The 'Prince of the Humanists': Erasmus

Desiderius Erasmus (1469–1536) was born in Rotterdam and became a priest in 1492. In his youth, he went to a school of the 'Brothers of the communal life', a kind of revival movement in the Netherlands founded by Geert Grote. This 'Modern Devotion' originated in the 14th century in reaction to

---

3. Humanists with a more thorough knowledge of history have no problem admitting that renaissance humanism had a completely different character than the present secular one. An example of this is Peter Derkx, *Humanisme, zinvol leven en nooit meer ouder worden* ('Humanism, a Meaningful Life, and Never Again Growing Old'). Peter Derkx is professor of humanism at the University of Humanistics in Utrecht (The Netherlands) and presents a very correct and respectful rendition of the mutual history of Christianity and humanism. But too often, the debate is not as serene on an academic level and too often things are said that are historically incorrect.

the degeneration of church life and aspired to a practical devotion and spirituality. Later, Erasmus studied and worked in many places throughout Europe (The Netherlands, England, Belgium, Switzerland, Italy, Germany . . .). He thus came in contact with all kinds of renewal movements which greatly expanded his view. He was a broad-minded and open man who could rise above the many boxes of church life at that time.

In his book 'Praise of Folly' (1511), with his sharp pen, he already derided the abuses and derailments of the Church in his time: the debauchery and greed of the high clergy, the abuse of power by the Church, the obstinate hunt for heretics, the dark jargon of philosophers and scholastic theologians, their bizarre subtleties and hair splitting, superstition among the people, the veneration of the saints, confession, fasting . . . His first reaction was against all the inhumanities committed in God's name: how can the inquisition, the religious wars, the burning of heretics and witches be consistent with a God who is love? The Church was in a real crisis in his time, and Erasmus was terribly shocked by a figure like Pope Julius II who came to power by large-scale bribes and had children with various mistresses, and who was more concerned with excessive parties,  war campaigns against Venice and grand buildings for which he needed mountains of money.

Another aspect that Erasmus inherited from the Renaissance and applied extensively was the saying *ad fontes*, 'back to the source'. Because he had studied Greek (which was quite new at the time) he could go back to the source of the Church and Christianity, namely the Bible. Therefore, in 1516 he made a scientific edition of the New Testament from the basic language and from the most reliable manuscripts. In its preface, he describes Christianity as a wide river that was polluted by all kinds of tributaries, but if we want to know what the pure water looked like, we need to go back to the source: the words of Jesus and his apostles. Erasmus founded a school in Leuven where students, in addition to Latin, had to learn Greek and Hebrew so they could study the Bible in its original text. This also was innovative at that time and caused clashes with other professors who assumed the Catholic dogma that Latin was the holy language.

Erasmus undoubtedly launched the idea of tolerance. He disliked theological disputes and even more so, bloody quarrels because of religion. Erasmus is sometimes called a 'biblical humanist' because he wanted to reconcile the biblical message with a humane (men-loving) attitude. He pleaded for a tolerant and evangelical Christianity inspired by the Sermon on the Mount. Erasmus was undoubtedly a great soul, a cosmopolitan, someone who transcended his time in many ways, and in that sense, he represented many beautiful values of modern Europe. For this reason, the 'Erasmus' program of exchange between European universities was rightly named after him.

When, however, modern humanism refers to Erasmus as its founder, we must put this very much into perspective and place it in the right context, otherwise we run the risk of distorting history. With a retroactive effect, it is too easy to put all kinds of ideas into his mouth that he actually never had. Firstly, Erasmus never used the word 'humanism', not for himself nor for others (this word only emerged in the 19th century)! Secondly, Erasmus was a faithful Catholic throughout his life, moreover a priest. In no way can he be regarded as a forerunner of secular, anti-religious humanism. When some of the Italian humanists began to rave about the classics, and even began to choose this paganism, Erasmus strongly and fundamentally disapproved. He even satirized and ridiculed it as a foolish imitation that showed a complete lack of historical understanding. He also wrote in 1525, for example, that in his young years he had a strong aversion to sacred literature and preferred to read classical poetry ('inventions of poets'), 'but now there is nothing better than studying the Scriptures'.

Finally, Erasmus was also a child of his time and understood the term 'tolerance' very differently than we do today. He did not address freedom for the individual but freedom in science and ideas. We do not find the modern concept of tolerance (freedom for the individual) with Erasmus, or the idea of 'freedom of religion' or respect for all religious convictions. Erasmus has, for example, made very fierce anti-Jewish statements and, at one point, called the Jewish religion the 'worst plague and bitterest enemy of the teachings of Jesus Christ'. We must not overestimate his broad-mindedness either, or place him on a pedestal where he does not belong. Present-day humanism would much like to pull Erasmus into

> *"A Carpenter made humanity, and only by this Carpenter can humanity be restored."*
> *—Erasmus*

its camp but ignores (consciously?) the deeply-Christian fundamental convictions that propelled him.

1.4 The 'Enlightenment'

The term 'Enlightenment' is a well-known and established concept in our western culture today and marks a definitive transition (± 1690–1800) from one historical era to another. The word itself indicates a reaction against the 'dark' Middle Ages, but what is it exactly about, and is this term truly correct? Were the Middle Ages really as dark as alleged today, and is the Enlightenment as 'luminous' as claimed?

During the previous centuries, the Church had a quasi-monopoly over all of Europe. The idea of theocracy was generally accepted: God ruled over all, and the Pope was his stand-in on earth. Therefore, the Church had the last word in all areas of life, not only in religion but also in philosophy, culture, and science. Everything had to be theocentric and subject to ecclesiastical authority. The Church was the undisputed moral authority; though there was regular criticism of her, it was about the misuses and abuses, not regarding her position or mandate. We should not have a skewed understanding of this as if everyone in those centuries slavishly did everything the Church proclaimed. In practice, the people, even the kings and emperors, ignored much of what the pope said, and much happened that could not see the light and that was outright contradictory to the Christian faith. The practice was often very poor, but the theory and the institution in itself were hardly questioned by anyone[4].

3. Humanism as a movement appeals to Erasmus, but if Erasmus could see what happens today in institutions named after him, he would turn in his grave. In the 16th century, humanism was a plea for a more humane Christianity; today it is an anti-Christian, anti-religious ideology. Claiming that Erasmus is the father of (modern) humanism is historical falsification.

---

4. Even the great reformers (Luther, Calvin, and Zwingli) and all their forerunners (Wycliffe, Waldo, Hus, Savonarola, Erasmus) expressed very sharp criticism of the Church, and this from the Bible, in order to prove that the Church made mistakes because she was 'not Christian enough'.

In the Renaissance, a first call for more freedom arose. Free-spirited citizens and thinkers experienced the interference of the Church as curtailing, sometimes narrow minded and unhealthy. Artists asked the question, "Should all art per se be religious? Is it a sin to depict the beauty of man or of nature? Does not the 'pagan' art of ancient antiquity have something beautiful to offer?" Scientists wondered, "Do we not have much to learn from the (pagan) Greek scientists and philosophers like Aristotle?" And philosophers felt the need to freely use reason—also God's gift, or not?—and discover what that would lead to. There was much admiration for the classics, their development, science, and knowledge, their free-spirited nature; it seemed like a culture with more freedom. And it was a real discovery that there were more cultures possible, not just the Christian one!

However, in the beginning the Church resisted strongly. Freedom of thought was too dangerous and would undoubtedly get out of hand because man is naturally a sinful being. Reason had to remain subject to revelation, because faith was regarded as a superior way of knowledge, and reason was limited and fallible. Science could not teach anything that went against revelation, and the earth had to stay in the center of the universe, 'because the Bible taught it so'. A critical attitude toward the Bible or the Church was unacceptable because faith cannot be understood by reason; there are mysteries that transcend our understanding. The latter sometimes led to obscurantism: 'The darker the better', or 'If it is incomprehensible, it must come from God' (according to the motto *credo quia absurdum* ('I believe because it is absurd').

At the same time, some things that the Church taught or did were manifestly incorrect; everyone with common sense could see that. In reality the Church could hardly keep up her claim of infallible guide. There was an ongoing huge tension with those who demanded the right to 'free thinking'; Copernicus (1473–1543), Vesalius (1514–1564), Galileo (1564–1642), and many others experienced this personally. Although the Council of Trent officially stated in 1563 that the Bible was infallible only in matters of faith and morality and not in the area of science, Galileo continued to invariably have problems with the Church.

Despite all this ecclesiastical resistance, the movement of freedom could not be stopped. On the contrary, several centuries later, the Renaissance led to the Enlightenment. The sciences had developed tremendously since the 16th century and proved their worth: they had brought real changes and progress. The invention of the compass opened unprecedented possibilities for sea transport which led to the discovery of new countries and continents. The invention of gunpowder brought tremendous military predominance, which led to many conquests. The printing of books led to the massive distribution of books, ideas, and knowledge. Medicine made great leaps forward and gradually overcame diseases and epidemics. Physics discovered many natural laws and the existence of electricity . . . Because of these discoveries, boundaries were definitively shifted, and new horizons opened. Socially too, there were many changes: welfare increased, the beginning of capitalism emerged, the bourgeoisie emancipated itself from the nobility, cities became more independent and the culture came into the hands of laymen. The Church lost its grip on society and criticism could be expressed more and more openly.

The main feature of Enlightenment is therefore an optimistic rationalism. It had a very high confidence in the power of the intellect, combined with a belief in unrestricted progress, whereby man would solve all its problems one by one. It was believed that the rapid development of mathematics and physics (Newton) would lead to unlimited growth, also for other sciences and other areas of life, which would be built on that sure foundation. There had to be room for unconditional freedom of thought; philosophy and science fought for their independence and autonomy, thus pitting themselves against tradition and authority. No Church or Revelation (the Bible) could stand in the way of free research, but nor could former 'authoritative' philosophers or scientists such as Aristotle. The power of reason was deemed more reliable than the traditional authority, which had proved to commit great blunders in many areas (think of geocentrism, the *horror vacui*-hypothesis etc.). Only reason and experience (the empirical, hard facts) were counted as sources of reliable knowledge. When there was an epidemic, for example, instead of turning the eyes toward God in supplication, one had to put one's shoulder to the wheel and develop medicines.

> 4. The Age of Enlightenment was characterized by optimistic rationalism: a great confidence in the power of the mind, combined with a belief in unlimited progress, whereby mankind would solve all his problems, one by one, without God's help. Although we are now 300 years on and humanity's problems are only increasing, humanists naively continue to profess this 'dogma'.

Disease was no longer a punishment from above, but the result of physical contamination. Thunder and lightning were no longer the result of the wrath of God, but an explainable electrical natural phenomenon. The old motto, 'You must believe because we say so' seemed to work less and less. By all means, the Enlightenment thinkers experienced their revolution as a great liberation, as the "Ausgang des Menschen aus seiner selbtverschuldeten Unmundigkeit" (the well-known description of Immanuel Kant in 1784: "the Exodus (Outcome) of Man from his self-indebted Immaturity")!

However, how should we evaluate all this? This call for freedom is very understandable; we are all children of our times, right? But there is always a danger that we judge the past with the standards of centuries later, which is not right. Was this urge for emancipation right or not? Is it a sin to give man, next to God, also some attention? Is it sinful to make a painting of a beautiful man or woman? Must it all per se be about the Church and the Bible? Is God so jealous that He wants all the attention for Himself and does not grant man anything? Does glorifying God automatically mean that one should despise humanity? Of course not! These questions and false contradictions arise from a narrow and unbalanced image of God.

---
5. Humanism has voiced much justified criticism of the Church, and this was necessary and liberating for the Church itself. But not all criticism was and is legitimate; it is historically unfair to judge the Middle Ages with the standards of centuries later. And it is far too easy to simply blame the Church for all what went wrong in the Middle Ages.

The Church certainly worked stiflingly on the cultural, philosophical, and scientific life. She interfered with many things that were not her domain, paternalizing and condemning. Many church leaders were perhaps also afraid of new ideas. Did they feel threatened that these new scientists and thinkers would be smarter than them; did they fear losing control? There must have certainly been narrow-mindedness and rigidity, and especially fear of losing power. But blaming the Church for everything that went wrong in the Middle Ages is also too simple. In all cultures, the traditional authority and ruling class is conservative; it wants to protect the existing order. This is 'of man', not 'typically Christian' even though it is

often stifling, oppressive, and unjust. In retrospect, it is all too easy to say, 'We would not have reacted like that'. This is also naive and testifies to little self-knowledge. Realism also compels us to say that not every change is an improvement, and that every progress also brings necessary loss.

We must therefore make the same comment as in the previous chapters: when modern humanism appeals to the Enlightenment as its cradle, it distorts the historical facts and makes the thinkers of that time ventriloquize. For apart from one exception, none of these great enlightened thinkers or philosophers were atheists! Isaac Newton, 'The' scientist of the Enlightenment, was a deeply believing man, and his discoveries about the laws of nature and gravity in the universe did not lead him to less faith in God, rather to more awe for the Creator[5]. From him also comes the famous statement, "The more we know, the more we discover we do not know much yet." Also, the great enlightenment philosopher, Immanuel Kant, was a believer in every fiber of his soul. For him, faith in God was evident, even a philosophical necessity (a 'postulate of practical reason').

Nevertheless, 14th and 16th century humanism and the Enlightenment began a movement that, centuries later, led to humanism in its current (secular) sense of the word. For the first time (in art and culture) man, and not God, was at the center Although, no . . . this is put far too strong and is not historically correct: 'at the center' is not the right expression! It was a reaction to the fact that art could only be about God and that the Church dominated and monopolized everything. Man and the earth were also entitled a place beside God and heaven, or not?

> 6. Humanism in the 14th to 16th century was a plea for permission to give attention not only to God (theocentrism) but also to man, for example in art and science. Centuries later, this shift of focus from God to man continued to 'slide downwards', and humanism in its current form has an exclusive focus on mankind to the exclusion of God (anthropocentrism).

Certainly, the tracks were changed; the focus definitely shifted and had begun to 'drop down' from heaven to earth; could this shift still be stopped? The door was set ajar, but how far would the door be pushed open? As often is the case in history, the pendulum swung all the way to the other side. The focus was no longer on 'God alone' but on 'God and man'. How long would it take for it to be on 'man and God' and finally on 'man alone'?

---

5. Newton still believed that 'in case of emergency' angels had to correct the course of the planets to avoid collisions.

1.5 The search for a 'reasonable religion'

One product of the Enlightenment was the rejection of the dominance of the Church over reason. In reality, this went in the opposite direction: reason was gradually placed above religion. It must be said that much irrationality had invaded medieval religion and pagan practices had mixed in with the Christian ones: a big 'clean up' was indeed much needed. However, some enlightenment thinkers thought that reason was in the best position from which to create a 'pure religion': a reasonable, universal, clear religion with a small core of logical, insightful dogmas (the belief in a Supreme Being, the necessity of virtue, the immortality of the soul, and an afterlife with reward or punishment). If everyone would believe in this new 'enlightened' religion, all religious wars and conflicts would end resulting in universal world peace! 'Reason' now became the 'neutral' referee between and above religions.

Some thinkers (such as Immanuel Kant) found that, in this context, Christianity was the most reasonable religion of all. But they often shifted to a rationalistic, heavily toned-down version of Christianity whereby all 'irrational elements' from the Bible or church doctrine had to be filtered out. This evolved into deism (Christian Wolff), the vision that God (Latin: 'Deus') created the world, but otherwise leaves her to her own devices like a wound-up alarm clock. God does not interfere in it actively because the laws of nature rule everything. And one more step: God may not even break His own laws, otherwise He would be inconsistent. Because He can no longer intervene in the laws of nature, there is no place for miracles, the supernatural, and prayer (because then you would ask God to change the course of the world). The Christian faith thus becomes ever 'thinner' until there is only a kind of moral teaching left.

From the same requirement of 'being reasonable', others drew the opposite conclusion. Freethinking, secular humanism, freemasonry, and atheism are, in later stages, also the product of this process. The oldest forms of freethinking, in England at the end of the 17th century (John Toland, Anthony Collins, Matthew Tindal), were also far from atheist. They remained Christian, but positioned themselves 'freer' in the faith, e.g. more rationalistic and deistic. God's existence remained evident throughout this period. Slowly, here and there a lonely individual appeared who directed the principle of rationality against religion as such and threw it out completely.

This quest for a 'reasonable religion' did not amount to anything but took all possible directions. Reason has, after all, not a criterion for judging a religion as such (see chapter 2.6).

1.6 The French Revolution

The ideas of the French Revolution are closely linked to those of the Enlightenment. You can even say that here, many of the ideas of Enlightenment were transformed into political currency for the first time. It is important to note that the French Revolution (July 14th, 1789) was not in the first instance directed against the Church or religion, but against the French absolutist king Louis XVI, who behaved like a god, and against his untouchable privileges. However, the power of the royal house was so closely connected with that of the nobility and the Church, that anti-clericalism (the hatred of the 'clergy' as the ecclesiastical priestly class) went hand in hand with this. France was already familiar with fierce criticism of the Church by big names such as Diderot and Voltaire. The arrows of the revolution thus aimed against the monarchy and aristocracy, but in its wake also against the Church, her power and her possessions. The whole institution of the Church was regarded as an accomplice, as part of the plot to keep the multitudes poor and ignorant.

The battle against the Church was fierce at times. Under the regime of terror of Robespierre and Danton, Christianity was even abolished for a while (1792), the so-called 'de-Christianization'. To erase all traces, the Christian calendar was replaced by a revolutionary calendar (22-9-1792), and Christian feasts by republican, secular parties. To replace religion itself, the 'worship of reason' was introduced (1793). The 'goddess of reason', in the shape of a sculpture of a young woman, was placed in the main church of Paris during the big 'celebration of Freedom'. Several churches were transformed into a 'temple of reason', where the new (secular) republican values were celebrated and propagated. After a short while, Robespierre (who was rather deistic) abolished this cult and replaced it by the 'cult of the Supreme Being'. But a few months later, Robespierre himself ended up under the guillotine (1794), and the radical wing won the upper hand again. All over France churches were closed and all religious orders were dissolved. There was a ban on ecclesiastical processions and bell-ringing. Thousands of massacres of 'suspicious' priests took place. It was a very chaotic time; it was unclear who fought whom, with much infighting between rival revolutionaries. A regime of terror took place with much arbitrariness, mutual settlement-reckoning, executions-without-trial, and mass executions...

The consecutive governors did not know what to do with religion and devised different formulas to introduce a kind of state religion. For example: 'theophilanthropy' (a kind of 'natural religion' of Jean-Baptiste Chemin-Dupontes, 1796), 'theism' (a kind of open masonry), 'culte décadaire' (a pure moral, non-religious cult, 1798). However, these new religions died as soon as they had sprung up. In 1799, the successful general Napoleon put an end to the chaos by a coup d'état. All of France breathed a sigh of 'enlightened' relief! In 1805, the republican calendar (which was changed eight times because of mutual conflicts) was abolished again.

A critical analysis of the French Revolution is highly interesting. Here, for the first time, the Enlightenment ideas were translated into political reality. When they were transplanted from the study room into harsh reality, from the sterile lab to be tested in the dirty world, they did not prove to be viable at all. The French Revolution is generally presented in Western history books as a liberation, but the reality was much rawer. The crowd of people that stormed the Bastille was in fact used (misused) by the bourgeoisie for its own purposes and they hijacked the revolution later for their own interests. It was a period of great chaos with little 'rationality', of much arbitrariness, terror, bloodshed, injustice, corruption, and civil war. As with many revolutions, we see that the 'opposition', once the old king was expelled, fell apart in countless splinter groups, each attempting to seize power and massacring the rivals. The main reason for confiscating church possessions was not ideological, but purely to fill the bankrupt public treasury. Churches and abbeys of inestimable historical value were sold very cheaply to the corrupt revolutionary leaders (who enriched themselves) and often demolished to sell the stones per kilo. Robespierre, for example, was executed by these leaders because he was not corrupt. During the period of 'terror' (1793–1794) approximately 500,000 people were thrown into prison, and 100,000 executed (7,000 under the guillotine and 25,000 shot).

Although the French Revolution was a failure on a political level, and much of the 'Ancien Régime' was restored afterwards, it still meant a decisive turning point in history. The privileges of the nobility were abolished forever, and the rupture between Church and State was accomplished. Through Napoleon, this revolution flooded a large part of Europe, and several later revolutions introduced its acquisitions in other countries. The relationship between religion and society had drastically changed, and the clock could not be turned back.

There is little reason to boast of 'the values of the French Revolution'. The highly praised 'freedom, equality, and fraternity' were actually a watered-down version of Christian values, and in practice they turned out to be a catastrophe. The French Revolution was successful in what it broke down, but not in what it built up, neither in politics nor in philosophical-religious areas! It has definitively separated Church and State, but made no substantive constructive contributions, and did not provide a better alternative.

In the context of this book, it is especially instructive to see what happens when people want to take over from God and want to dictate what He can look like. This tells much more about these people than about God Himself! These ideas illustrate the new spirit of this age. Previously, religion interfered with science and claimed authority over it, now we see the reverse happening: science is interfering with religion and imposing its rules! But the result, the 'improved version', is neither religion nor science! Experimenting with religion may be interesting, but it is even more interesting to see that none of these 'reasonable versions of religion' catch on. None of them has followers, nor lead to an organized, successful church that overcomes the ages. Why?

By its nature, religion is not reasonable. One cannot 'make' it, assemble it with pieces of philosophy and spirituality and well-intentioned values. It is of a completely different order. A man-made religion has no higher appeal and cannot inspire. And then there also arises endless divisions about how exactly things need to be done. They are naive attempts by people who confuse two areas and thereby create a lot of semantic confusion. This era, which claimed to be so rational, was—to say the least—a very naive one! Today we may smile a little about this, but this period started a certain thought movement which is still stubbornly present today.

1.7 How 'Christian' were the Middle Ages actually?

The Enlightenment opposed itself against the dark Middle Ages, which are usually described as 'Christian'. But what is 'Christian' actually? The only valid standard with which to judge this is, of course, the founder: Jesus and his words in the Bible. This is an infinitely high norm, and the comparison is extremely sobering for the Church. From that viewpoint, the Middle

Ages can hardly be taken as a model for what 'Christian society' should look like; it is full of holes, cracks, and distortions.

From the time of the first growth of the Church, the danger of counterfeits was already lurking. When emperor Constantine converted to Christianity (313 AD), a mixture of spiritual and worldly power began. And when emperor Theodosius (380 AD) made Christianity into a state religion, it became even worse. There were times that faith was enforced with violence; a spiritual battle was fought with earthly weapons. Christians would discriminate and prosecute Jews[6] and heathen. Whilst Jesus shed his own blood, his followers shed that of others. Can the 'good news' of the gospel get more perverted?

On the outside, the Church conquered the world, but from the inside it was the opposite; 'the world' conquered the Church by secretly sneaking into it. 'Strange elements' invaded its DNA: worldly power and its entire arsenal of temptations. Prestige, power, and wealth can corrupt the very best. You can also ask serious questions about the 'Christianization' of Europe (4th to 10th century). Europe became 'wholesale' Christian by mass conversions, but how much did the people understand the new religion? Underneath remained much sorcery and magic, often only covered with a thin Christian sauce. Whole people groups were forced to convert by Charlemagne. However, conversion out of fear and by force has no spiritual value, just as rape has nothing to do with love. This conversion method is so far from what Jesus taught and did, and from what his apostles practiced. 'God's work' was done in a very 'human' way and as such, actually abnegated and destroyed.

It is an illusion to believe that all people in the Middle Ages were active and involved Christians. For example, The Fourth Lateran Council (1215) stated that every Christian should attend church at least once a year. What does this say about the average church attendance at that time?! Luther is known to have said that "less than one in one hundred Germans is a true Christian; the rest are no better than the Turks." And Calvin said, "All people have a seed of God in their hearts; with one in one thousand this is germinating a little, with none coming to full growth." In other words, true Christianity can be seen at most with a couple of small groups or individuals, and even then only in part.

---

6. The history of centuries of anti-Semitism and persecution of Jews is a dark, black page—even chapter—in the history of the Church; how she could come to slaughter the people of her own founder and apostles shows a very dark side.

It seems that there is not only a law of physical gravity on earth but also a law of spiritual gravity. People can have the sincerest good intentions, but there is a force that constantly draws us down. It calls for ceaseless effort, discipline, and hard work to keep the norm, and even then, we don't get it—and this applies to believers and nonbelievers, to individuals as well as organizations.

If we were to judge the Church in comparison to other regimes of that time, the conclusion may be that she did not 'do so badly, not as badly as barbarism on other continents', or maybe even quite well. But the 100%-assessment standard, the one of Jesus, is the only right one in this context because the Church calls herself after Jesus. What percentage of the kingdom of Heaven was realized at that time? 50%, 5% or 0.5%? No one can answer that question, but smugness and self-overestimation are surely not Christian virtues. It is safer and more modest to bet on a number between the last two. Compared to the heavenly norm of God's kingdom, it was very poor on earth, even a mess. Honest self-examination is extremely important for the Church. Too often she was not open to any self-criticism because of her aureole of infallibility. But only in this way can we do justice to the criticisms of humanism, and to the pain of the many victims of the Church. The strong points of humanism are namely where the weaknesses of the Church are brought to light and denounced.

The errors of the Church are judged more heavily than when a non-believing organization makes the same mistakes. And this is partly right because the Church pretends to represent God and priests to be 'men of God'. If they lie and abuse people, it is indeed twice as bad as when someone else does this. The anger of people toward the Church is justified to a great extent! When so many people turn their back on the Church today because she did not do what she preached and did not realize what she promised, then this is understandable. Expectations were not met and people were disappointed. If the Church cannot acknowledge this openly, she will never regain the people. She, who was the undisputed moral authority for centuries, will also have to be the example by sincerely and humbly acknowledging her deep mistakes.

1.8 Abuses in the Church at that time

The young community of first Christians, as we read about it in the book 'Acts of the Apostles', was a sparkling movement, full of vitality, enthusiasm, and spontaneous love; the life bubbled from within! In the course of centuries, this movement evolved into an 'institution' with all its consequences. The fact that 'structure' can suffocate life is a well-known phenomenon. The outer form that was intended as a tool became an obstacle. Jesus envisaged a radically alternative form for his church, "Whoever would be great among you, let him serve you, and whoever would be first among you, let him be your slave." (Matt 20: 26–27). But the Church became an institution following the model of the world, and the Church leaders ruled over the people. They kept the believers small, ignorant, and dependent. They did not enable them to grow into adulthood. They served themselves and not the people.

The Church not only became rigid in its structure and sociological form, but also the message of the gospel proclamation itself changed character. The 'good news' promises happiness, peace, blessing, salvation, 'living in abundance' (John 10:10), in other words, a full, best, and true life. And yet, so often outsiders associate the Church with being strict, gloomy, sorrowful, hostile to the world, without fun and humorless!? Jesus preached

true freedom (John 8:36), but the Church created a stifling system of laws and rules. The emphasis shifted from the inside to outer religiosity, routine repetition of rituals without any content. All attention went to the beautiful church buildings of stone, but the inner, spiritual building was skinny and weak. The outward things (chapels, crucifixes, amulets, statues of saints) were intended to support the faith, but too easily became a distraction, or were they compensating for inner poverty? The focus was also on the afterlife, which did not challenge believers to live here and now as Christians, and to make the earth better. Sometimes it even became an excuse to let injustice on earth persist. It was, by all means, not in line with Jesus' view that God's kingdom is 'in your midst' (Luke 17:21), but more 'above and later', very far away in a dreamy future.

The Church also often presented an unnecessary, exaggerated negative image of man. The emphasis was so much on his badness and sinfulness that one lost sight that he was created in God's image and likeness, and that God found His dearest creature 'very good'. It brought an especially heavy and gloomy atmosphere of 'life as a valley of tears'. Spirituality in the

Humanism

Middle Ages could sometimes be alienated from the worldly reality. People dared not enjoy anything anymore, fearing they would receive less of a reward in heaven. The glorification of suffering became something unhealthy and morbid, while Paul explicitly condemns self-chastisement as 'fleshly' (Col. 2:23). It is a form of masochism and an attempt at self-justification. Also, the hostility against women, the body, and sexuality is a non-biblical element that infiltrated from Persian dualism which invaded early Christianity through Greek philosophers (certainly through Augustine and Plotinus), and has done much harm. God was also portrayed as very high and very far away from people. In theology, God's inaccessibility and unknowability was much more emphasized than His proximity and His desire for relationship with people. God was kept at a distance.

The blossoming of popular devotion introduced mass amounts of paganism and superstition. The former worship of many gods was replaced by the worship of saints, etc. The legends of saints might have had a very small historical core, but around this, wild and outrageous stories were spun so that in fact it became a form of deceit 'for God's sake'. Around the core of faith, many side issues were built, a whole periphery that moved the attention away from the core and became a smoke screen. The extensive trade in relics (full of cheating and forgery!) is a poignant example of this. How can dead remnants receive more attention than a living God? The financial interests behind it were unfortunately too big. This blend of religion and popular culture gave faith the character of a fairground or a spiritual flea market. It has led Christianity to the verge of magic and idolatry—according to some: over the edge.

> 7. Many of the attacks on the Church have their origin in the fact that the Church built too many side issues around the core of the Christian faith, and declared them to be sacred, eternal, and infallible as well (e.g. devotion to the Saints). Because of this mixture and externalization, she became weaker and her message cloudier, and thus gave much 'cheap ammunition' to her opponents.

The fierce reaction of humanism against the Church after the Middle Ages is very understandable if you see what the Church often made of the gospel. The mixture of religion with pseudo-religion, the hypocrisy that resulted from it, a tangle of foolish side issues and manmade rules ... It has given such a distorted and crippled image of what Jesus originally intended, which disgusted and repelled many people. It was, under the influence of the law of spiritual gravity, a massive descent to a lower level, and testified to a low level of spiritual maturity. The Church was authoritarian. The effect of authoritarian education, however, is that if the parents are not around, the children cast off all restraints and turn completely in the opposite direction. When looking for causes for church abandonment, the Church can look deeply into her own bosom.

The Middle Ages wanted to establish a kind of perfect theocracy but did this in such a way that today 'theocracy' has almost become a curse word because people immediately associate it with its worst expressions, such as fanatic intolerance (especially in extremist Islamic groups), obscurantism, and rigorous repression. And yet, we cannot say that this descent of the Church was inevitable and necessary. It must be possible to escape the law of spiritual gravity, just as a hot air balloon can also take off.

> 8. Humanism is an unpaid bill of the Church of the Middle Ages. If the Church had done better at presenting the message of the Gospel and putting it into practice, a humanistic movement would never have been necessary (just as a Protestant Reformation would not have been needed).

The errors of the Church were systematic, constant, and fundamental; they should never be minimized. The fact that she tries to deny, conceal, or give a 'right' context to her own mistakes is—according to human standards!—not even unusual. Every institution or group does this. But it is true that if one institution could or should be different, it is the Church. The people could expect this from her who set herself up as 'The' moral authority.

1.9 How 'dark' actually were the Middle Ages?

The mistakes of the medieval church should not be minimized. Yet, another question must be asked as well; were all the attacks on the Church appropriate? Were they in proportion or out of perspective? What was the motivation and intention behind them: destructive or constructive? Were the arrows on target or shot in the periphery? The criticisms can be focused on very different things: religion in general, religion as a system, God Himself (or a certain image of Him), the Church as an institution, the excesses of the Church, the doctrine or certain parts thereof, the content or the wrapping, church leaders as a person or as a representative of the institution,

mistakes of individuals (which were also condemned by the Church!) ...
All this is often intermingled. But confusing Church and God is of course a major logical error (even if the Church herself promoted this). When someone hears a journalist make a mistake, he is not going to also blame the media minister, or throw his TV set out the window. What does one diagnose as the cause of a disease, and what as the remedy? Was the Church the cause of all the problems in the Middle Ages, or her human executors? Often, humanists conclude that in the Middle Ages there was 'too much God', but you can equally say, 'No, there was just not enough God'! It went wrong because the Church did not do what Jesus said; there was too much of man! God abhors, more than anyone, when injustice is committed or condoned in His name and people are terrorized or killed. The corruption of the very best is the very worst. That religion was greatly abused is very clear, but this is the downside of the enormous positive strengths that religion can evoke. There are strong parallels between faith and sex. Faith is also something very personal, intimate, sensitive, delicate, and you must throw yourself into it! You cannot practice it halfway, and if it is abused, it is extra painful. The solution, however, is not to throw out God, not even to throw out religion. There is also no one who pleads to abolish sex, is there!?

> 9. In its criticism of religion, too often humanism identifies the Church with Christianity itself, and even with God (something which, by the way, the Church herself has also provoked). A person who throws out God and the Church from their life because of the mistakes of an institution or individual believers is like someone who throws out their television because the responsible minister or a journalist make a flagrant mistake.

> 10. Humanism points the finger at Christianity as a source of oppression, abuse of power, and hypocrisy, but fails to discern that all these wrongs were committed by *people* (and human institutions) who failed to live out God's commandments. The God of the Bible, more than anyone, abhors injustice, exploitation, and any type of abuse. This accusation therefore proves the opposite: man is the cause of all religious malpractice, not God or faith.

We often hear the criticism that 'all religions' are a source of war and bloodshed, but here too we must ask if this is correct. Firstly, religion is usually not the real reason for the conflict, but rather functions as a pretext or a smoke screen. Secondly, atheist regimes have already shed much more blood than all religious wars together (see chapter 2.9.1). Thirdly, wars are being conducted today for money, power or oil; is this then more civilized and noble? Even if religious justification stops, wars just continue. Man is the source of all wars. We can certainly critically consider the Church and religion, but to lump it all together is oversimplified and absurd.

Criticism of the dominance of the Church institution is understandable, yet almost every institution is dominant. Each government needs a 'hard hand', and each regime contains a certain dose of intolerance, oppression, violence, and injustice. During the Middle Ages, there was no part of the world with any culture or regime that knew religious freedom! It is not honest to condemn the Church for generally-human faults, and it is also not correct to judge her with 21st century standards.

> 11. Humanism has (or creates and spreads) a very narrow understanding of religion, as if all religion is necessarily restrictive and oppressive, as if religion is just stupidly submitting to irrational dogmas, slavishly nodding, turning off one's brain . . . It cannot imagine that the Christian faith can be extremely liberating, enriching, and joyful. It is never intellectually honest to compare the worst form of the other to the best form of oneself. Humanism first creates a caricature, and then professionally deconstructs it, thinking that in this way it has defeated Christianity.

When the Church and faith are criticized, a certain caricature is usually attacked. But whoever makes a caricature, and then systematically breaks it down, does not prove anything. The arrows do not hit the opponent, but just a self-made straw doll that looks like him. Much criticism of the Church and Christianity is not well-founded but is more often the stereotypical parroting of clichés.

It is also striking that the criticisms were almost never directed toward Jesus himself. His words, deeds, and examples keep standing in the midst of a rain of arrows. When the Church is tempted to boast in itself ('See how well we've done'), she enters the danger zone and makes herself vulnerable. If she would only boast about her founder, it would look very different.

When evaluating the pros and cons of the Church, we must always take into account the psychological mechanism that negative things (emotionally) remain 'ten times' stronger and longer than the positive ones! Criticism of the Church is therefore only honest and in balance when all the good things of the Church are at least named as extensively. The Middle

HUMANISM

Ages also produced very beautiful things, including science and art, architecture, education, health care, innovation, and many freedoms were given. Furthermore, we must judge any period of history with appropriate mildness, taking into account the living conditions at that time which were much more difficult and limited than today.

When comparing belief systems, it is not right to compare the best version of one with the worst version of the other, e.g. pure, loving humanism and irrational, intolerant Christianity. You must compare the pure form of both, and the malformed versions, with each other. Another common mistake is that double standards are often used. Some things (such as faith and church) are examined super-critically (so that nothing remains) and other convictions are accepted indiscriminately naively and are eagerly consumed[7]. With one the holes in the sieve are very small, and with the other they are super-sized.

Today, due to centuries of one-sided imaging, the word 'medieval' is almost an insult, and is synonymous with obscurantism, intolerance, and oppression. Modern man has a certain aversion to that era, whereby he says, 'We never want to go back there at any price'. But to exaggerate the mistakes of the opponent and repeat them constantly does not prove that I am right. Often perception and imaging have a greater weight than content itself.

Much criticism has been focused on the Church regarding a hunger for power and money and be motivated by self-interest. This may have been true on a regular or partial basis, but then this question may also be reversed: what was the underlying motivation of the critics? Was it pure, upright, noble, and free from any self-interest? An authoritarian father can react out of lust for power, need for recognition or fear, but a rebellious son is not necessarily

> 12. The rise of humanism is very understandable as a reaction against the monopoly and dominance of the Church, where the Church made herself indispensable, and claimed authority over areas that were not hers (e.g. art and science). And so, what could have been a fruitful, open, and mutually enriching ideological dialogue became a bitter and unhealthy power struggle which was no longer about substance, but about all kinds of worldly interests surrounding it. The Church has certainly been guilty of fighting a spiritual battle with worldly weapons, but later on, humanism did no less.

---

7. You can see this for example very strongly with all 'alternative' religions which come from the East, the New Age movement...

right. His rebellion can also be driven by laziness, selfishness, narcissism, immaturity, and short-sightedness . . . Honest self-examination must be done in both camps.

> 13. Criticizing the Church is not difficult to do: the standards of Christianity are so high that no-one on earth is able to live by them. We need to bear in mind that even the best churches and well-meaning Christians are only able to put a small part of the gospel of Jesus into practice.

The ideological discussion between humanism and Christianity (regrettably) rarely happens serenely or substantively. It was and is almost always mixed with power factors. The context was never free from a conflict of interest, for the one to retain their power or funds, for the other to conquer them. This muddles a real dialogue!

We must further notice that we can never set 'Enlightenment' as opposite to Christianity because the whole Enlightenment took place in a Christian context. All those fighting against the abuses of the Church and for the emancipation of science and art were Christians. 99% of the 'enlightened thinkers' were believers! The 'seeds' for their fight for freedom came precisely from the Christian faith itself.

If we ask afresh whether the attacks on the Church are deserved or unjust, the answer is probably both! Yes, when comparing her with the standard Jesus sets. No, when comparing her with other regimes at that time! Although no objective measuring bars exist here, we can assume that the 'darkness' of the Middle Ages has been heavily exaggerated, and the 'light' of the Enlightenment at least as much.

> "The gospel has in itself a bacterium that is hostile to the Church."
> —Dietrich Bonhoeffer

1.10 How 'light' was the Enlightenment?

Believers as well as unbelievers can appreciate the positive accomplishments of the Enlightenment, but a one-sided 'glorification' is completely out of balance. A positive point is certainly that there was more freedom. Without freedom, there can also be no pure religion; forced and imposed faith is by definition improper faith. More room was also made for man, and for his 'ordinary' earthly life. The monopoly position of the Church was broken and space created for alternatives: just as in the economic world, 'competition' leads to quality improvement. Superstition, in its hundreds of forms, was gradually reduced. Superstition is like a tumor that grows fast and takes away much energy but does not produce any fruit. In order for faith to remain healthy, the wild shoots need to be continually trimmed back to the core. There also came more tolerance, thereby ending the countless religious wars and controversies of the 16th century. Humanism had to remind Christians of this biblical value. Certainly, after the French Revolution, the worldly power of the Church was severely restricted. She lost much of her possessions, yet this had a positive effect as the Church began to engage more with spiritual affairs again—her true calling! Humanism, practically speaking, has often functioned as a catalyst, as a bringer of new ideas. For the Church and Christianity this had a whipping effect.

14. In some respects, the humanists of past centuries applied the Christian values better than the Christians themselves, and as such they acted as a 'wake-up call' for the Church, causing great discomfort and were a catalyst for many good innovations. Thanks to their sharp criticism, a lot of abuse of power, superstition, inconsistency, hypocrisy, and a mixture of worldly and spiritual power was exposed.

Now for the opposite side and critical remarks: what progress and what light did the Enlightenment bring? As we said, it created much freedom, but this is ambiguous at least, because freedom can surely also be abused. It can also lead to more licentiousness, immorality, crime, social degradation, new tyrannies, and can undermine the quality of life. Most clearly, we see the progress in science, research, knowledge, technology, and the improvement of living conditions. The 'blessings' of the Enlightenment are evident on a material and physical level, but more knowledge and comfort do not automatically lead to better lives! The question here is, "What did the Enlightenment produce for us in the areas of beliefs and morality?" The Church has been fiercely

15. Humanism in the 16th century— quite rightly – opposed the inhuman practices that were taking place in the Middle Ages in the name of God, but it didn't introduce any new values. It actually reminded the Church of her own values (such as love and tolerance).

attacked, but what alternatives did the critics offer, and especially, were they better? Does the 'illuminated' person behave more 'illuminated' and has he become morally better? Here the fruit is much more difficult to pinpoint. Has the darkness of the Middle Ages been cleaned out or was it mainly shifted to other areas (other gods or idols)? The Enlightenment has sought a more rational religion but was very naive in this. It constructed, above all, a superficial image of God, an image as general as possible so that everyone could find themselves in it, and thus a vague, abstract container concept, empty, and not inspiring. Also, morally, the Enlightenment did not provide new, better, higher, loftier values. It only secularized the Christian values, cut them off from God, and thus weakened them (replacing love by tolerance for example).

Another phenomenon typical of the Renaissance and Enlightenment is fascination with the antique culture. Because in the Middle Ages ecclesiastical art could only find its inspiration in biblical stories, worldly art sought this from an 'alternative' source, the Roman and Greek myths. The science and art of Rome and Greece are certainly at a high level, but what about their religion? Humanism wanted emancipation from the 'old, primitive' Bible and sought inspiration in . . . pagan antiquity, a religion that is even older and even more primitive. The historical reliability of Bible stories was questioned, and they threw themselves wildly on myths known to be fabricated, irrational stories. It is very ironic that humanism wanted to focus on man, and ultimately took Greek and Roman gods and half gods as their 'muse'. The 'great spirits' of antiquity such as Socrates, Aristotle or Cicero were elevated to role models, as secular alternatives to the whole series of saints.

When we look at Greek-Roman antiquity, we need to distinguish between its cultural and spiritual aspects. The culture (art, buildings, sculptures) can be grand, but the spiritual, moral, and religious content can be very low at the same time. In the Greek world of gods, there are no absolute moral principles! These are clearly gods made after the image of man, projected and enlarged with all their human imperfections on Mount Olympus. If Zeus was a human being today, he would be put behind bars for life for rape, excessive violence, abuse of power, fraud, betrayal, and a coup. He is the image of a whimsical, immoral potentate that cannot control himself, and fights without any shame for his absolute rule. Glorifying the Hellenistic culture is a moral anachronism!

The 'enlightened' spirits ignored (consciously?)—as Friedrich Nietzsche rightly pointed out—the dark, irrational, sublunary aspects of

Greek religion and culture: the bacchanals, orgies, human sacrifices, the glorification of war, the absence of morality... Roman civilization was exalted, but it was forgotten that it eventually succumbed to its own decadence, corruption, and internal division. It may have been of a high quality in cultural terms, but morally and religiously, there are hardly any lessons to be learned, on the contrary!

In the arts, there was free play with Greek gods and goddesses because it was 'harmless', non-threatening. It was after all an extinct religion, a kind of toy religion. But this irrational obsession with pseudo religious stories was a strange twist for 'enlightened' thinking and remained a sort of intoxication until the 19th century. It is one of the signs that in the whole of European culture the focus was lowered from the supernatural to the terrestrial. The earthly and human had become more interesting than the heavenly and divine. Therefore, we can also ask serious questions about the word 'renaissance' which means 'rebirth'. Jesus used this word first and meant the spiritual birth as a child of God through the Holy Spirit (John 3:3–8). The Renaissance referred to it only as a cultural, esthetic innovation. The second, in the long run, overshadowed the first completely. The cultural revival led to spiritual impoverishment, or at least camouflaged it.

The Enlightenment suffered and suffers terribly from self-overestimation in her naive faith in progress. Calling yourself 'illuminated' is already quite pretentious. It betrays a certain sense of superiority which says, 'Those others are still in the dark; I am already further ahead'. But this illusion of unrestricted progress painfully burst apart when the 'most enlightened' continent, Europe, drove itself into destruction by two world wars. Unprecedented barbarity with new demons raged across Europe, darker than ever. But are these lessons of the past really learned when European leaders today still speak proudly about 'the values of the Enlightenment'?

> 16. Humanism, the Renaissance, and the Enlightenment turned to classical (Roman and Greek) antiquity for inspiration as 'an alternative to the Christian stories', turning a blind eye to its dark, irrational edges. The Christian concept of God and the Bible stories were rejected as naive, unhistorical, and irrational, but instead, bizarre myths, contradictory images of God, and immoral gods were embraced. The Enlightenment considered the Bible as primitive but took refuge in even more 'primitive' forms of religion. They preferred 'toy gods' above a real God.

The Enlightenment time, in conclusion, was a reaction to the 'dark' Middle Ages. But you can also turn it around: only through the Middle Ages could this new era arise. If the Middle Ages had been truly dark, the Enlightenment would never have been possible. Only in the Christian world did Enlightenment break through, not in Islamic or Hindu cultures. Precisely because of the freedom that Christianity brought, protest became possible against (the abuses of) church authority—even in the name of that ('primitive') Bible upon which the Church was based! He who scolds the one on whose shoulders he stands, also cuts himself off from his own resources.

We must also note that the Renaissance and the Enlightenment at their time concerned only a small elite group of wealthy citizens who had the luxury of much free time. Even though these were highly developed people who often brought renewal, every elite is subject to the danger of being alienated from the people and from 'real life'. This consideration very much downplays their ideas and experiments.

One easily and proudly speaks today of 'the values of the Enlightenment'. If you think, however, they are very difficult to define. And they are actually, one by one a weakened version of Christian values. If indeed 'light' came, then this applied surely to knowledge and science, but did it also to the areas of morality or spirituality?! For we can say that in the Renaissance, spiritually, a reversed Copernican revolution took place. There where formerly God was central in all society[8], man placed himself, against all logic, in the center of the universe. This massive shift took place unnoticed and progressively, and yet was fundamental for the whole culture. Its consequences cannot be overestimated: foundational beacons were shifted, basic concepts redefined, the perspective reversed (see 3.1.3).

17. The Copernican revolution rightly caused a fundamental shift in the old worldview, stating that the earth revolves around the sun and not vice versa. But in that same period, a reverse Copernican revolution took place in the spiritual domain: man placed himself, rather than God, at the center of the universe. This defies all logic.

---

8. In medieval society, the 'theoretical framework' was that God was central to everything; in practice it was, however, very different, and very far removed from the 'kingdom of God' (see 1.8).

2

The Humanistic Vision

2.1 'Modern' Humanism

The concept of 'humanism' has evolved greatly from the 14th and 16th centuries, until today when it has acquired many meanings, even opposite ones! In Erasmus' time, it stood for a more 'humane Christianity', today it sometimes means 'anti-Christian anthropocentrism'. It is useful to describe and analyze this evolution.

As we saw earlier, the term *humanitas* first appeared in 14th century Italy. The intention was that, in the area of education, more attention would be paid to 'human subjects' instead of to only sacred subjects. It had a cultural, esthetic meaning, not a religious one (and even less an anti-religious one). For these first humanists, the thought to turn against God did not even come to mind. At the time, theocentrism was widely accepted as a 'logical' starting point, and the Church had its obvious central place in European society. Erasmus' plea really was, "Can the Christian faith once again become more humane, as it was meant to be in the beginning?" Humanism was certainly a quest for more room for man (in art and science) next to God. Theocentrism does not have to crowd out man, right?

The word 'humanism' itself only shows up in the 19th century and in a completely different context. In 1808, the German philosopher and theologian Friedrich Immanuel Niethammer wrote a book in which he devised the concept of 'humanism' to indicate a particular movement in education, namely that of J.J. Winckelmann and Wilhelm von Humboldt. Niethammer opposed their educational ideal because, according to him, it paid too much attention to education as an end in itself, namely literary and ancient heritage. This concept of 'humanism' ('pedagogical humanism') had a clear educational meaning, not at all a philosophical one, let alone an atheist interpretation (Niethammer was a believing protestant and very active in his church).

It was not until the 19th-20th century that 'secular humanism' emerged with its explicitly non-religious meaning. It emerged from the circles of organizations of free-thinkers (although free-thinking and humanism certainly do not coincide!). Again, in the early years, these were rather deistic by nature, certainly not yet predominantly atheistic. At that time, it was still 'too dangerous' to openly confess atheism. This movement, however, continued to present itself increasingly as a fully-fledged non-confessional philosophical alternative to organized religion. It targeted the ever-increasing group of church-leavers and tried to unite and represent them. In other words, this form of humanism (which today carries the upper hand) is very recent as a movement and has a very different nature than all the previous ones.

An unambiguous, exact definition of 'humanism' cannot be found; it can be defined very differently. Because of this, we hear about 'Renaissance humanism' (Petrarca, etc.), 'Weimar humanism' (Niethammer), secular or modern humanism, atheistic humanism. Then there are also the variants such as social humanism, religious humanism[1], ecohumanism, planetary humanism, transhumanism, etc.

The situation is again very different from country to country. In countries dominated by the Roman Catholic Church (especially France), secular freethinking ('la laïcité') is strongly anticlerical and anti-religious, rationalistic and a bearer of Enlightenment ideas (just as irregular freemasonry). In more Protestant countries (England, The Netherlands, Germany), it is more open to religion-in-the-not-dogmatic-sense-of-the-word (just like regular freemasonry). In the United States, however, humanism is strongly atheistic, in reaction to the strongly religious society.

On the one hand, we cannot stress enough that modern humanism is almost the opposite to what

---

1. In 'religious humanism', 'religious' does not refer to organized or confessional 'religion' but an acknowledgment of and awe of higher cosmic connections, and an openness to the unfathomable mystery of existence.

Petrarca and Erasmus meant; they would abhor it. On the other hand, it is the logical consequence of something they started; the theocentric focus diminished and slowly became more and more anthropocentric. A seed was planted for more freedom and attention for man, and this continued growing. Here we can compare the Church with a father who gives his growing children more and more freedom—and that is how it should be in good education. But this freedom also includes the risk that some children will choose to turn their back on their father, even definitively.

Humanism was and is, if you look at its numbers of members, a very small group, but its social influence is much bigger. In some respect, it changed the whole spirit of this age. When some people call it the 'new state religion', they point to the fact that current social rules about religions and churches are determined by the atheist-humanist paradigm (more about this in chapter 2.10.1 addressing secularism). It can never be indicated exactly where and when this happened, but in the delicate relationship between God and man, at a certain moment, the balance can turn from 50.1% to 49.9%. This happens with an individual who slowly evolves into unbelief (or vice versa), but the same applies in a sense to a whole culture. It cannot be linked clearly to one particular influential person (politician, thinker, scientist, artist) or event (a book, congress, new law) neither to a population evolution (for example that only 49.9% of the people go to church), but 'suddenly', in the spirit of that time, the criterion of humanity is more important than that of divinity. It is very subtle at first, but God really gets second place from then onwards! He finds Himself on a slippery slope, because after the 49.9%, His relevance will continue to decline, and He will get third, fourth, fifth ... place. God is no longer the guarantee of humaneness and reasonableness, no longer the foundation, the infinitely high standard, the superior intelligence, the obvious authority who can enforce His laws. Now, man becomes the judge and creator of values! He sets himself up as the Supreme Court. This does not mean that the Bible and its values are immediately thrown out, but the texts of the Bible that no longer fit in this way of thinking are now 'critically' reviewed, called 'secondary, culture-bound, historical', and thus no longer normative. The point of decision has shifted, subtly, but essentially. Man is no longer accountable to God, but God must meet the requirements of man. In other words, God is not allowed to be God anymore. In a culture, this is of landslide importance!

2.2 Humanism as ideology.

Only in the 20th century did the concept of 'humanism' evolve into a separate non-religious philosophy of life that wants to offer a fully comprehensive explanation for all the questions for which religion also gives answers. Humanism sees itself as an 'enlightened variant of Christianity', a totally secular version. 'Humanistic' and 'human' are thus substantially different, even though in daily language, 'humanism' can sometimes be used as a synonym for 'humanitarian' or 'philanthropy'. To suggest that only humanists are humane is an insult to all other groups of people, the same as saying that only socialists are social. It is impossible to see 'humaneness' as the exclusive claim of humanism; every ideology has a high regard for this. The term 'ism' points out that one principle is made dominant, and here we arrive at the ideological aspect. The underlying mindset makes the real difference.

Humanism as an ideology, however, is very different from religion, and this makes a comparison difficult. To begin with, it has no founder and no common starting point. There is no central authority, and so nobody who can make the claim on behalf of all humanists, 'This is true humanism'. There are only minimal common convictions ('belief content'), but even these are not fixed; there is a continuous mutual discussion on foundations and principles. Furthermore, they can be defined individually and very diversely;

> 18. To the extent that humanism presents itself as a secular alternative to religion, as a fully-fledged, all-encompassing explanation that can provide all answers to life's questions which believers seek in religion, it serves as a de facto religious system and exhibits all the corresponding characteristics of such a system.

everyone has the right to interpret or apply them in his own way. On the one hand, humanism is not religious at all, on the other hand it is indeed a belief! In sociology one distinguishes between a substantive definition of religion and a functional definition[2]: according to the first, humanism

---

2. A substantial definition is based on content-related characteristics (for example: faith in God or supernatural beings), a functional one depends on the functions it performs. According to this latter definition, atheistic communism clearly has religious characteristics; they have, for example, 'an infallible book' ('Das Kapital' by Marx or 'the little red book' by Mao), Marx counts as the new Moses, the official party ideologists are the recognized prophets who can give the correct interpretation of 'the book', the party leader is the high priest, the ideologists paid by the regime are the 'evangelists', the deceased great leaders are the 'saints', the grave of Lenin is the central place of pilgrimage,

is not religion, according to the second it is. Though its content is not religious, it does take over almost all of its functions; it gives its members what religion provides for its followers. You could say you are comparing 'apples and pears', but you could also say 'coconuts and peanuts'.

In common public use, humanism comes across as an extremely friendly and humane concept, but as an ideology, it can become as fanatic or militant as other ideologies, and thus also imperialistic and intolerant. To investigate the core points of humanistic thinking, I refer to some quotes from the Declaration of Principles of the 'Nederlands Humanistisch Verbond' (Dutch Humanistic Union) of 1985[3] (emphasis in bold made by me).

The central point of belief, of course, is 'belief in man': man is by nature good and has the capacity to do all he must do. In doing so, he does not need help from God or gods. He can trust in his own abilities in all areas and thus is essentially optimistic. Humanism considers man "as *meaning-giver, and creator and bearer of moral values*" and "*. . . is convinced that values and norms find their origin, foundation, and completion in man.*" It is thus man, and man alone, who creates values and norms, and gives meaning to life. Man is the center of the universe, the standard and the plumb line, and each person for him or herself; no one can impose values or norms on another. There is no authority from above or beyond. Man is autonomous, that is, his own legislator, meaning-giver and boss over his own body and life. Humanists "*. . . cannot accept that life is led and protected by forces outside of nature, or that the so-called supernatural could give meaning to the natural . . . They choose to live without readymade answers, without the comfort of an afterlife and without gods.*" A humanist is principally focused on the 'now-life', life here and now: this is all there is, and this finiteness must be embraced as something positive. His goal is free self-development, not hindered by restrictive authorities. However, a humanist is not a narcissist; responsibility, respect for others, and tolerance are highly valued. Dignity and equality of every person are the guideline for all ethical action. 'Freedom, equality, and brotherhood' are also of course the red thread.

The only recognized means of acquiring knowledge is reason; a person must, in everything, think critically and rationally and grow up to

---

they believe in a (secular) paradise etc.

3. Cited from *Humanisme vandaag* ('Humanism today'), EPO, 1987, a publication of the 'Humanistisch Verbond', pp. 9–20. Of course, not all humanists will accept every word of this, especially because this Humanistic Alliance is outspokenly atheist. Some might weaken or give nuance to them, but generally speaking, it is representative enough of the big lines of thought.

assertivity. *"The Humanistic Alliance' regards free research as the only acceptable method of searching for truth in order to find answers to the questions man may have regarding the meaning of his existence . . . It rejects every enforced authority, all so-called revealed truths and dogmas in whatever domain, as well as the inhibitions, indoctrination, and any means of pressure on the free development of man and society."* "*A freethinker is the one who does not allow his thinking to be guided by dogmas and statements of authority . . . He does not accept any revelation or teaching authority no matter the ruling body they may originate from. After all, he cannot accept that certain institutions or individuals could offer privileged access to the truth."*

The first thing that stands out is that this text is very 'anti' and aggressive, very much generalizing, fierce in tone, and pretty emotional for people claiming to be guided by reason only. It is especially heavily loaded with assumptions and unprovable statements; none of these core beliefs can, to begin with, already be rationally (!) proven. They are, however, firmly postulated as 'dogmas' that cannot be questioned! Each of these bold core words deserves to be critically scanned; 'critical' is surely a feature of humanism, is it not? The rest of this book will engage with this. To begin with, the belief in man and the trust in his own abilities are already very absolute statements that require much faith! Hence the humor in the believer who says, 'I do not have enough faith to be a humanist'. The claim to be 'reasonable' and to be based solely on science is already undercut at step one.

The text clearly reacts against God, gods, faith, church, dogmas . . . but in its phrasing appears to have a very distorted image of these, an image that a believer cannot identify with at all. It is based on an artificial enemy portrait and aims its cannons at self-made caricatures. The text associates faith with '*inhibitions, indoctrination, pressure, and means of pressure*', and suggests that one cannot wholeheartedly and consciously choose to believe and find freedom in this. The Bible is presented as a book full of dogmas intended to be imposed on others, instead of a report of testimonies of people who have found happiness and peace with their Maker. The language used displays a fair share of suggestion, one-sidedness, deception, and manipulation. The text is furthermore highly contemptuous towards believers and pretty hurtful; a believer is someone who is 'happy with ready-made answers', who would rather not think for himself, who is not brave enough to stand on his own feet. Faith is like a 'pacifier' for him where he sucks out (false!) comfort, an illusion in which he occasionally has to flee to survive . . . so much for respect for those who think differently.

Because humanism seeks to offer a comprehensive explanation, it automatically functions as a religion: it has its own (unprovable) dogmas, own god (man), own confession of faith, own prophets and ministers, own evangelists and martyrs, own rituals and festivals, own holy places and temples. Here also, you find those who are convinced, those who hang on and those who fall away. There are moderates and fanatics, which means intolerant 'fundamentalists'. And also here, we find a (sometimes intense) fight over which of the many groups represents 'true humanism'.

But some still say there is also 'Christian humanism?' Certainly, there may be people and groups who label themselves this way, but what does this expression mean? It suggests that 'humanism' is the core word, and 'Christian' an additional feature. Being 'man oriented' ('human + ism'), however, is the reverse of being 'god oriented'. Placing man at the center of everything is diametrically opposed to the message of the Bible. According to the Christian view, 'placing oneself at the center' is precisely the cause of all misery in the world. We will look at this in greater detail in chapter 3.3, but in our opinion, this is an inconsistent use of concepts.

2.3 'Believing in man'

2.3.1 What does 'I believe in man' mean?

Let us address the central belief of humanism: 'I believe in man'. At first, this seems like very beautiful, noble, positive, and radiant optimism. But if we look at it more critically, we must say that it is a very general sentence and it is not clear what is meant by it. If you say to someone in an everyday situation, 'I believe in you', then this is a splendid saying that can greatly encourage the person and give them 'wings'. But if you elevate this to the level of a central 'dogma[4]', on which you build your entire faith and life, it becomes a statement of a completely different order. There is a huge difference between

---

4. I realize the word 'dogma' can be very unpleasant for humanists, because humanists are 'allergic' to dogmas, but this is not meant to be hurtful. Nevertheless, 'faith in man' functions just as much as a belief statement in the Church and is on the same level.

hammering a nail in the wall to hang a frame and hammering a nail in the wall to hang your whole house! To test this 'nail', we need to exert some pressure on it, just as the LPG gas tank of a car during car inspection is put under extra high pressure to ensure it can take it.

What do people mean exactly when they say, 'I believe in man'? A Christian can also say 'I believe in man'. If he gets a chance to explain this, it would mean he believes a person has the potential to make good (or better) choices; that his 'good self' can be victorious . . . Or, that despite everything, he still finds man lovable, worthwhile. But this is no guarantee, rather more a question of 50-60-70% . . . He is expressing hope rather than a certainty. But if a humanist says this, it is on the same level as when a believer says, 'I believe in God'. It has a much heavier weight; on this 'nail' he must hang his entire world vision.

Let us first try to determine what a humanist does not mean. He does not want to say, 'I believe that man exists' (in analogy with '. . . that God exists'). He does not mean, 'I believe that man is almighty, only good, all-knowing, and perfect' (again, in analogy with God). Finally, he does not state 'I trust man 100%, I would build my life blindly on him'. Therefore, whoever says 'I do not believe in God but in man', is, strictly speaking, talking complete nonsense. It is obvious that 'I believe in God' and 'I believe in man' are statements of a completely different order, just as 'I love my wife' and 'I love ice cream' are.

19. 'Believing in man' is often postulated as an alternative to 'believing in God'. The word 'believing', however, has a completely different meaning in these two statements, just like the word 'love' does in 'I love my wife' and 'I love ice cream'. No one believes that man is almighty, only good, all-knowing, infallible, and perfect. This kind of proposition creates a lot of semantic confusion and ideological fog in discussions.

However, what a humanist does mean is something like, "I believe that man is good in his deepest being." Here we come closer to the core of the humanist creed, but not entirely. For, in fact, the Bible believes this too; man was originally made in God's image and likeness; he was perfectly good in paradise. And this good image of God in man has, even after the fall, not completely disappeared (though it is soiled and cracked). So here we do not really see the big difference with Christian belief.

The humanist can also mean, "I believe man can and must solve all his problems himself." Here we are coming closer to the difference, because indeed a Christian does not believe this. We do need to qualify this however. If this suggests that Christians are dependent, weak, and passive, and when in trouble just lift their eyes to heaven powerlessly and pleadingly... then this is a heavily distorted image. A Christian will certainly confess that man cannot solve all his problems himself, but... does a humanist claim this, and does he really mean it? Practical life shows a lot of opposite examples (more about this later). But neither does a Christian have the experience that 'God removes all the problems on his path', just as a mother clears all the obstacles for her toddler. God just helps him to become mature and strong, and to learn how to bear his own burdens. God continually helps the believer to recognize his own responsibility and choices, and certainly does not make it easy on him! Whenever man falls, God certainly helps him, but does not carry him the rest of his life. He restores man's ability to stand on his own feet again. A Christian also needs to learn to solve his own problems.

> 20. 'Belief in man' is presented as the distinctly characteristic principle of humanism in contrast to Christianity, but this is a misrepresentation. The God of the Bible has more faith in man than we could have ourselves. He thinks very highly of man and still today continues to give him a very high level of trust and freedom. Furthermore, Christians also believe in the original goodness of man (as presented in the Garden of Eden)!

Finally, the humanist also intends, 'I believe that man is the center of the universe and can and must determine his own values and standards.' At this point however, the roads completely separate. Yet this statement raises the most pressing questions! What does it mean 'man at the center': the center of what? The center of the universe? We all know that neither the earth, nor our sun are the center of the universe, how could these puny, mortal little minikins then be the center? It is completely unclear what is meant by this. And if man were the center of everything, who are we talking about then? Is it about me? Or about my neighbor? Which 'closest'? But there cannot be seven billion centers in the universe? Does this refer maybe to the whole of 'humanity'? But these seven billion people still have seven billion different opinions, visions, and values, and barely

> 21. Humanism is unable to clearly define what 'believing in man' exactly means. This leads to the most diverse and contradictory interpretations, whereby in reality, there is no common calibration point whatsoever.

make a whole!? Is this then maybe about a concept of man, as a kind of Platonic idea, an ideal person? But then this 'ideal' man must be an idealized, fantasized person, and this image will clash with the hard and often raw reality. Who, by the way, will define this concept and image? Every man will of course do this for himself! If each person interprets this image of what 'man' means for himself, then that is of course topnotch circular reasoning. The humanist has no answer to this question; he has no 'bottom' under the concept of 'man'. Those who dig deeper find only loose sand. This track of thinking leads to nowhere; it ends up in a void, a black hole. And this is the central dogma of humanism!

2.3.2 Man as 'measure of all things'

The statement 'man at the center' only really makes sense in the context of the processing of knowledge (epistemological), meaning that man is indeed 'the measure of all things'. This is probably also how Protagoras intended it. From a philosophical viewpoint (knowledge theory), this is also true. In everything I do, I in fact start from myself, from my eyes, and my brain. Nobody else can know how I perceive and experience things. No one can 'think' in my head, no one can memorize a text in my place; no one else can make decisions in my place and believe or reject a truth. Even when I look at a fellow human being, I have an image of this person in mind (which may not be how he really is). It is even impossible philosophically to prove that the images in my mind correspond to the outside reality. 'I'm a prisoner in my own head', we could say (also called solipsism), who could even be completely misled by my senses and ideas. By all means no one can live my life in my place; no one else can be 'me'! Only I can be 'myself' and even if I would want to, I cannot be someone else. In this sense, I am indeed the center, the beginning and the end of my own little inner world. I am even doomed to do it myself! This because nobody can do it for me! In a negative sense, we can also say that for the most profound decisions, we are all alone.

In this sense we have to say that every person (humanistic or religious) in fact determines his own values. These values come to him through upbringing, other influences or indoctrination, but only he decides what to accept and what to reject. He opens or closes the little inner door and makes a selection. In our innermost being we are sentenced to freedom; even not choosing is a choice! This also applies to a believer because God also gives freedom to the believer! By definition God does not indoctrinate, manipulate or coerce. This is in principle against His nature, for He is love and made man to be free. He does not intrude but leaves a startling amount of room for man. Even if a believer decides to believe and submit himself to God and His values, this is his own free choice!

Man, therefore, is inevitably the center of his own little inner world. But surely, this is something completely different from making 'man is the center' the core dogma of a real-life philosophy. In our own head, the steering wheel is indeed in our hands (and yet, still very limited: see chapter 2.8.1). This, however, is by no means the norm for the rest of the world. It says nothing about the outside world; my 'decrees' have no consequences for anyone else. The most I can say is that I am indeed central to my own (small) most individual universe! Therefore, according to humanism, there are seven billion mini universes in which seven billion people are 'creator and absolute ruler'.

Therefore, the ultimate consequence of humanism is: there is no center of the universe at all! The throne is empty. Humanism leads to total subjectivism. If I'm central in my own world, then this world is like an uninhabited mini island. And an uninhabited island is just like a prison; total freedom is at the same time the pinnacle of loneliness. It sounds very nice and promising that a person can determine his own values and standards, but when you think about it, it proves to be yet another meaningless statement (see later in chapter 2.8.1).

22. The slogan 'man is the measure of all things' is a misinterpretation of what the Greek philosopher Protagoras meant by it, and as a philosophical principle it is absolutely untenable. This would be the same as all the planets in the cosmos declaring themselves to be the center of the universe.

The statement 'I believe in man' can of course only be understood as a reaction to 'I believe in God'. And again, it is very instructive to investigate this opposition; are they truly opposite to each other? Do Christians not believe in man then? It is true that the Church has often portrayed a one-sided, negative, and gloomy image of man as being sinful and corrupt (see ch.1.8). This however was a distortion of the biblical image of man under the influence of Persian-Greek dualism. The Bible portrays God as One who does believe in man! He created man Himself and sees His own image in man, just as a father when he looks at his own child. God has also given man much space and autonomy[5] and continues to do this! He respects (!)

---

5. A powerful story to illustrate this is that of the prodigal son (Luke 15: 11–32).

man's choices and freedom, even at the tree of knowledge of good and evil. Man disappoints Him countless times a day, but He gives him new chances and opportunities each day. He forgives seven times seventy times[6], much more than any human being would do! God believes infinitely more in man than a humanist does! He intentionally planned and designed man. And even if it goes wrong, He stands in the gap for him as for His own child and waits confidently until he returns without ever forcing his free will.

One more comment about the word 'believing' is needed here. It is clear that 'believing' means something completely different when referring to faith in God or believing in man. In the first context, it means: total trust, surrender, building upon Someone much bigger, the Source of everything, the almighty Creator. It is 'hanging your house' on a divine nail; consciously connecting yourself to Someone outside of you! The humanist, on the other hand, who says, 'I believe in man', knows very well that man is a volatile and unstable being, easily influenced and tempted. This 'believing' certainly does not have the characteristic of 'unconditional trust'. When we look at the practice of everyday life, we see that it is even very conditional and limited: how many people would you entrust your bank card to with the PIN code? How many of your immediate fellow men do you consider to be 'absolutely trustworthy'? 5%? 0.5%? 0.05%? If you were going to cross a bridge over a ravine, which is 5, 0.5 or 0.05% reliable, would you take the steps? In fact, you really cannot measure this 'faith' with the same weight as faith in God. At best, it is a derived and diluted variant of this that indicates an intention, not a rock-proof certainty. (In chapter 2.13 we will explore more deeply the subject of 'faith', what it is and what it is not, to try to eliminate some confusion and misunderstandings).

---

23. 'I believe in man' is a beautiful and noble statement at the level of interpersonal relationships, but when you transpose this to the level of an all-encompassing life-explanation and make it an absolute calibration point for norms and values, this statement becomes ludicrous. And in daily life, it also turns out to be a hollow slogan: humanists have as many locks, alarm systems, and security cameras as anyone else.

Humanly speaking, the father (who represents God here) is a 'fool' to give his youngest son all the money and then let him leave. The freedom he gives to his son is phenomenal; no human father would do this. He shows deep trust that his son will eventually come back.

6. When Jesus tells us to forgive each other seven times seventy times (Matt 18:22), it means that God certainly does this Himself and even much more.

The Humanistic Vision

Finally, when humanism trumpets its 'faith in man' as its deepest conviction, it seems as if it brings something new to the 'market of world views', as if it launches a new and original product. The fact that humanism arises from Christianity cannot be denied, but what did it do with it? Actually, it did not add anything, but only removed things from it. Belief in human dignity and uniqueness is a thoroughly Biblical value, and absolutely not innovative to Christianity. It is actually a part of the Christian faith that has been made the main part. Man, who, in Jesus' view, gets a place after God[7], is put in the first place. The order is swapped: what is secondary becomes primary. The question is, of course, whether the second floor of a house keeps standing when you remove the first floor. Or whether the tree will continue to bloom if the roots are severed (more about this later too).

Conclusion: 'Believing in man' is a beautiful, noble pronouncement on the level of interpersonal relationships, but if you transpose it to the level of a total world explanation, making it an absolute benchmark for truth and morality, it becomes an empty statement without content or substance. It is an unsecured bank check.

2.3.3 Man: champion of unreliability

'I believe in man' certainly sounds positive and optimistic and is in any case better than 'I do not believe in man'; cynicism, nihilism, and pessimism help no one to move forward. But what about the actual everyday practice? Does a humanist really mean this, and does he live out his belief, or is it a hollow slogan? Is this just a good-looking formula to show off on his business card, or does it work out very well in the harsh, resilient  reality? Does a 'man-believer' for example, entrust his wallet to any person on the street? Does he believe everything that people tell him? If so, why is he so critical of everything? Why do we actually protect ourselves more and more, with locks, alarm systems, and cameras, with security codes and passwords on the internet?

---

7. When Jesus is asked what the first commandment is, He answers 'to love God', and immediately He adds as an 'equivalent': and 'love your fellow man'(Matt 22: 37–39), in that order!

We could write an encyclopedia about how unreliable mankind has been in history, the mess he made of things in all areas of life, and this in all areas: private, family, social, national, and international. Even in our most individual universe, we are not consistent. We cannot even trust ourselves and are sometimes afraid of our own thoughts or reactions, and . . . we 'deceive ourselves'! We cannot even live up to the most elementary moral value of honesty. We are full of immaturity and often startled by our childish reactions. The fact that we hardly dare to expose our true self to others, shows how little we trust each other! It is very challenging for us to be trustworthy in relationships, friendships, and marriages.

> 24. Humanism claims to believe in man, yet there is no more volatile and less reliable being on this planet than a human being. The one who is the very cause of all the mess is the least likely to solve those problems! "If the fault is in the system, even the best solution is still part of the problem." If man is the measure of all things, then that is the most stretchable, subjective, self-willed, and unpredictable measure that exists, and full of conflicting interests. The human administration of justice is the best illustration of this.

On the larger scale of society and politics we see this distrust, as it were, structurally built-in. For example, humanism has a high priority for democracy, as a kind of guaranteed recipe for good governance. Democracy, however, was originally designed to prevent the abuse of power by absolute monarchs. It is, in other words, the result of fundamental distrust in human beings, namely the near-certainty that he cannot handle too much power. It is an overt and structural confession of human unreliability. Democracy builds as many safeguards as possible against misuse in its system, but the more 'consistently' this happens, the more the system slows down. The pace of the machinery increasingly slackens, just

> 25. Humanism asserts that it has a lot of faith in mankind, and claims democracy, for example as one of its most important 'achievements'. The driving force behind democracy, however, is precisely a great mistrust of man, namely the near-certainty that people will abuse an excess of power. Therefore, democracy builds in as many safeguards as possible against misuse of power, to the point that society becomes stuck in a multitude of control mechanisms and bureaucracy, and democracy no longer works.

like a computer with five-fold antivirus software. We see the same in the whole of legislation, the legal system, bureaucracy, and the over-regulation of the economy. Also, on the highest level, that of world politics, we see that irrationality prevails. We trust no one so completely that we would dare to make him 'president of the world'. The whole history of fascism and Hitler (who was democratically elected!) teaches us terrible lessons about the potential of (modern) man to be misled, even of a whole nation. How can someone, after Auschwitz, still sincerely claim to believe in the goodness of man?

We do not claim here, however, that man is always completely bad. We do not want to fall into the medieval error of depicting humanity as sinful as possible, as if God were exalted by humiliating humanity. We could also write an encyclopedia of acts of extraordinary goodness, signs of generosity, manifestations of selflessness, and truthfulness, exceptional friendships, bravery-unto-death, and self-sacrifice. However, if 'faith in man' is the foundation of the humanistic house, it must be resistant to earthquakes, even against earthquakes of twerlve on the scale of Richter. The slightest vibration though, is already sufficient for man's shameful descent.

People who say they believe in man do not truly realize what they are saying and negate this conviction in their actions each day. Man is the weak link in the system, in every system, even in the best system and at every level. If he is the major cause of the problems, how should he solve them?

Humanists accuse believers of believing in something that cannot be proven, but how 'provable' is the goodness of man? It may come across as a witticism, but it does have a certain truth; from the statement 'God is good', you can never prove scientifically that it is true or false, but of the statement, 'man is good', you can absolutely scientifically and experimentally establish that as false. As said before, to believe in the goodness of man, you need so much more faith, excuse me, you must even systematically ignore what you perceive daily with your own eyes! The one who is optimistic about humanity, consciously closes his eyes to the many terrible realities from the lowest to the highest level. It is a blind faith and therefore a dogma in the fullest sense of the word, because it does not rely (1) on the facts, (2) on the requirement of rationality, and (3) may not be questioned. And even if it may be questioned, it will never be abolished because it is 'the' axiom of humanism.

> "There are two things that are infinite, the universe and foolishness of man; but of the first I'm not entirely sure."
> —Albert Einstein

Humanism claims that all thinking must be subject to the facts alone, but despite billions of facts contradicting it daily, this belief untouchably stands its ground! Sharp atheistic criticism of faith in God says that believers have 'lost contact with reality', and dwell in the world of myths, but does this not apply as much (or more) to 'belief in man'? The tenacity with which humanists continue to proclaim this is completely irrational, and highly astonishing for people who pride themselves in a (self) critical attitude.

2.4 The humanistic and Christian image of man[8]

2.4.1 The 'value' of man

Humanism speaks of the dignity of man and refers hereby to the conviction that each person is unique and valuable in himself, regardless of age, gender, race, origin or conviction. This is beautiful, but where does this 'value' come from, and what concept of man undergirds this? The value of a thing is determined by its own qualities, but even more by external factors: 'the demand' for it or its scarcity. There is no objective standard for this, but it is extremely subjective and fluctuating (just like the stock market). The value of a human being can even be zero euro when nobody gives a cent for your life (often the case in war situations!).

According to the humanistic concept of man, the value of a human being is solely determined by man. There is no authority outside or above this. Firstly, this is a circular argument, secondly it is prejudiced and full of conflicting interests, and thirdly, man himself has no objective criterion for this. If you were to look at a human being purely materialistically, its value would simply be the price of its weight in meat (just like a cow). But it becomes even more difficult. If man, from a humanistic point of view, is merely a product of stupid, blind coincidence and purely material evolution, what then is his higher value compared to the stone or plant next to him originating from the same big bang? In the humanist discourse, you read on one hand texts about the nobility and dignity of man, and then texts about his animal nature and the 'banality' of his existence. 'We are no more than a conglomerate of molecules and cells'. The value of man suddenly evaporates through these 'scientific analyzes' to less than zero.

---

8. In this chapter the underlying images of man and God are dealt with very briefly because these philosophical backgrounds will be further elaborated in a subsequent book.

In the Christian concept of man, his value is clear: he is made in the image and the likeness of God (Genesis 1:26). He is even given dominion over the entire planet, thus sharing in the royal character of God. Man is an 'original creation', no serial work. Because he is a unique and precious 'handiwork', he is priceless. Divine origin alone determines that man has 'value in himself', regardless of his 'usefulness': a baby also has this intrinsic value. There is namely an 'objective outsider' who has established this value. And even if a person has strayed far from his origin and is broken and soiled, God still sees that intrinsic, infinite potential, and His own image.

The humanistic explanation of the origin of man snatches man down from his royal throne and strikes him to the ground with a hard blow; the disillusionment is complete. He becomes a naked monkey who has even lost his tail as well! This is deeply cynical, and just one step further is nihilism (see also 3.2.4).

2.4.2 Images of God

It may seem strange to insert a short piece about 'God images' in this chapter about images of man. The reason is that someone's image of man is closely associated to his image of God. You cannot understand the Christian concept of man without a clear understanding of the corresponding image of God. But this also applies to the other party; an atheist also has a God image, namely one that he rejects (yet this he does have in mind). A Christian has the lifelong assignment to honestly investigate his concept of God, and continually adjust it. But a humanist or atheist has a similar obligation. When rejecting God, he must be honest enough to investigate whether it is possibly a childish image of God 'from primary school' that he threw into the rubbish bin. It is certainly true that the Church or Christians have often transferred half-hearted, mixed-up images of God. They still have a lot of work themselves to get to the bottom of their own message. What someone's God image looks like is very important because it determines the person's life purpose. Whoever reveres a war god

> 26. Humanism is usually based on a (the rejection of) a wrong view of God. To a large extent, the churches and Christians are responsible for this as they have presented a distorted/half-hearted/mixed image of God. Christians who criticize humanism cannot do so in an honest way without first looking deeply into their own hearts and taking their own responsibility in this.

will become warlike. Whoever honors a God of infinite love will also strive to become like Him.

In the search for the right God image, it is essential to realize that God is always bigger than we can imagine. Something we can understand in our league cannot be God. A simple but very strong illustration of this is when we look at the immense universe with its stunning distances and incomprehensible energies. The God who made all this must be so much bigger than all this! And this applies as well to all His other characteristics: His goodness, love, mercy, power, holiness, faithfulness, forgiveness. We systematically underestimate Him. And He is not only very big and very far away, but He is also very near in His love. It is revolutionary and mind-blowing how

Jesus depicts God's paternal love in the story of the prodigal son (Luke 15:11–32). This story radically redefines God and religion. It greatly stretches our frame of mind. Only those who believe in an exceedingly loving God are capable of extraordinary love. One of the most difficult qualities of God is His justice, because the (often hard and unjust) reality seems to contradict this. Not only atheists clash with this, also believers struggle with it. But if God were unjust and could make mistakes, then, by definition, He is not the God in whom Christians believe. God must be perfect, or He is not God. Whoever cannot reconcile this (yet) with 'the facts' has still work to do to refine his God image.

2.4.3 Afterlife or here-and-now

Humanism strongly opposes any belief in eternal life after death. For them, 'heaven' has the character of a fantasy fairytale world in which man seeks comfort. And this is not only useless, it is even negative because it is an 'escape' from reality. For when you focus on a castle in the air, it prevents you from putting your shoulder to the wheel in life here. However, when the focus is on the here-and-now, this makes one live more intensely in the knowledge that you only have one life, here and now. It forces you to make the most of it.

In Christian faith, on the other side, the idea of eternal life is a core element. It has, however, also become problematic for many believers in these modern times due to the many childish images and popular stories (rice pudding with golden spoons or little devils with goat legs). Also, the fact that 'hell' in the Middle Ages was seriously misused to terrify people did not help either to get a balanced picture. Christians still have much homework to do to get a mature and spiritual understanding of this.

Humanists also consider every idea of 'heaven' as an 'external motivation' (reward) to behave well. But this is not what Christianity teaches. Also, the believer must go through the process of internalizing God's moral standards and make them his own; if not he stays in kindergarten. Humanism actually creates a false contradiction between the afterlife and the here-and-now; either you focus on one, or on the other. In other words, whoever is heavenly minded is useless on the earth. Belief in eternity however, actually gives eternal value to our smallest choices on earth. If someone gives a cup of cold water to 'the least of mine', it is as if he does it for the King (Matt 25:31). An eternal perspective makes a Christian live more intensely; his motivation gets so much stronger. Countless Christians found exactly in this the necessary strength to change something in this world for their fellow human beings, even to sacrifice their own lives. Life on earth is not just a test, it is Life itself, the 'first phase' of eternal life.

> 27. The humanistic concept of man creates a false contradiction between the afterlife and the here-and-now. The perspective of life after death does not reduce the value of earthly life, on the contrary, it gives an eternal value to our smallest choices (e.g. to feed a hungry person).

On the other hand, whoever must expect everything from this earthly life will create a strong rigidity. Whoever knows and lives only for this short earthly life will automatically become 'short-sighted' and only be capable of short-term thinking. He wants to maximize 'profit', but very soon this will be filled in materially. 'Seeking happiness' is by definition self-directed. Only those who believe in a higher life can let go of short-term interests and are not even afraid to lose or lay down their earthly life.

2.4.4 The view on good and evil

The traditional (Christian) perspective on good and evil is found in the story of the fall (see Genesis 3:1–24). Is this a naive fairy tale, an irrational, outdated myth, or was it rejected because it was incorrectly and superficially understood? The many folkloristic versions of it did not help to grasp the core of it. And yet, it is a very subtle story, with a surprising logic when we make the intellectual effort to move into the mindset of the culture of the time.

For a humanist, regardless of whether he believes in this story, the choice of Adam and Eve to eat from 'the tree of knowledge of good and evil' is a very good choice, even a 'must'. Man must after all, know himself, and not blindly obey and remain dependent. He must be independent, self-conscious, stand up for himself, and on his own feet. The parallel is sometimes drawn with the Greek myth of Prometheus, that 'brave rebel' who blessed humanity with the forbidden fire. According to the Bible, however, eating from this forbidden tree was the most stupid choice ever, which opened the door to all evil in the world. These two visions collide head-on.

> 28. To a humanist, Adam and Eve's choice to eat from the tree of the knowledge of good and evil was a very good choice, even a necessity. People must be independent, self-conscious, and autonomous. But if there were a set of scales which could weigh how immeasurably heavy the cost humanity paid for this choice (all the cruelty, pain, sadness, despair . . .), and how slight the 'advantage,' then this choice of 'man' would clearly be the biggest blunder ever!

The story of the fall is the answer to the question of how a perfectly good God created a perfect world and yet, today there is so much evil. It happened this way for the 'weak spot' in God's creation to be the freedom of man. But God had no alternative, otherwise, man would have been a puppet

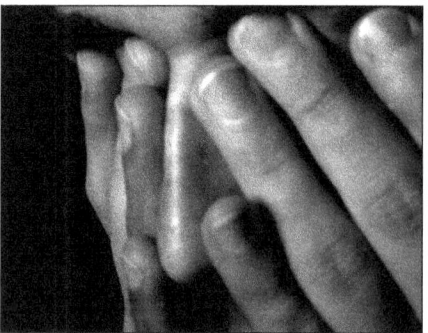

in a doll's house, and this does not look like God. God therefore took the very high risk of giving man freedom, but then love always takes risks. When God forbade Adam to eat of the tree, it was not to keep him small and stupid, but to protect him from an evil he could not (yet) bear. By himself he was too weak to handle that knowledge. The core of the problem was that he wanted to have that knowledge outside of God, independently from God. But if God is life itself, independence is actually tearing away from the Source of Life, and thus taking a step towards death. Adam's choice was stupid and destructive; it had no advantages, only disadvantages. The price for this deceptive independence was an immeasurable amount of pain, despair, misery, and torment poured over humanity and it still is today.

In general, humanism does not have a 'standard' explanation of 'evil', where it comes from and how to solve it. The concept is usually ignored and swept under the carpet. Either it is ranked under the category 'ignorance' or as a natural necessity (survival of the fittest). In both cases, its moral scope is minimized: evil is a kind of 'mistake' or an 'accident'. Humanism has no words to name the truly dark side of humanity; it closes its eyes to it.

According to the Bible, evil is not just a 'mistake', but the heavier sounding word 'sin' is in place here. 'Sin' is again one of those old-fashioned words that was deleted from our vocabulary in the last decades because we do not like it. It is indeed gloomy and loaded with negativity, especially as it communicates debt (and this, we want to avoid at all costs, don't we?). But can you explain the reality of evil without this concept? The Bible believes in absolute evil, in the figure of a 'pitch black' devil. Whoever depicts the devil in the popular manner of a 'rascal' has not understood anything. Lucifer revolting against God was really insane, irrational, the epitome of foolishness, the result of pure blindness. There is no moral or rational 'glossing over' whatsoever. Therefore, sin is never innocent; sin is not 'sweet' or 'nicely exciting'. Ask a girl who was raped. Sin is when a person lives below his level, sets his goals too low and wastes his possibilities. Sin always leads to lesser life. It focuses our eyes on something that resembles the real thing, but that is lower and especially cheaper, with inferior ingredients. It is almost always 'instant' or 'short-term thinking': the quick enjoyment, gaining money without too much effort. With sin, the focus often shifts subtly and unnoticed to 'self': it begins with (misplaced) self-love, but after a while turns into self-contempt and self-hatred. When God has been removed from the center, everything gets out of balance, and all relationships get out of tune. Man gets into a tangle with himself, with his fellow human beings, and with nature. That is why the Bible says as radically as possible, 'You must hate evil' (Psalm 97:10, Amos 5:11)! The only correct attitude is to loath it with all your heart, with every fiber of your body. Sin, moreover, costs society vast amounts of money, tens of billions: the fight against crime, the army and defense, police surveillance and security, justice and prisons ... A sinless country would be endlessly prosperous. The price we all pay for being-our-own-boss is completely out of proportion!

Humanists (and liberal Christians) deny the existence of the demonic or make it into something 'figurative'. This is a risky strategy, like ostrich politics: "As long as we ignore it, it is not there, or it doesn't bother us." In the name of 'the goodness of man', all the facts that contradict this are ignored. But in every war underestimating or not seeing the enemy is a life-threatening mistake. Humanism has no explanation for the blind rage that blows at times across whole nations and continents, such as unreasonable nationalism (which gave rise to the horror of WWI and fascism). And if it does not see it, it certainly has no cure for it! Finally, humanism believes in the goodness of man, but has no reasonable ground whatsoever to believe or hope that goodness will be victorious. It can just as well go the other way with man!

---

29. Humanism is dangerously naive. Being optimistic about humanity means consciously and systematically closing one's eyes to countless terrible realities. A General who, out of naivety, underestimates the enemy, will send many of his people to their death. Anyone making such an unforgivable mistake would be summarily dismissed and condemned by history. Anyone who assumes the goodness of man (as a dogma, an axiom) denies the reality of the demonic (for example spiritual blinding, addictions, irrational nationalism, and racism, blind rage . . .) and so gives it free rein.

2.4.5 Man: naked monkey or 'god'?

When humanism puts man at the center of the universe and makes him the highest principle and measure of all things, it gives man the status of a 'god'. He is characterized as autonomous, sovereign, free, and rational. He is the creator of values and norms, of meaning and purpose. This actually sounds very dogmatic and bloated because (believing in) the goodness of man cannot be empirically or scientifically proven. But also, if humanism wants to be purely rational and based on (materialistic) science, then man is just a monkey fallen out of the trees! So, what's up with 'man' then? Humanism swivels back and forth between these two but cannot connect them.

At the same time, the Christian view is more elevated and realistic. The origin of man is divine and so is his ultimate destiny. Yet, the Bible also emphasizes human sin and man's depravity and lostness. We can safely say that humanity is morally bankrupt; too many facts illustrate this. We still might succeed in giving ourselves a 'morally good feeling' when we compare ourselves to the 'average' human being. However, measured by God's standard of 100%, we fail grossly and systematically. Man is his own biggest enemy and a danger to himself. Too often he is like the alcoholic who denies his addiction and therefore cannot get out of it. To put it simply, man truly needs to be liberated! An outside arm needs to pull him out of his own swamp. Christians are not doomsday-thinkers or pessimists, they are just realists. They do not like gloomy self-condemnation and guilt feelings, but they love honesty and truth. In essence, man must stand naked before God in order to see himself in an honest mirror; there is no other way to an objective self-evaluation. Admitting to our failure is that indispensable point of honesty, as well as the first step towards liberation. Admitting our weakness is not being weak but being strong; it was a brave step for the prodigal son to return to his father. And it restored him from feeding pigs to a true son, with all the corresponding privileges as well as a big party. God's restoration of man is much more wonderful than he could ever dare to hope! The Christian view of man puts the finger on the painful wound, but with the intention of curing it. This is much more realistic as well as hopeful.

2.5 Materialism versus idealism[9]

In the context of the discussion about images of man, it is important to ask the following question. Which of these two worlds is most real, the world of ideas, or the world of matter? Which one determines and dominates the other? The Christian view is almost certainly to be found in the camp of idealism: the material world originates in God. Naturally, atheism and humanism are at the other, materialistic side of the spectrum. In general, they deny the existence of a real other-worldly dimension up there with God, spiritual beings or angels.

This however, greatly influences someone's image of man and the world. How does Christianity see this supernatural, spiritual world, and how does it avoid escapism and sobriety? And how does materialism

---

9. In this more philosophical chapter I only briefly mention these points, and will elaborate them gradually in a subsequent book.

explain non-material things? Does humanism escape the banality of a materialistic view of life?

2.5.1 What is the 'spirit' and spiritual poverty?

The traditional Christian concept of man defines him as having three parts, 'layers' or areas: body, soul, and mind. This can seem somewhat simplistic, 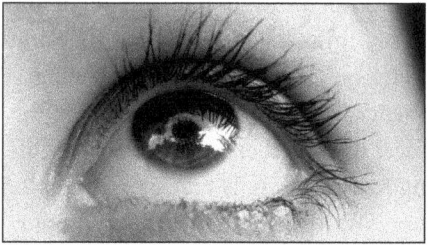 and yet it has an important core of truth. The first area, the body, is of course easiest to designate; it is visible and can be located. Nobody has trouble acknowledging that this is a 'hard reality'. The other two, however, are not as tangible or measurable, and much 'vaguer'. The soul can be best represented as the whole world of the personality, our psyche: our character, talents, intelligence, the will, the emotions and romantic love, passions and ambitions . . . When, however, we try to describe the spirit and its specific domain, it becomes even more subtle. Our spirit is, by definition, volatile just like air or wind. The Hebrew word *ruah* and the Greek *pneuma* have these three meanings: spirit, wind, and breath. Adam came to life when God blew His 'breath of life' in his nose (Gen. 2: 7). The spirit can be regarded as an awareness of transcendence: 'There must be more'. You can compare it with an antenna: the ability to capture signals from God. Or like a sensor in a camera, it is a kind of sensitivity. The spirit in man seems to have the least 'weight', yet it is the most essential, the most determining. It does not matter what you *have* or what you *do*, but it is about who you *are* when all that is secondary falls away. This is where it is decided what kind of person you are, your deepest life choices and attitudes. And when the spirit is healthy and functions well, the soul and the body will also benefit from it.

Each person potentially has a spirit. Otherwise he could never have an awareness of God. But whoever only lives for this material here-and-now world is, according to Jesus, spiritually dead (Matt 8:22). He is stuck in the bottom layer of 'life'. And whoever is dead does not realize he is dead, just like anyone who sleeps, does not realize he is sleeping. This spirit-asleep state must at some time get 'activated'. Therefore, a human being must be born again (John 3: 1–8); first, a seed of the Spirit of God must 'fertilize' our human spirit (as a sperm fuses with an ovum). It is something deeply tragic when the most important dimension of a person never comes to fruition.

In the practice of human life, the spirit is severely and systematically malnourished; it is not taken care of or cherished. Most people hardly spend 1% of their time and attention on it. By the 'law of spiritual gravity' our attention is automatically pulled down, drawn to our body. But if our spirit, just like a muscle, is never used and trained, it gets weaker and thinner until it dies. Many modern people suffer from spiritual anorexia. Physical poverty is a known phenomenon, emotional poverty too, but spiritual poverty is even worse than these. Some very 'successful' people even commit suicide. Nothing is as distressing for a human being than the feeling of no purpose, of living in total futility. When the spirit is not fed, the soul will also pine away. You can also compare it to spiritual illiteracy. For many secularly educated people, the term 'God' has no more content than 'Santa' or a 'Martian'. In a spiritual conversation, most people just feel like 'a bull in a china shop'. Their cognitive intelligence is perhaps more than enough, as well as their emotional intelligence, but who deliberately develops their spiritual intelligence?

It is crucial whether you see man as a one, two, or three-dimensional being. It impacts strongly the perspective from which you approach yourself and your fellow human beings, but also hundreds of daily choices. Materialism denies or minimizes the spiritual dimension but gets into much conceptual trouble and has no longer any words to name the most essential aspirations of man. Furthermore, when the spiritual aspect is silenced to death, the spirit also dies off.

2.5.2 Philosophical materialism and 'flat' materialism

Philosophical materialism is a reaction to (exaggerated) philosophical idealism. It comes from sober, 'down to earth' thinkers, mostly people who highly esteem the sciences and thus prefer to deal with the perceptible and tangible rather than 'vague', invisible realities. There are roughly two variations: (1) The spiritual is considered subordinate to the material, or as secondary, but is not denied (e.g. Karl Marx). (2) The spiritual is negated: only the bare materialistic

exists, the atoms and molecules, and the rest is nonsense, figments. However, when thinking consistently through this, philosophical materialism is, in both versions, contradictory in itself. As this theory itself is non-material, it has therefore no reality value whatsoever. Materialism, in fact, is based on a methodological error. When a scientist would aim his microscope at the starry sky, concluding, 'I do not see any stars, so stars do not exist', he makes a conceptual mistake. Tools that work perfectly for one domain of knowledge are useless for another. One jumps here from one level to another: out of a scientific observation, a philosophical, spiritual conclusion is drawn.

> 30. Whoever proclaims science and reason to be the only valid approaches to knowledge will naturally arrive at a materialistic worldview and a denial of the existence of a spiritual, higher, invisible world. However, this is a conceptual mistake; if you look through a microscope, you will never see stars or the 'bigger picture'. The type of glasses you wear determine what you do and do not see.

However, a materialistic worldview has a major impact on someone's concept of man! It reduces human beings to the level of animals, as well as plants and stones, even to a 'temporary and somewhat denser mist of atoms and molecules'. All the ideas and theories in man's mind, all the so-called free decisions and moral choices, become just products of chemical processes or electrical signals in his brain. Gone is all his freedom, autonomy, self-determination, rationality, and morality! This approach is as hard as concrete and as cold as iron. It does not inspire us to make the world a better and warmer place. It is each for themselves, the brutal battle for bare survival, to eat or to be eaten. There is no meaning, purpose or destination, nothing higher. Everything comes from nothing and will return to nothing. The ultimate consequence of this is that whoever personally views man

> 31. Humanism almost automatically results in a materialistic approach to life because all happiness needs to be realized during this earthly life and a spiritual dimension is not acknowledged. So, humanism has no 'sensor' to see the limitations and the dangers of materialism, nor can it define it as 'sin' and certainly does not have 'antibodies' for it. Materialism leads to an impoverishment of every aspect of humanity: love is reduced to chemical reactions in the brain, friendship and idealism to calculated survival strategy, well-being to welfare and happiness to pleasure.

in a purely materialistic way, will eventually treat him as such as well. Stalin treated millions of his people as 'negligible quantity'.

Also, philosophical materialism almost in itself leads to 'flat materialism', a lifestyle whereby someone lives purely for the material: eating, drinking, sleeping, money, sex, pleasure, possessions... It is the worldview of a person who has concluded that the best thing one can do is enjoy the here-and-now, the 'carpe diem' of epicurism. 'We are sure of this life, not of what follows'. Or even flatter, 'My wallet is my god'. The problem with flat materialism is that it (1) aims at the short term and not the long term, (2) focuses on the most primary needs of a human being and not on his soul or mind, and (3) is automatically very self-centered because own needs take precedence over those of others. Happiness gets reduced to pleasure, love to sex, well-being to welfare... Humanism, of course, does not propagate flat materialism, but (1) opens the door wide to it, (2) has no argument to stop people who choose this 'downward road' and (3) has no 'antidote' to cure them from it. Although it may call people to idealism and altruism, there is no power or credibility behind this.

2.5.3 The spiritual world: castle in the air or 'the' reality?

One of the most critical questions in this discussion is whether there actually exists a spiritual world. Is this a fairy tale or is the spirit world real, and the original reality? Let us first clarify that science by definition cannot help us in this choice for or against because it is limited to observable realities. When atheism claims to have science on her side, then this is actually intellectually dishonest. Everyone would agree that it is not easy to know this spiritual world. However, to then conclude because of the challenge that it does not exist is another conceptual error. Is this difficulty due to the spiritual world or to us? Is that world blurry, or are our glasses blurred?

> 32. The denial of the existence of a higher spiritual world conceals a widespread error of thought. It is true that nothing can be 'proven' in that realm and that there are hundreds of conflicting opinions. However, because of the difficulty in getting to know this dimension, many then conclude that 'therefore,' it does not exist. It is precisely this difficulty which truly reveals our human incompetence in this field, our insensitivity to such subtle matter. The problem is not with that spiritual world, but with our dirty glasses or the calluses on our soul.

Whoever really wants to get to know the invisible spiritual world must adapt to its laws (just as science has to do this with every area of knowledge). You cannot study God as you study a frog. God is not an 'object', but the Subject of subjects, the One from whom we derive our 'person-hood'. He is not even subject to physical laws (such as gravity), or bound to space and time or to three dimensions. You cannot approach Him as a neutral, objective researcher, because knowing Him has everything to do with yourself. According to how someone positions themselves towards God, he or she will get to know Him or not; our openness or closed-ness, softness or hardness, love or selfishness, holiness or sinfulness are decisive.

Whether someone can believe in a real spiritual dimension has to do with whether he has an adequate picture in his mind, free from toddler-like or mythical images. Here then we have the problem that the human language is far too limited to describe these realities (read, for example, the visions of the apostle John in the book of Revelation with, for example, the streets of translucent gold . . .). Still, a multitude of images and comparisons can help arrive at a true and mature image of the 'above'. When Jesus speaks of the kingdom of God or heaven, He makes it clear that you cannot locate this  geographically (Luke 17: 20–21). It is not defined by a location but by the presence of God Himself. The kingdom is where the King is, not vice versa. It is His 'light circle', His sphere of influence, His radiance. Therefore, you must imagine heaven as 'the fourth dimension' which is everywhere 'within reach'. It does not take up any space, just like 1000GB of digital data does not make a USB stick heavier. In order to get a very small idea of God's greatness, we can study the immense size of the universe, the gigantic energies in the stars, and then realize, God created this whole physical world with one word (Psalm 33: 6, Hebrews 11: 3)! When even the smallest creatures in heaven, the angels, appear to a human, he is filled with fear and trembling. Angels are not chubby and rosy babies as depicted by Rubens, but their voice sounds like a trumpet or a mighty waterfall. In this heavenly world, colors must surely be more intense than on the earth, shapes sharper, smells blissful, and sounds perfectly harmonious. It is vibrant with energy and beauty, with purity and unity, with life and ultimate ecstasy. A human being almost dies under such intensity; it is greater than the biggest 'kick' on earth. For a believer, God is the focal point of everything, where all lines converge, the 'logical' endpoint of truth and goodness, the ultimate meaning of all meanings and the purpose of all purposes. Only God can view the world from an Archimedean viewpoint and has the only objective perspective.

In short, if we want to get an adequate grasp of the spiritual world, then this must be much more real than the earthly world. Compared to that world, the present one is only a shadow, an appearance, a lean decoction, a bad copy, like a ruin in the face of a magnificent cathedral. However, these eternal powers are already at work on earth for those who learn to walk according to its laws. "For truly I say to you, if you have faith as a grain of mustard, you will say to this mountain, 'Move from here to there,' and it will move. And nothing will be impossible for you." (Matt 17:20). Jesus is talking about forces here that even the best Christians could hardly imagine.

Humanism ignores or minimizes the higher dimension, but if you 'cut it out', nothing really works anymore. It is like playing football without a goal; why would you still devote yourself to something anyway? It is like a hot air balloon where the air has leaked out; what remains is an empty bag. What is left is skinny and bald and empty; 'It has lost all its spirit. Everything has become extremely pointless, meaningless, and worthless. The spiritual needs of man are as real as his sexual needs; somehow, he always seeks something or someone to adore. His spiritual 'drive' is undeniable and cannot be wiped away, and if this does not focus on God, he will take anything in his surroundings to idolize.

2.6 Science, philosophy, and reason[10]

2.6.1 Science versus religion: real or false contradiction?

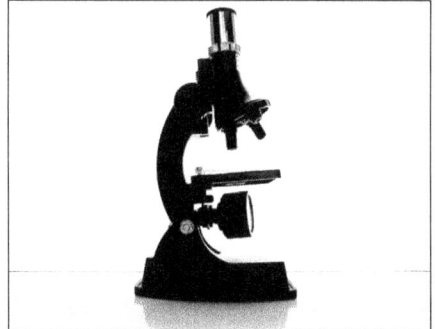

Science and religion are often depicted as enemies or opposites. In the course of history, there has certainly been much of tension between both, even until today. In the Middle Ages, the Church often went outside her boundary and interfered with science, but today

---

10. This chapter is too short and compact to be really good, but will be treated more thoroughly and completely in a next book.

scientists equally cross their boundaries and want to dictate what religion can say, believe or do (think, among other things, of 'reasonable religion'). Yet, this contradiction is fake, and this tension is based on a misconception of science as well as of religion. The Church often made the mistake of interpreting certain (poetic, picturesque) depictions in the Bible too literally as a kind of scientific description. It is not the Bible that clashes with science but a too limited interpretation of it. The Church has indeed regularly counteracted science, but the other side is also true. It is precisely in the Christian world that scientific research got the necessary space to develop in a way that is unseen in other civilizations such as Hinduism or animism.

There is still the misconception with many people that science replaces and decreases God's place, as if a believer only needs God for those things that man cannot scientifically explain (yet!)! Thus, God gets the function of the 'hole filler' of the universe. This too is a childish image; if God is truly God, He cannot be threatened by man, just like the sun cannot be threatened by a space mission coming its way. Yet, this notion still stubbornly remains with many who 'believe in science'. "If only we could better explain the ultimate mechanisms of the universe, or if only we would discover this or that primeval particle . . . we could prove that everything occurred naturally." Here science crosses the borders of faith again!

Actually, you can as well claim that due to scientific discoveries God's place just got bigger. Thanks to, amongst other things, the huge space telescopes, we learn that God's creation is billions of times vaster than we ever knew. Furthermore, because of the discoveries in the micro cosmos, we can now see a second 'infinity' in the other direction. The world of the miniscule (cells, DNA, atoms, and molecules) also turns out to be gigantically more complex, ingenious, and phenomenal than thought. A believing scientist can praise God so much more for His greatness, wisdom, and creativity.

Furthermore, another false contrast is often created between 'the certain and exact knowledge' of science, and the 'vague, irrational beliefs' of religions. However, the philosophy of science gives much nuance to this; science is not at all as clear, rational, certain, 'exactly proven' as is claimed aloud. In science, you find masses of mistakes and blunders, guesswork and exaggerations, unfounded hypotheses, even manipulation and forgery. All types of human mistakes are found here, just as within the Church because everywhere man is the weak link. In every area of science there are 'believers' of a particular theory, and 'non-believers', opposing camps that fight each other fanatically. In the media, whenever someone shouts 'science has

The Humanistic Vision

proven that . . .' this usually needs to be heavily qualified. This expression is very regularly misused—sometimes unconsciously yet sometimes also consciously—and acts as a knockdown argument in a debate.

A third false contradiction is created between scientists and believers. It is sometimes vocally claimed (but more often suggested) that you cannot be a scientist and a believer at the same time. But the facts contradict this; all fathers of science (Newton, Kepler, Bacon . . .) were convinced Christians, and today you find this as well amongst top scientists and Nobel laureates. You could equally ask the question, "How can you be a scientist and believe in love?" Or, "How can you be a scientist and believe in the goodness of man?"

When people say, 'I do not believe in God, I believe in science', they are making the same mistake of mixing soul and spirit levels. It is impossible to make science compete with religion because (1) they are on different levels (physical vs. spiritual), (2) they have a totally different focus (material life improvement vs. giving meaning and salvation), and (3) they have a different method; the method or way of knowing on the spiritual level is not superior or inferior. They are just different and adapted to the 'study object'. The claim of transposing 'my method as the only right one' on other areas distorts the whole discussion. The statement 'God created the world' is of a completely different nature than a scientific explanation; they do not compete.

> 33. Humanism creates a false opposition between faith and science. 'Faith' is presented as something totally irrational ('to believe in something which science will never be able to prove'), although it stands perfectly as an extension of knowledge and science. Faith is not something bizarre or difficult, but something quite natural. We exhibit it continually in our daily lives (as well as in science!) as we 'trust' an authority or an expert, and this is generally a very 'reasonable' thing to do.

When we look at the relationship between faith and science from below, we see contradiction. However, when viewing them from above, we see harmonious transition. From God's point of view, they can never conflict with each other because only one truth can exist, and with Him, all partial truths come together and complement each

> "Newton discovered a law of nature. However, he did not at all conclude, 'Now I do not need God anymore', on the contrary, a law presupposes a Lawgiver!"
> —Prof. Dr. John Lennox

2.6.2 Scientism: must science save the world?

Scientism is a philosophical viewpoint dating from the Enlightenment, namely that science will solve all problems, including the social, political, philosophical, and spiritual . . . Let us clarify that this is certainly not a scientific statement: scientism is a belief, an ideology. The slogan *scientia vincere tenebras*[11] ('overcoming darkness by science') shows the same semi-religious connotation. It is a paraphrase of Jesus' claim to be 'the light of the world' (John 8:12) that drives out the spiritual darkness of sin and evil. Science is being 'remodeled' from a useful instrument for material progress into an ideological battle weapon. This battle was first against all superstition, but then expanded against every belief and religion.

> 34. The slogan 'We believe in science' is one of many examples of semantic confusion in this debate. Christians believe in science as well and thank God for it. The difference however is that humanism expects science to deliver answers of an ideological nature (an all-encompassing explanation, including salvation and redemption), and so, it uses science to promote its concept of a god-less society. In this way, science becomes a tool, similar to a ventriloquist's dummy.

When people say, 'I believe in science', we must ask the same critical questions about what they mean, just as with 'I believe in man'! Does science have a status of divine infallibility? Humanism strongly opposes a privileged position of Church or religion, but in fact gives this to science. As if the latter offers an 'objective viewpoint' and is an irreversible authority. Science, however, is a neutral tool such as a knife or a computer, and these can be used for good and for bad. Science has certainly brought some 'light' (insight and progress), but on the other hand has also brought new darkness's: addiction to technology, pollution of nature in every area, deregulation of the climate, a gigantic war industry . . . to the point that the very survival of our planet is threatened! A semi-religious exaltation of science is naive and dangerous.

---

11. This is the slogan of the 'Vrije Universiteit Brussel' ('Free University of Brussels') which is founded by freemasonry as a free thinkers university.

The Enlightenment reproached the Church for being too controlling and dominant, but ... in the vision of scientism, science will control everything, the whole of society on every level. In science fiction films, we sometimes already see portrayals of such total control. Religion in the hands of tyrants is life-threatening, but science is even more so. 'Restrict yourself to your own business' is applicable to science. Science is great as an instrument for technological progress and improvement of material living conditions, but not as a foundation for an all-encompassing spiritual explanation to life. Just as glue is very helpful to paste together two objects but is not for repairing a broken marriage relationship. When science has the pretension to explain the origin and purpose of everything, it makes itself ridiculous. Rigid scientism leads to bad science and a poor life philosophy.

> 35. Science is great as a foundation for technological progress, but not as a foundation for philosophy and spirituality, just like glue is very good for sticking two objects together, but not for mending a broken marriage. This is of a totally different order. But since the time of Descartes, the confusion between these two differing levels has been an immovable notion in the western spirit of this age.

2.6.3 Miracles vs laws of nature

With the rise of Enlightenment, the sciences and the search for a reasonable religion, faith in miracles became more and more problematic. Deism taught that miracles were not only impossible, but even undesirable. They are impossible because natural laws are universal and cannot allow exceptions, undesirable because God would be inconsistent and violate His own laws. Numerous attempts were made so that Biblical miracles were either spiritualized ("they are not meant to be taken literally but only as a spiritual lesson") or explained causatively and naturally. But these explanations were usually very much forced, were not very convincing, and created other—maybe even bigger—explanation problems.

> 36. Many humanists think that miracles are contrary to the laws of nature, but for a believer of course that cannot be true. Faith does not go against the laws of nature, but relies on higher (spiritual) laws, just like a rocket can escape the force of gravity and take off by a stronger force.

The big question is, are miracles truly contrary to the laws of nature? Some miracles, for example, are in line with nature; a miraculous healing is often a kind of 'accelerated recovery process'. In other cases, it is as if a law of nature is 'overruled' by higher laws, spiritual laws that are stronger than gravity. When Jesus walked on water for example, He seemed to, without effort, be standing 'above' it in a relaxed way. For those who 'can get hold' of even a small fraction of God's creative power and are familiar with the higher laws of the spiritual world, this is child's play. According to Jesus, the law of faith makes everything possible, even moving mountains!

And why would miracles be undesirable? Most miracles are for salvation, healing, deliverance, help, power, undeserved grace . . . For the one who receives this, it is, on the contrary, absolutely not unwanted. Only for the theoretician who watches from a distance and rigidly sticks to a deterministic and closed worldview, is it perhaps unwanted. Also, in this world a king can grant amnesty to a criminal; he sets the law and justice aside and gives grace. Why then should not God?

When we talk about miracles, we also need to mention that, for a believer the whole of nature is wonderful and full of miracles. Each baby that grows from one cell in the mother's womb and at birth emerges as a 'perfectly finished product'. . . every insect that is an incredible example of top technology . . . they can and must continue to amaze us because there is so much we cannot understand! But above all, God lives in the world of the miraculous. He Himself is the One of all wonder. If God is God, He is absolutely free, and He is under no law that would restrict Him—unless He chooses for it Himself. God can, from the 'fourth dimension' intervene in the laws without breaking them and without anyone seeing it. He can 'influence' a human being without forcing his free will.

In some church movements, there are many beliefs regarding the miraculous that are naive and even unhealthy, and that would not endure a critical testing. On the other hand, countless inexplicable healings occur today in our world that have been verified by doctors, and that puzzle science. Stubbornly not wanting to believe in miracles can also be a prejudice, the result of a particular paradigm. Wanting to per se reason away the biblical miracles is the result of wanting to force an external worldview, or a rationalistic framework on these stories. But perhaps this framework must be critically questioned! Are the stories 'inappropriate' to our 'enlightened thinking', or is this rationalistic paradigm 'unsuitable' for these stories? Or, is this paradigm simply unsuitable (see 2.6.5)?

2.6.4 Should philosophy save the world?

When it comes to spiritual questions, the search for meaning or 'higher' goals, the humanist does not turn to religion, but to philosophy. This is namely the world of ideas, logic and reason, reflection on all the big questions of life, which is strictly rational and secular. A non-religious person will live out all his desire for meaning and purpose here. Just like science, philosophy has also known tension with the Church. In the Middle Ages theology was at the top as the highest science, and philosophy only gained a place as 'handmaiden of theology'. But philosophy also emancipated itself and became free and autonomous. As a result, a large part of philosophy got stuck in this anti-attitude. Therefore, it wants to keep as much distance from religion as possible and is in fact very secular and often hostile to religion,  or at least very skeptical. In the meanwhile, however, philosophy has committed all the mistakes it accused theology of: appointing oneself as the sole referee, as highest science, as well as subordinating and despising the other. They could be best neighbors, but now there is a concrete wall with barbed wire; an anti-religious or at least a supercritical attitude is very common in philosophy.

But if secular philosophy wants to take over the role of former religion (namely seeking ultimate answers), it seeks to deal with matters for which it is incompetent. If it claims to work only with reason, indeed it cannot judge supernatural or spiritual matters. This is because of the limitation philosophy imposes on itself! The philosopher can, as a matter of principle, not answer the truth question, otherwise he is no longer a philosopher, but gives himself the aureole of a prophet. He can think of a thousand answers, but no theory can stand above another. Philosophy is brilliant in asking critical questions, but absolutely poor in giving answers. And in reality, it is much less rational than it would desire; every philosopher has his pre-philosophical, pre-rational assumptions he brings from his education or culture.

Nevertheless, philosophy has something very beautiful; how can 'love of wisdom' be in competition with God or Church? 'Wisdom' is a very important theme in the Bible and is highly honored; several of its books are categorized as 'wisdom literature'. However, this is about a much 'wider' wisdom that is not separate from life. Whether someone is truly wise is seen by his walk of life, not by webs of clever thoughts. It is not about an intellectual power display but about the art of living. In comparison, philosophy uses a very narrow, one-sided notion of wisdom. When philosophers create a god image, Blaise Pascal calls that 'le dieu des philosophes'. This is a very rational, abstract, and emotionless image, but, he says it has become a god after their image and likeness!

Approaching philosophy as an alternative to religion is unfair to it. It is of a totally different order. You would do injustice to Socrates by placing him next to Jesus because Socrates never claimed he came from God to give his life to save humanity; Jesus, however, did. And if we soberly look at the facts, we must note that philosophy has never saved the world; it cannot even 'save itself'! No philosopher has had 2.2 billion followers.

Philosophy seeks wisdom, but who introduced the rule that it can only use reason in this search at the exclusion of other cognitive powers (heart, intuition, spiritual sensitivity)? At the very least, this (people made) rule can be critically questioned! Precisely this limitation to the 'rational-only' has often made philosophy so dry, alienated from life, incompatible with common sense, and non-inspirational. In its worst form, it is a favorite hobby of an intellectually elite few who feed their snobbism with it.

The Christian viewpoint says philosophy is beautiful, useful, and meaningful if it remains within its domain. But if it allows its ambition to get inflated (semi-religious) and its 'instrument' to shrink (narrow rationalistic), it can never do what it promises or find what it seeks. It is irresponsible to seek wisdom merely with reason! This can only lead to bad

---

37. In the late Middle Ages, philosophy emancipated itself from its 'supporting role' as the handmaiden of theology—understandably and to some extent rightly so—but now it behaves as the boss who despises or ignores theology and faith. This can be understandable as a temporary backlash to restore balance, but those who are still stuck in this view after five hundred years have a problem. Most of the history of Western philosophy is permeated with this false contrast between wisdom and religion, while in the Bible (e.g. in Proverbs and Ecclesiastes) 'love for wisdom' is in fact highly praised.

philosophy, without wisdom! And if it wants to play the role of a religion, philosophy is stuck in an eternal existential crisis with itself.

2.6.5 Rational, rationalistic, reasonable or wise?

The highest, ultimate and only valid way to knowledge for humanism is rationality. This is also very logical because when man is placed at the center of everything, he only has his own reason as a guideline to evaluate everything. Enlightenment believed—in a very naive way—that reason would bring 'light' in all areas in the way of progress and freedom, humaneness and peace.

Today, several centuries further on, we see that rationality has as many downsides as benefits. We must continue to acknowledge that 'common sense', logical thinking and critical thinking can help in settling much irrationality and unnecessary misery in this world, even in the field of religion. But rationality is not the answer to all our problems; on the contrary, it can even make them worse. In fact, our highly esteemed rationality has been debunked as an illusion by many philosophers and thinkers these last centuries, or at least highly relativized. Reason does not even succeed in unequivocally defining 'rationality', and if it could, it would play its own referee. Whoever sets 'reason' as the first and highest principle ('-ism') makes one (partial) aspect into an absolute, and creates much one-sidedness, many misunderstandings and conflict. The big questions are (1) how narrowly or broadly do we define 'rationality', and (2) which place does reason get in which areas? In practice, each thinker still uses his own criteria, and the more rigorously and strictly he does this (the smaller 'the holes in the sieve'), the less certainty remains. This already applies to science and philosophy, but even more so for a life view.

> 38. Humanism appeals to rationality, but often fails to recognize the difference between 'sensible' and 'rational'. Rationalism and intellectualism are inherently unbalanced and can be very unhealthy and narrow-minded. They are crippling to creativity and human relationships, harsh, cold and deadly, blinded and arrogant, driven by (subconscious, irrational) fear, self-protection or the need to control. 'Reason' is like a whore (according to Luther): she lets herself be used by anyone who wants her.

Consistent rationalism is unthinkable, unlivable, and undesirable. It is physically and materially impossible for a human being to exclusively address all areas of his life in a rational manner. Reason is also certainly not that infallible guide it claims to be. We daily make wrong calculations and reasoning errors, as well as false conclusions. Our arguments are constantly intertwined with emotions and unconscious motives, and contaminated by our own self-interests. It should scare us how easily man (or humanity) can be misled, even misleading himself. At one time, Luther called reason a whore: giving herself to anyone who will pay. She sells arguments to the highest bidder, both left and right. "Tell me what you want to prove, and I will fix the evidence."

Rationalism disregards a great deal of the reality. Reason is efficient for a small part of reality, maybe 10-15%, but it goes seriously wrong whenever its methods are applied to other areas. The rational is usually only the proverbial tip of the iceberg. The whole world of emotions and subconscious thoughts is 'stronger than our self', and when our intellect fights non-rational forces, it usually loses! We so easily believe what we want to believe and are barely able to investigate our deepest beliefs in life. Also, in real life almost nothing works in a rational way; just consider for example society and politics. Or regarding relationships, approaching them in a purely rationalistic manner would be like a bull in a china shop. For example, someone getting married for purely rational reasons would completely miss the point. Reason turns out to be a good adviser, but not a decision maker.

Imagine if it were possible to build an exclusively rational world; what would this look like? Rationalism leads to an artificial, unnatural world, straight, tight, geometric, functional, bare, uniform, impersonal, cold, not cozy. Is this what we really want? In a rational and efficient administration, everyone becomes a number. There is a general discomfort with our self-made, cool society! Rationalism destroys so much more than we think! Life is split, dissected, stifled. The Bible, on the other hand, places love far above knowledge. Knowledge analyzes, decomposes, and kills, but love builds up, believes, and creates life (1 Corinthians 8:1–2).

Humanists and atheists repeatedly emphasize the opposition between reason and faith and drive them apart. This happens, however, because they use an extremely narrow definition of reason and an ultra-narrow image of faith. They like to portray religion only at its worst, as if faith is just a stupid submission to irrational dogmas, a slavish nodding out of fear of damnation and an oppressive clergy. The widely distributed poster of the 'Humanistisch Verbond' (Humanistic Alliance) with the famous statement of Henri Poincaré exemplifies this: "Thinking should never submit, neither to a dogma, nor to a party, nor to a passion, nor to an interest, nor to a preconceived idea, nor to whatever it may be, only to the facts themselves, because for thought, submission would mean ceasing to be." Poincaré shows in this statement that he had a very superficial  and confused notion of faith and religion, as if it is impossible for faith to be an inner, free, conscious conviction. Poincaré's statement is itself very dogmatic, absolute, black and white, unqualified, and is proclaimed in a 'prophetic' rather than a rational way. If you require strict rationality in the field of religions, you can analyze everything to pieces, but you can do that as well with humanism!

For a believer, there can be principally no conflict between reason and faith because all intelligence, knowledge, and science is in God and originates from Him. God who created man with great intelligence, wants us to use it fully, just like all our talents. An inflated reason, however, is a badly functioning reason, just like a 'swollen' puzzle piece no longer fits in with the other puzzle pieces. Thus, reason becomes very unreasonable, and 'rational' becomes very different than 'wise'. It is not the intellect that is in the way of faith, but conceptual categories that are too limited, boxes that are too narrow-minded.

2.6.6 A higher rationality

Religion is certainly not rational in the narrow sense of the word, but that religion is irrational or anti-rational is not true either. Certain requirements of rationality, such as inner consistency, moral consistency, consistency with scientific and historical facts, also apply to the area of worldviews and religion. Manifest and flagrant contradictions with the facts are unacceptable for a religion that also acknowledges the mind as 'created by God'. God is absolutely not irrational—as atheists usually imagine—if so, why would He have given us reason, and made the laws of nature rational? Opponents of religion often equate 'non-rational' to 'foolish and stupid' or 'proven incorrect', yet it is not that difficult to recognize that a different kind of rationality applies to the area of religion and worldview than to the field of mathematics and theoretical physics. We enter here into the domain of spiritual beings (also man by the way!), where each person has a unique individual identity and a free will. Whoever cannot appreciate the finesse of the spiritual world had better declare themselves 'unauthorized' and stay away from this area.

In every religion, there are a number of things that are non-rational, that may seem irrational and clash with human logic. This is also a serious struggle for a believer, but in the end, he will say, 'These things have a higher reason'! In order to capture this 'higher logic', man must be able to view things from a higher perspective. God's thoughts are, according to Isaiah 55:8–9, so much higher than our human thoughts, as high as heaven is above the earth. A good example of this is the story where God asked Abraham to sacrifice his son (Genesis 22). 'Seen from below', this was completely illogical, even contradictory and cruel. But from God's perspective, there was a perfect logic; it was the ultimate way to test Abraham's faith, his 'doctoral degree' in faith, so to speak. God did not want to test his intelligence but his willingness, his dedication, and love. Many apparent 'irrationalities' fall under the category of 'God's Higher Education'.

Inherent to the spiritual world is the idea that religious belief is not rationally provable ('no compelling evidence'), otherwise, people would not have the freedom not to believe something. In the area of spirituality, there must be maximum free will; the choice for or against does not then reveal our level of intelligence, but what kind of person we are.

Western 'Greek' thinking assumes that real truth must be abstract, impersonal, general, the same for everyone. But this clashes with the very nature of a spiritual world. The starting point of the biblical worldview (or, Hebrew thought) is thus an intelligent and loving Person who created the world; personality, therefore, is at the core of all reality. Identity, uniqueness, free will and morality, relationship and love are much more fundamental core categories than the mathematical-logical ones. First there was a person, then mathematics and logic. This is the philosophical view behind the words of Jesus, "I am the way, the truth, and the life." (John 14:6), and the movement of personalism.

A rationalist actually thinks he can draft the rules that should apply to God, but what authority do they have? Whoever argues that 'only reason' can define here, actually says, "Only I am the boss and determine the laws here." Between the lines, he also suggests he alone has the right criterion to judge everything correctly. The very first preaching of Jesus, the first word He spoke in the gospels, was: "Repent . . ." The Greek word here (*metanoia*) indicates 'change of mindset'! In fact, Jesus says to every human being, "Your mindset must be changed, your paradigm renewed, you should not look through the glasses of your own psyche but see the bigger picture!"[12]

Humanism presents religion as lower-than-rational, while Christians see it as higher-than-rational. A human being naturally thinks too much of himself, with himself central to his own world, and that is precisely the reason why we constantly clash with each other as 'loose planets'. To impose the requirement of rationality on religion is itself highly irrational and very selective! The fact that religion precisely transcends our (limited) reasoning is exactly its liberating power, its reason for existence.

2.6.7 What is 'believing' then?

'Faith' is often depicted by humanists in the most negative way, as something completely foolish, irrational, and blind, 'evidently incorrect'. For them, faith seems to be something very weak and childish, a flight in a dream world, a kind of self-deception.

However, we must stretch the notion of 'believing' to a much broader understanding if we want to transcend the level of caricatures. It is namely something we all do continually every day. We believe the weather forecast, the news on TV, we trust our chair will not fall through, that the baker's bread is not poisoned . . . A certain amount of faith is needed every time we are not 100% sure about something, which is the case in 99.9% of life's situations. There are thus hundreds of forms of secular faith: a politician believes in his ideal, a businessman in his product, an investor in the stock market, a general in his strategy . . . In the area of interpersonal relationships (friendship and marriage), 'trust' is everything, a 100% guarantee does not exist. This also applies to science, though to a lesser extent, yet still much more than is generally admitted. A scientist trusts the textbooks, the leading experts, his instruments, the consensus, and the paradigms . . . There are countless things he believes on the authority of others. Creating a

---

12. Beware: I do not want to suggest here that a 'conversion' as the Bible sees it is just a new intellectual 'insight'. It is about a much deeper turnaround in the heart of a person, a choice of will that changes his whole life attitude and behavior deeply.

false opposition between belief and knowledge is thus meaningless; they go in the same direction. There is nothing wrong with trusting an expert more than ourselves for some things, on the contrary, it is reasonable, and we do it constantly, especially in our daily lives, but also in science.

Faith is far more than an (alternative) method of knowledge, a theoretical assumption. There is a huge difference between 'believing that God exists' and believing that the galaxy GN-z11 exists (which I cannot see with my eyes either). The second has no consequence for my life; the first makes all the difference in every area of life. If God exists, He has an impact on all my goals in life, large and small, my standards and values, my thinking and feeling, ambitions and plans. The dimension of 'trust' enters here because God is a person. Belief has a cognitive and a relational aspect. But how then does 'trust' function? Totally irrational? Not at all! Faith is never just 'a jump in the dark' or 'a cat in a bag'. Even though there are no compelling rational arguments, there are enough (rational or other) arguments that

make this choice 'responsible'. We only trust people we have first gotten to know more or less thoroughly. This is not rational, but certainly not irrational either in the sense of 'foolishness'. Presenting 'faith' as if it means that (totally illogical) revelational truths have to be blindly accepted and swallowed is a heavy distortion of what happens in reality. Actually, someone can only be convinced of God's existence (or His goodness) when the person recognizes this in his own experience, life, and surroundings. Someone who passes from unbelief to faith is more likely to say "At last, I have seen the light. Now I see things in a correct perspective, and the existence of God becomes the most 'logical' that there may be."

Knowledge is limited to visible and measurable facts; faith however has to do with a spiritual world that is fundamentally invisible and immeasurable. If we cannot rely on our own senses or understanding, we can only rely on someone who in our view is an expert. We can compare it with a pilot who must fly in the fog; he cannot trust in his own senses, only on 'external sources'; his tools and the air traffic controller! Certainly, it will sometimes be terrifying for him to not be in control, but it is all he can do!

The Humanistic Vision

If he says to the air traffic controller, 'I do not trust you', he is a big idiot and, because of his stubbornness, endangers the life of all passengers.

'Believing in Jesus' is in line with this, and thus for a Christian, very 'reasonable'. Of all spiritual teachers and wise men that walked the earth, Jesus can easily claim to be 'number one', if only because numerically He has the largest number of followers and His book is the best bestseller in the world. He certainly qualifies as 'the reliable guide'; this is not 'foolish' for a believer, on the contrary, it would be crazy to trust oneself more than Him.

One last aspect of 'believing' is that science can describe reality, but faith can change it. Faith is: being visionary, seeing the bigger picture, being able to rise above the naked (often depressing) facts. Only those who can first see how this world could be different (namely from God's perspective), can receive strength from there to bring real change. Belief is not a flight in an imaginary dream world but finding refuge in the real world in order to adapt the fake earthly realities. Faith does not only look at reality differently but transforms it. It does not observe safely from the fence but engages self. Whoever says to a fellow human being, 'I believe in you', gives him wings; belief does something, accomplishes something, brings the best out of someone. Jesus extrapolates this to the infinite. "For those who believe everything is possible", even faith as small as a mustard seed can move mountains (Matt 17:20). Those who want to change deep-rooted degenerate conditions also need supernatural faith to be able to persevere; faith heroes such as Henri Dunant (founder of the Red Cross), Father Damian, Martin Luther King, Mother Teresa, and many others have drawn from divine sources to accomplish what they have done.

> 39. Faith is often presented in a one-sided way as an 'alternative method of knowledge' (e.g. I believe there is a God), but is much more than that: faith is visionary, sees more and further than others do, and from that viewpoint finds the inspiration and perseverance to change the grim reality (think of 'faith heroes' such as Henri Dunant, Father Damian, Mother Teresa . . .). Faith achieves things, moves mountains, accomplishes the impossible.

2.7 The main principles of humanism

2.7.1 Humanism as a framework for meaning: life questions, goals, and transcendence

Humanism presents itself as a non-religious framework for meaning. It claims to provide a full-fledged secular alternative to religion, as well as answers to all major life questions. This claim is found in three variations or grades: (1) the more humble humanists regard their 'life view' as equally good as others, of equal value; (2) the more militant make it clear that a secular interpretation is better, gives more logical answers or is of a higher moral standing; (3) the 'fanatic' exclaim that all religions are deceitful and dangerous, and that only an atheist alternative is valid, reasonable, and humane.

But still, there is a problem with those questions about the meaning of life because they really belong to the 'spiritual dimension'. If humanism strictly assumes that all comes from man, the here-and-now and rationality, then it inevitably is very much in the line of materialism. Then all the questions regarding meaning are completely pointless for there is nothing higher nor any transcendence; all answers must be found within this world. Therefore, the humanistic answer to the question of the meaning of life can be summarized in one sentence: 'Every person determines this themselves'. There is no God or external authority that can define this for us. No one can therefore get it wrong, because there is no 'right plan'. 'Everyone has his own opinion! Period'.

The humanistic answers to the big questions of life such as '*Where do I come from*'? or '*Where am I going*'? are, 'I do not know' or 'Nobody can say that' or 'Nowhere' ... These answers leave man pretty much in the cold. 'Believe what you want!' is basically the same as not giving an answer. Also, regarding the question '*What is the purpose of life*'? it is put completely into man's hands. "There is no meaning and purpose: just what you make of it." Again, humanism does not provide something substantial, the framework

is just empty! This may seem like fun, freedom, and happiness, but just imagine this as a football field where the twenty-two players have put twenty-two goals; everything falls apart and nothing makes any sense.

The Humanistic Vision

Man, however cannot help but ask the why-questions. The purpose of life cannot be eating and drinking, getting up and working, sleeping and getting up again . . . He has a very strong need to know why he is doing what he does, and after every why-question he asks a new why-question. How then could we just ignore the ultimate 'why'? It is as if transcendence is already in our DNA. Everything in us shouts, 'There must be more!' Man wants to transcend himself in a bigger purpose! A feeling of meaninglessness is one of the worst tortures for a human being: it can even give him a disgust for life (an expression of Sartre, 'la nausée'). The last why-question however ends up for a humanist in a vacuum. The 'footballer' no longer asks, "Why do we actually play football?" This 'difficult' question is mostly avoided because it gives an uncomfortable feeling; everyone senses that something is not right, but a demure silence prevails.

Still, humanists try to find the purpose in life on a purely human, secular level, such as 'being happy', or 'being a good person'. Higher goals may refer to 'humanity' or 'my people', a collective entity that supersedes an individual and for which he could possibly give his life? Or abstract ideals such as 'justice', 'truth', equality', freedom', democracy'? They are undoubtedly very well-intentioned attempts, but there is hardly any unanimity and no criterion in terms of content. Still, man sits in his need and hunger . . .. The quest for meaning and purpose happens so-to-say in a spirit of openness and broad mindedness, but one possible track is already definitely taboo; the God-hypothesis is rejected in advance. That area is sealed with a wall of reinforced concrete. Systematically, humanism does not speak about Jesus; the discourse must be secular. It is a limitation that humanism imposes on itself, but in so doing, it turns the issue of the question for meaning into a dried-up river.

40. Humanism presents itself as a non-religious meaning-of-life ideology and claims to offer a fully secular alternative to religion. But in practice, it does not give any answers to life's great questions because each individual must personally determine the meaning and purpose of life, and all transcendence is rejected. Consequently, humanism leaves people looking for solutions within themselves in an otherwise empty framework.

According to the Christian perspective, 'the meaning of life' can only be found outside of our self. Self-made goals are not 'credible', or inspirational, not something we could give our lives for! The 'unreachable high' of the words and values of Jesus is what makes them extremely challenging and expands our consciousness. No one has trouble recognizing that the physical universe transcends us infinitely, but why do humanists deny this stubbornly with regards to the spiritual world? In the Christian view, transcendence is before man (our origin), after man (our eternal future), constantly present above man (God's constant proximity), and even in man (God's Spirit in the heart of the believer). Without this transcendence, life is boring and there is nothing to 'look forward to'.

Humanism offers people as it were, a large 'build-your-meaning-yourself' package, but in the box is only a note saying, 'Build your own package'. There is not even an outline of how it should be, and, if there are rules, everyone has the right not to agree! The humanistic framework for giving meaning has (extremely) stretchy lines, or should we say, 'There is no frame at all'? Whoever 'cuts off' life from all transcendence, from any higher goal, reduces it to a game! A game has its goal in itself: to relax. If you lose, nothing is seriously lost because it does not have real consequences. For a believer, life is not a general rehearsal, it is the real thing! And it also has consequences for eternity: it is about (eternal) life or death. This makes it infinitely valuable.

2.7.2 Separation between Church and State

Separation between Church and State is an important principle for humanism. The historical background is sufficiently known. Before the French Revolution, the Church ruled over Europe and in the spirit of the theocratic ideal, claimed authority over all areas of society. This led to monopolization, abuse of power and unhealthy interference in someone else's domain. Nowadays, the separation of these two in the western world is an almost obvious achievement that nobody wants to reverse. Still, some fundamental questions can be asked here, and there is also much semantic confusion and negative imagery about this. Far too often a horror image is still painted; "If Church and State are not separated, there is total religious dictatorship, complete intolerance and darkness, and an end to all modern freedoms." But is this correct?

This picture is actually based on a historically distorted image of the 'ancien régime' because previous to that, Church and State were never completely mixed. Even in the Old Testament there was a clear demarcation of the powers of 'king and prophet', and in the New Testament Jesus says, "Render to Caesar the things that are Caesar's and to God the things that are God's." (Matt 22:21). A healthy separation is also better for the Church itself; mixing with worldly power (as in the Middle Ages) distracts her from her true vocation and brings in too many worldly influences.

This contraposition suggests, however, a fundamental hostility between both, as if the Church will always be a threat to the State, which is very unjust. The Church is often a support and complement in areas where the government is not competent or has no 'weapons'. The civil government is not there to give moral or spiritual guidance. The State can punish people for their crimes but does not help them to repent of their selfishness and resentment. Only religion has the 'instruments' for moral laws to be internalized in the hearts of people. There is no reason why Church and State cannot work together harmoniously and respectfully as 'good neighbors'. They could as well build a friendly hedge as a demarcation instead of a concrete wall with barbed wire on top. There are many forms and ways in which Church and State can get along well because there are countless interfaces where both meet and have to work together: legislation, education, media, subsidies... There are enough examples of countries where a 'majority church' or even a state church is tolerant to other churches and religions. We should also not forget that the State can also 'seek to influence and control (far) beyond its boundaries'. It can also go beyond its authority, be dominant and intolerant, interfere with religion and church, and curb these. The atheist regimes of the 21st century amply proved this.

> 41. Separation between Church and State can be a sound principle, depending on how one defines it. But militant humanism confuses 'separation of Church and State' with 'separation of faith and politics', and therefore tries to silence believing politicians and citizens. Secularism tries to force religion back into the corner of private life and Church, but this shows it has a substantially different definition of 'religion'. For a believer, God is Lord over all areas of life and can never be put in a corner or in a box.

Confusion of concepts arises when some want to extend the separation of Church and State to a separation of God and politics. Then it is misused as a slogan to choke the believer's voice, to turn religion into a taboo subject, and to push faith into an ever-smaller corner of 'church and private life'. In this way, it becomes an instrument for a different agenda, namely that of secularism wanting to ban God and faith completely from society (see 2.10). But for a believer it is essential not to separate his faith from the rest of his life. God is Lord for him, also over his daily life and work. Often, believing politicians drew their greatest inspiration and perseverance from their Christian convictions and ideals (e.g., Abraham Lincoln, William Wilberforce, Martin Luther King . . .).

2.7.3 Critical sense and rationality

Another important principle for a humanist is to be critical. This, of course is strongly linked to the requirement of rationality (which we discussed sufficiently in chapter 2.6). A critical attitude undoubtedly has many positive aspects: it can inspire much innovation. Critical spirits dare to walk new paths, and this sometimes leads to making surprising discoveries. Authority should be questioned because it is not by definition right! Historically, criticism even helped to purify religion of popular belief and superstition, irrational traditions or skewed Biblical interpretations. The cliché image is too easily sketched that, in the area of religion, everything must be accepted without questioning and whatever one ('the institute') tells you should be blindly believed. This creates (yet another) false opposition between 'believing' and 'being critical'.

A critical approach is important and indispensable in every religion, otherwise it gets stuck in kindergarten phase. Everyone who is honest in his belief must also critically investigate it; if it cannot pass this test then it is not strong enough. "Examine all things. Firmly hold on to what is good", Paul says, for example (1 Thess. 5:21). Naive credulity may be what some churches have preached, but it is not in accordance with authentic and mature faith as the Bible means it.

Critical observation, however, can easily swing to the other side and does not automatically lead to something better. Ultimately, a critical approach cannot be sustained and is unlivable with. It is impossible to question everything in your life in every area all the time. Everyone who boasts about his 'critical attitude' is at least inconsistent and selectively critical. Chances are very high he also measures with two sizes and two weights. The critic actually fundamentally has a suspicious attitude; he constantly thinks that others did not do their homework properly (that is why this clashes with the other fundamental principle of humanism, 'belief in man'!). Secondly, he is very arrogant because he is convinced he knows better. Being critical can become for some a kind of 'fashion' or 'sport' and can stem as much from irrational wounds and the inability to trust.

There are however many areas in life where we can and must trust others; practically, we do it hundreds of times a day and this is not wrong. We seek experts in many areas and trust them more than ourselves! Why should this be so strange in the domain of religion and belief? For a Christian, Jesus is this kind of 'expert' in the supernatural world. When we are in a swamp, deciding to trust 'the Guide' more than our self is a very wise thing to do. And so, the step of faith is not the end of all 'critical thinking', but a 'rational' choice!

The main question here is how much do you value critical thinking and in what areas? And are you critical enough about your own criticism? Christians believe namely that humanists are not critical enough, certainly not of themselves! By making critical thinking a main principle and thus giving it too high a place, it gets out of balance and can become a 'loose cannon', and even counterproductive and harmful. It can ask a thousand questions, but does not provide answers; on the contrary, each answer is critically analyzed until there is nothing left. Critical thinking is excellent in pulling down but does not build up.

2.7.4 Active pluralism

Humanism has always fought against the monopoly of one religion or church. But what does it propose as the alternative? The answer is not unambiguous because humanism is not a uniform movement of like-minded people. On the one hand, there are the militant humanists or atheists who consider all religions to be dangerous and fight them continuously. What they actually want is to replace one monopoly with an opposing anti-religious monopoly. On the other hand, there are the more moderate, broad thinking humanists who can recognize the good in religions and see them as a valuable life view. They plead for an open society where all views on life can peacefully co-exist side by side, usually called pluralism. Between these two viewpoints, there is a continuum of many shades. Broad-mindedness and generosity are undoubtedly beautiful values, but, how far can you go in this and how does it work out in practice?

Firstly, we must note again that two concepts are being mixed in this debate; many people confuse pluralism with plurality. Over perhaps the last century, Western Europe has thoroughly changed in the area of life-approaches. Due to secularization, the group of non-believers has grown, extensively, and through migration, religions and Christian churches of foreign origin entered and gained a place and space to live, freedoms and rights. Plurality of many spiritual views is thus a fact in our society. However, pluralism is an '-ism', a principle, a kind of ideology, which believes that this multiplicity is good, or that it must be like this. Pluralism says something like, "All religions are equal, all paths lead to God, they each have a part of the truth, they all have a certain richness and are complementary, and they must work together or merge into one." However, you can already sense that again this is a new religious view beside or opposing other religions. In practice, this view comes out of the New Age movement, which is more influenced by the Orient than the Occident. The statement "All religions are the same and lead to the same God", comes from Reform Hinduism (a modern, liberal flow in Hinduism in the 19th and 20th centuries). It presents itself as a kind of overall vision for other religions, but these do not recognize themselves as part of it. Instead of uniting and reconciling religions, it creates a new vision, and therefore even more confusion and division. In practice, it is syncretism (a mixture of different religions) and eclecticism ('shopping' from the many religions such as in a supermarket).

> 42. The word 'pluralism' is currently regarded as a beautiful ideal, but many people confuse pluralism with plurality. The plurality of many ideologies in our society is a fact, but pluralism is an ideology which believes that this is how it should be: that all religions lead to the same God, that all of them have a part of the truth and that they should all work together or merge into one. Only this is a kind of meta-religious assertion, which in fact is not acknowledged by any religion.

In practice, 'pluralism' means for most people that you need to find a healthy and open attitude in dealing with this multitude of worldviews, not in an aggressive or narrow-minded way, but with tolerance and with an open view. This seems evident to all, and you cannot call this typically humanist. Christians will also always plead to approach those who think differently as a human being and engage in conversation. It is a sign of mature faith to have a strong conviction and at the same time give the other the space you would also like to have. That this is not so easy in practical reality, we see enough in multicultural societies.

When, however, pluralism says, "You must believe or acknowledge that all life-approaches are equivalent", then this is a problematic statement. It sounds pious and peaceful, but does it really make sense? Is everyone really equally right in the area of beliefs? Thousands of religions and sects exist in this world, some of which are clearly public deception, manipulation by a power-hungry sect-leader, utterly dangerous, fanatic, anti-rational, totally not credible... No sane thinking person can be serious to say he finds them all equal. This would be precisely the end of all critical thinking!

This interpretation of pluralism also has something contradictory. How can you be convinced of your own opinion and say that the other is 'equally right'? Also, what about fascism, neo-Nazism, and open racism? Was Hitler indeed as equally right as Churchill? Or what about negationism and anti-Semitism? And all forms of fanaticism and extremism? Are suicide terrorists as noble as peacekeepers? 'All religions are equal' is a cheap, hollow phrase, a feel-good slogan. It seems a nice magic formula to put an end to all religious wars and divisions in one blow, but unfortunately, it does not stand, and does not work in practice either. What one means by 'God' is sometimes diametrically different from the other. Their god images are as compatible as if you would try to mix iron and clay.

But humanism goes one step further; some say they advocate active pluralism. 'Passive pluralism' in this context means to 'forcibly tolerate' the other visions because there is no other way; you grant them their space. Active pluralism, however, means to actively promote the living space and rights of others (with whom you actually do not even agree). It implies you rise above thinking in boxes and take selfless steps to seek the benefit of others. Let us be honest and realistic, no matter how beautiful and noble this principle is, there are very few that succeed in doing so. Some rare exceptions highlight how terribly difficult this is for a human being. How would this function practically for a humanist? Does this mean he is going to contend that Jehovah Witnesses also receive recognition and subsidies from the government? Or will he join demonstrations of radical and extreme Muslim groups to build mosques, or racist groups to get room for free speech? Where is the boundary? In practice, it will always prove to be a very selective pluralism, depending on how the other groups fit into one's

> 43. The view that all religions are the same and ultimately lead to the same goal, would seem to be a 'higher' vision, a lofty and superior insight, but is in fact only one opinion alongside (not above) other ones, which does not even take other views seriously. The creation of a 'universal religion' leads to a kind of man-made 'religious Esperanto', that doesn't enthuse anyone.

own box. Whether or not in reality humanists will be actively pluralistic remains to be seen in each case and for each person. And then, there can no longer be any contemptuous, mocking, anti-religious comments in their publications . . .

Pluralism is an overrated principle; it emphasizes the existence of many opinions side by side but says nothing about how they should co-exist. In practice, 'pluralism' is used as an argument for opposing views. Some argue, for example, that everybody should freely express their religious convictions, e.g. with outer symbols (headscarves, kippahs, crosses . . .). Others, however, for the same reason claim that 'in public spaces' everyone must remain neutral and hide his conviction out of respect for others. In this way, pluralism erodes into a meaningless concept.

2.7.5 Free research

The principle of 'free research' is of paramount importance to humanism. Historically, this results from a reaction against the constraints imposed on science by the Church in the Middle Ages. For religious reasons, certain issues could not be investigated or published. The counter reaction was therefore, nothing or no one, no dogma or institute may limit research. The motto here is total freedom for the scientist.

It is and remains true that religion should not be afraid of scientific research as long as this is done honestly and objectively, without an ideological agenda. In principle, the discovery of new material facts or laws can never be a threat to faith, for it is namely something spiritual, of a completely different order. But the discussion can sometimes become fierce when one poaches on the other's territory, or when crucial moral principles are touched on.

What exactly does the principle of free research mean? If we take it as an absolute and go the full extent, then Josef Mengele (1911–1979), the notorious camp doctor in Auschwitz, applied this perfectly. He did not allow any religious or moral constraints to stop him from executing cruel experiments on humans as on guinea pigs. The same question can be asked regarding animal testing or experimentation on human embryos. Who pleads for truly 100% free research? Nobody! Everyone acknowledges there are limits to what is humanly responsible, but believers and non-believers put these in different places. Until what age is an embryo a 'thing' and from what time does it become a human being? Everyone agrees there must be legal statutory standards to protect society against unscrupulous scientists and companies that smell huge amounts of money in this industry. The Christian restraint in this is not as much influenced by 'irrational, dogmatic revelations', but rather by moral considerations, namely (greater) respect for (God-given) life.

Humanists thus in practice accept restrictions—fortunately—on free research; moral principles and human dignity are important. But where exactly is the boundary, and who determines this? Humanism has an *absolute* belief in the individual conscience of the researcher. Again, each scientist determines his own values and standards, which always shifts the boundaries—as we also see in practice. Putting much emphasis on free research means that this process *automatically* continues. This is a slippery slope, and humanism will only with hesitancy call this to a halt and even then have no authority whatsoever.

The principle of free research also tends to give science a 'carte blanche'. It seems as if scientists get some kind of infallible status as 'the new priests' who must solve everything, and therefore are allowed more freedom than others. They are 'the experts', and their competence automatically applies to the moral area as well, or at least no external moral authority may restrict their freedom.

Again, we must say that 'free research' is an overrated principle and in its absolute form untenable. By all means, humanists mean that research must be freer than what believers mean: they move the boundaries further out, but no one can decide how much further. What the consequences are and how this clashes with its other principles, we will see in chapter 3.2.1 (on medical ethics).

> 44. Humanism proclaims the principle of free research, but if it used this principle consistently, it would also need to approve the Nazi experiments of Joseph Mengele. This principle gives scientists a kind of infallible status, as 'the new priests' who are to solve everything without any restrictions on a legal or moral level.

2.8 The (moral) values of humanism

In this book we are attempting to make a distinction between principles and values. Principles are, as one would say, the instruments or methods for achieving a goal; values are the goal itself. 'Values' refer to something that someone finds valuable, something worth pursuing. This distinction, however, is never watertight because what a goal is for one person can be an intermediate goal toward a higher one for someone else, and thus a principle. Furthermore, values are often understood as moral values (such as justice, honesty, solidarity, love), but some values are not strictly moral (e.g. autonomy or openness). Nevertheless, the latter do indeed have a moral component or moral consequences. The boundary between the two is, by all means, thin and fluid. Even so, in this chapter we want to make the transition to morality, and therefore we will look at what humanism indicates as its (moral) values.

2.8.1 Autonomy and self-determination

45. Humanism preaches the value of autonomy and self-determination: on a philosophical and moral level, it is totally (and fundamentally) opposed to any authority and every individual determines his or her own values and standards. But in all other areas of life, common sense recognizes the need for clear authority: in a family, football team, business, school, army, political party, government . . . How contradictory is it then to say that in the most important areas of life someone is free to do whatever he or she wants? It is like a country where everyone is king: this seems 'democratic', free, and fun, but leads to complete levelling and utter anarchy.

The requirement of autonomy is one of the most essential values of humanism and has far-reaching consequences! Man is namely the 'creator' of meaning and purpose, of values and norms in his life. This statement is, first of all, to be understood as a reaction against every authority imposed from the outside. The Church has always taught that God created the world and all its laws, determined the meaning and purpose of life, and ordained the moral standards and values. Therefore, accepting divine authority outside-and-above-ourselves is categorized by humanists as 'heteronomy'; the determining factor lies outside of us instead of within. In this way, man seems to be reduced to a slavish executor of 'someone else's plan', without any say in the matter. It is, of course, a question of whether this was indeed the image that the Church (in a blunt way) presented, and whether it corresponds with the biblical concept. In any case, this is the caricature representation that is usually spread and combated.

The consequence is that there are no objective standards or values outside of us. All meaning and purpose are determined by us! The humanistic counter-reaction accepts no higher authority whatsoever, from any religious book or institute, but then also not from any moral teacher or philosopher, nor any secular or humanist organization.

If this line of thought would be followed rigorously, of course this would lead to absurd situations. In real life, our autonomy is extremely limited; in every area and in every phase of our life we stand under many forms of (human) authority and must obey thousands of rules and laws imposed upon us from above. On an uninhabited island there might be autonomy, but as soon as a second person arrives there, it is over.

Take any area where there is social interaction, such as politics and justice, economy and business, theatre and orchestra, school and hobby clubs; nowhere can we enter a complex social structure and say, "I am setting my own rules here!" Even when people play a game together, rules are already required. With autonomy as a 'sacred cow', any team sport and any society becomes impossible!

Autonomy becomes even more problematic when reason gets involved with it (philosophy and science) seeking the 'seat of autonomy' in our brain. Since all our actions and reactions are directed by chemical processes and electrical signals, where then is this 'free and sovereign me'? It is simply physically untraceable and therefore unprovable! It is indeed a question of whether I control my thoughts and emotions, dreams and fears, passions and fantasies . . . or they control me! There are more things in life (and in myself) that I have no control over than the ones that I do have control over.

Autonomy is, strictly speaking, not even a moral value! It is a working principle for how to determine your values, namely 'freely and without interference from above'. Consequently, you can say that this value actually undermines all other moral values because moral laws lose any compulsory character. They can never be 'commands' because no outside agency has the right to impose anything on anyone. And one more step: humanism actually denies that universal moral values exist. There are no criteria left in order to say to someone that something is unacceptable. 'Everyone determines his own moral standards' is a perfect recipe for the greatest possible chaos!

Humanism reacted fiercely to the absolute power of an infallible pope, but in its world every human being is a pope! Compare it to a country where everyone declares himself to be king and acts as such! This may give a wonderful free feeling of 'omnipotence', but this power is limited to one little planet on which one person lives. This little world is no bigger than my brainpan.

> 46. The free-spirited human wants to be autonomous. But who in their right mind, wandering through the jungle of life, wants to find their own way without a map, and – out of pride—chooses to reject the guidance of an experienced guide? Life is not a game; it is not without consequences. Mistakes can be fatal, both for oneself and for others. In so many areas of life, people find it self-evident to consult an expert (e.g. for their car, computer, health, finance . . .) but when it comes to the most important decisions (i.e. what is the purpose of it all?), we think we know best and everyone is his own pope.

Going back to the question whether the Christian worldview teaches heteronomy, the answer is of course 'no'. Already the fact that God created man to be free proves the contrary. In as much as a materialist cannot really believe in freedom, a Christian does believe in it. According to the Genesis story, God gave Adam great autonomy to rule over creation. He is free to exploit, change, and adapt the planet, and does not need the agreement of the Boss for every decision. And even when doing it wrongly, God does not intervene indiscriminately to stop Adam. Even at the notorious tree, God did not intervene, but respected his autonomy to make a fatal choice. Also, the fact that a believer allows his life to be determined by God is not heteronomy, but it is his own free choice, and thus (another form of!) self-determination. Compare it to someone who allows his car to be guided by a GPS. It is 'I' who voluntarily decides to be guided, and I have good reasons for this, because the GPS knows the way much better than I do. God never takes over man's decision center; He wants to help and lead but will never take man's responsibility out of his hands.

The humanistic opposition to the Church as an 'oppressive moral authority' brought about a profound change in the whole culture, namely opposition against authority in general and the whole authority crisis in our society. For self-determination means: 'I reject all authority above me'. This resistance was most strongly expressed in Europe in the 1960s when the hippie and flower power movement questioned all traditional authority, from the father of the family to the President. Authority was examined super-critically, 'authority' became a dirty word and since then 'rebellious' has been regarded as something positive, as a sign of courage and masculinity. Anti-authoritarian education has since produced generations of insecure and spoiled children. Humanism has invariably no respect for authority and praises willfulness as a virtue. But when each individual obeys only the people of his choice, who he finds ok, society becomes ungovernable, people unmanageable and the world ultimately impossible to live in.

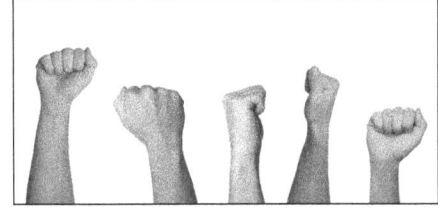

This resistance against authority expressed itself particularly by a general irritation against moral authority. Anyone who dared to uphold any moral standard was berated as a 'moral knight', just about the worst insult imaginable. Moral standards were reduced to the private sphere or the Church, and the public sphere was thus made amoral (or immoral). Whether this then is a delightful 'value-free society' or a derailed 'value-less' society, one can assess for themselves.

47. The humanistic principle of self-determination reveals a very strong distrust of other people, a negative outlook, and therefore little faith. The need to be absolutely free, the urge to not take orders from any authority, is so strong that it is irrational and resembles a 'ideological fear of bonding'.

The way in which humanism propagates autonomy is out of proportion, inconsistent, and unlivable. In most areas of life, people find it obvious to consult an expert (e.g. for their car, PC, health, finance . . .), but when it comes to the most important thing ("How should I live well?") we think we know best and everybody is his own infallible pope. Autonomy is not the reality, not preferable, not harmless, and not necessarily better. In practice, it means the undermining and disintegration of moral values.

2.8.2 Self-realization

According to humanism, the main purpose of life or life's mission is 'self-realization'. This is also logical because principally, one cannot think in any other way than from oneself. In the Christian viewpoint, self-development is also an important value; a human being cannot bury his God-given talents (Matt 25:14–30) but must develop them as much as possible for God, for his neighbor and for oneself. There are three differences between these two:

(1) Self-development can never be the highest value for a Christian because then the whole of life is only self-centered and has no social or moral value. It cannot be a final goal, only an intermediate goal at most, or a means.

(2) This brings us to another point where humanism and Christianity clash head-on. Jesus says we must lose our lives (Matt 10:39)! He consciously uses unusually sharp words and goes straight against our deeply rooted self-focus! When our attitude to life is, "I'm first going to develop myself, and if any energy is left, I'll do something for someone else", there will hardly remain anything for the other. If you do not radically choose for the other first, selfishness will always play the leading role. Selfishness should not be tackled with velvet gloves but needs to be radically 'crucified'. 'Losing your life' means essentially the willingness to submit your own ambitions to the higher goal, shift them (temporarily) aside for another, to die to one's own pet subjects or to one's own rights. In contrast to self-realization, Jesus promotes self-denial and self-sacrifice. This is certainly not the same as self-hate, self-torment or self-destruction, and has nothing to do with masochism, for Jesus' promise after this is, "Whoever loses his life will win it." The goal is to find a higher and real life. Dying to yourself is always difficult and painful, but surely liberating.

(3) The Christian vision of life also certainly has the purpose of the full development of the human personality, although not as the highest purpose! This however, also includes the whole spiritual domain: knowing God, the relationship with God (prayer), and developing all the 'spiritual virtues' such as holiness and service. This 'third dimension' tends to be completely ignored in the humanistic approach and so it misses the deepest core, that which makes man spiritual and very distinct from animals.

---

48. Humanism's ideal of unlimited self-realization constantly and inevitably clashes with its other ideals such as brotherhood and tolerance. It teaches people to focus so much on self that they are not able to realize real, selfless love.

Finally, we must make the same observation as when regarding autonomy. The principle of self-realization is certainly 'valuable' but is not a moral value; there is not yet anything 'noble' here. The development of all the human talents of someone can even be used for the most immoral purposes.

2.8.3 Freedom

Freedom is of course a very beautiful and worthwhile value. Often people are willing to go a very long (sometimes extreme) way to find or regain their freedom. This is especially very important for humanism; it is even the first great value of the French Revolution ('freedom, equality, fraternity'). This was in reaction to the (political and religious) lack of free-

dom and the oppression of the Ancien Régime and the Church. However, a number of critical observations or questions are needed here.

(1) The firm proclamation of this value creates another false contradiction as it suggests that religion and church bring a lack of freedom. No philosophy of life, by the way, has 'lack of freedom' or 'submission' on its banner or in its program. Everyone strives for it or promises it. How then is this goal unique to humanism?

(2) Total freedom, just like total autonomy, is an illusion. From all sides, we bump into limits to freedom in this life, both outside and within ourselves, physically, psychologically and spiritually. Everyone knows that freedom, in fact, is very limited.

(3) Every regime or form of authority inevitably implies a certain degree of 'oppression', even at the lowest level (a family). The promise of freedom was historically too often a fraud and deception towards the people in the mouth of demagogues or populists (i.e. the dictatorship during the French Revolution), even of dictators and sect-leaders. In this way, the slogan of freedom easily becomes cheap and meaningless.

(4) 'Freedom' is, again, no moral value; this concept has no 'content'. Freedom is not an end in itself, but has a goal, and must lead to something. A prisoner who, after years of imprisonment, is being freed and returns to his criminal environment has not yet understood anything about freedom. "What am I going to do with my freedom?" is the most important question for him and for any other human being.

(5) Freedom vs rules is again a false opposition because in principle all rules are meant to protect freedom, namely to protect the weaker from the stronger. This applies to all areas of life, and thus also to the moral area.

(6) Freedom is something very precious, which you cannot or should not grant to just anyone. This is the reason why criminals must be locked up because their freedom means a danger for others. Children also receive more freedom as they grow up, according to how much the parents can trust them to handle this. Unfortunately, with adults, this is not very different. Too many revolutions that were to bring 'freedom' degenerated in total chaos and anarchy, which was much worse than the previous state of affairs.

49. Humanism claims to strive for the 'freedom' of man, and naturally this means that it rebels against any oppression by a religious system. But every religion, ideology, political movement, revolution, therapy, sect . . . claims to bring freedom, and every system or regime brings with it a certain level of oppression! Freedom is one of the finest ideals on earth, yet so easily becomes a cheap slogan in the mouth of demagogues. And depending on which definition of 'freedom' one uses, people may or may not end up in another (more serious) form of slavery!

(7) Humanism associates Christianity and the Church as 'freedomless', but 'freedom' is actually an essential concept in the Bible. Jesus says, 'If the Son sets you free, you shall be free indeed' (John 8:36). Here, He actually denounces the fake freedom promised by many, and instead sets out true freedom (free from all forms of addictions and sins). Paul also speaks of 'the glorious freedom of the children of God' (Romans 8:21), and James about 'the law of liberty' (James 2:12). Whoever is 'mature in the faith', no longer lives under thousands of commandments and prohibitions. True, spiritual freedom is the purpose of the Christian life, but the road to it is hard work and long.

The Humanistic Vision

In short, Christianity and humanism have a very different view of what 'freedom' means. And whatever definition of 'freedom' is used, this determines whether or not people end up in another (worse) form of slavery!

2.8.4 Tolerance

Humanism brags about bringing tolerance, and contrasts this again with the intolerance of the Middle Ages. The religious fanaticism and the religious wars of the 16th century were certainly a disgrace to the history of the Church, and contrary to its own principles. Tolerance is undoubtedly a valuable feature and makes life in every area much more enjoyable. Yet, when we critically examine this value, we again encounter many unanswered questions. 'Tolerance' seems to have become the main dogma of this time. However, it is now being used so generally and ambiguously that no one really knows anymore what is meant by it. It is clear to everyone that you cannot and should not tolerate everything, such as crimes (child abuse, child pornography) or harmful ideas (racism, negationism . . .). There must be at least clarification about (1) what we mean by 'tolerance', and (2) what you may or may/must/should not tolerate.

(1) Tolerance can hardly be called an exclusive humanistic value, as it actually came forth from the Christian faith. Jesus himself was extremely tolerant; He endured mockery, incomprehension, false accusations, serious injustice, even inhuman pain, and punishment. He put up with all kinds of sinners (more accurately: He loved them), was humane and mild to prostitutes and tax collectors, and interacted with 'enemies' such as the Romans and Samaritans. Many humanists have an image of God as an intolerant, punishing God, but in practice, the God of the Bible is superhumanly tolerant. He endures billions of sins and insults each day, does not strike down sinners with lightening, and lets the sun shine on the righteous as well as the unrighteous (Matt 5:45). Christianity is very much for tolerance (Col. 3:13); it is as indispensable in interacting with each other as oil is in a machine.

(2) However, Jesus could also be extremely 'intolerant', and so can God. Namely, God hates sin, bloodshed, violence, and deception . . . As far as He is concerned, there should be zero tolerance for murder, rape, pedophilia, exploitation, in short, for any injustice and evil! Jesus was extremely

tolerant when he was personally affected but could get very angry when it concerned God's work. This was particularly the case with regards to sin that corrupts faith from the inside out, such as the hypocrisy and dual morality of religious leaders, the abuse of spiritual power in the name of God, or the commercialization of the temple. Abuse must make someone angry, otherwise it is a sin of indifference. Intolerance is namely the negative side of something very positive, the fact that certain things are holy to some people: "This, you cannot touch! This is a no-go zone!" Intolerance is in this case a sign of a positive commitment, passion or responsibility. Our modern day seems to sometimes call for demolishing 'all holy houses', so that ultimately, there can be no more taboos (the so-called 'taboo of the taboos'). This then, of course, is yet another taboo. Taboos, however, do have a function; they are a kind of protective wall around things that are regarded as sacred and delicate/vulnerable (such as children, marriage, sex . . .). In a society where nothing is holy anymore, nobody is safe! Therefore, believers are sometimes very intolerant. This is not necessarily because they are conservative, narrow minded or 'not yet enlightened. There are namely more things that are sacred to a believer!

(3) The reverse must be said, to tolerate what should not be tolerated is complicity and thus criminal! Tolerance does not always come from strength and bravery, but can at times be a sign of cowardice, laziness, and indifference. Permissiveness leads to child neglect. If you cross a certain boundary, tolerance becomes guilty negligence.

> 50. The highest humanistic virtue is that of 'tolerance', but this means both everything and nothing. It is impossible to tolerate everything (pedophilia, child abuse, rape . . .) because that is the same as culpable negligence. In practice, this principle is therefore applied selectively and arbitrarily. And as both sides in a conflict often accuse one another of intolerance, often the one who shouts first and loudest is perceived as the 'winner'.

(4) When in the media someone fences with the word 'intolerant', it is very two-faced or selective. The one who deems himself to be extremely tolerant probably has a blind spot for his own holy principles or (secular) 'holy cows'. Sometimes it seems like a competition; the one who shouts first and the loudest that the other is intolerant, wins the war of perception! In practice, when humanism is attacked, it often reacts defensively, fanatically,

The Humanistic Vision

and intolerantly[13]. Whether someone is truly tolerant, however, is only seen in difficult situations when sensitive convictions are touched. There are certainly Christians with blinkers and a short fuse, but you find these among non-believers just as well.

(5) Tolerance is not a strong value, in fact, it is a weakened version of (Christian) love. Tolerance is passive, love is active. A married man much prefers that his wife loves him rather than tolerates him. 'Tolerating' is, in the weakest sense of the word, granting someone daylight (with visible reluctance). This is not very noble and generous.

(6) Tolerance can 'tip over' when it is made into the overall dominant principle. The demand for tolerance can in itself become 'oppressive', namely, when you MUST tolerate it all and the counterparty does not even tolerate that you disagree.

(7) An emphasis on tolerance easily creates a new sense of moral superiority[14]: 'At least I am more tolerant

---

51. The humanistic virtue of 'tolerance' sounds very noble and exalted, but there is something arrogant about it. Those who 'tolerate' the other opinion indicate that they feel far superior to those who hold that opinion; that in a long-suffering way they tolerate their existence. In their heart, they look down on them, so in practice they don't consider them to be equal at all.

---

13. To give just one example of this: in an official brochure *Vrijzinnigheid en humanisme in Europa* ('Freethinking and humanism in Europe'), issued by several Belgian freethinking and humanist associations in cooperation with the European Humanist Federation, the first article is a text by Richard Dawkins, 'Tijd voor weerwerk' ('Time to stand up', originally published in *Freethought Today*), p. 8–11. A few quotes are: "My last vestige of 'hands off religion' respect disappeared . . .". "The great unmentionable evil at the center of our culture is monotheism." The God of these religions— Koran and New Testament are thrown on one heap for convenience—is called a "violent and vindictive God of Battles", the Bible is called "a barbaric Bronze Age text", and these three religions even "anti-human" (Dawkins quotes Gore Vidal, but does agree with him). Furthermore, he speaks of religion as a "hereditary delusion", a belief in "a delusional world inhabited by archangels, demons, and imaginary friends" which he calls "ludicrously tragic". His conclusion is: "Those of us who have for years politely concealed our contempt for the dangerous collective delusion of religion need to stand up and speak out." Dawkins is, of course, known to use as a fervent atheist his sharp pen against the religions, but in this official brochure of humanism, this article is taken over (without any correction or nuance!) Any respect is totally absent.

14. Atheist philosopher Maarten Boudry (University of Ghent) rightly points out that for centuries humanists have fiercely opposed what they call the moral 'superiority feeling' of the Church, but also this reaction ('at least we are tolerant, broad-minded, and

than you'. Tolerance can contain arrogance and be condescending. Whoever 'tolerates' clearly feels superior to the other and simultaneously noble-minded since they allow inferior opinions.

All of these arguments show that tolerance is unfit to be a general, dominant virtue; it is insufficient as a guideline. It is a nice value at the level of interpersonal contact, but inappropriate to be elevated as a guiding principle in approaching life and the world. Absolute tolerance, for which some seem to plead, sounds very progressive and cool, but is actually absurd. In practice, it is selectively handled, or not even applied at all. In this context, it is inappropriate to even call it a 'moral value' because it does not have a substantive criterion; whoever tolerates too much, risks causing much damage.

2.8.5 Openness and broad-mindedness

Humanism and freethinking are against closed thought systems, against authoritarian institutions that impede the freedom of research. Everything must be critically questioned and voiced. Humanism stands for an independent free spirit that accepts no curtailment. Still two comments here:

(1) Openness and broadmindedness are indeed beautiful qualities but are (yet again) not a novelty for Christianity. Jesus was a remarkably open person who stood above all confines, and could relate well with high and low, learned and simple, Jew and gentile. He never allowed Himself to be reduced to one party, to be hitched in front of one cart. The God of the Bible also stands above all parties; no one can say (exclusively), 'God is on my side and against you'. God is too big for one 'club' or institute. He is impartial, or better said, multilaterally biased, or even better, universally one-sided. He is for all people. Narrow-minded or closed Christians have a problem, or in any case have a thing or two to learn.

(2) In practice, however, humanism is not as open as it claims. Although in theory it advocates free research, any information from religious sources or from revelation is ruled out. A philosopher can search everywhere, except in the Bible (or Quran . . .). The fact that humanists do not accept religious authority is understandable from their point of view, but this taboo is expanded. Even making reference to a religious source is already

---

rational') feels as superior.

taboo. This does not only apply to science, but extends itself to philosophy and worldviews, to the whole of daily life. Searching for wisdom becomes restricted to the secular, human sphere. "You must seek truth as sincerely and broadminded as possible, but you may not pass through this or that door (revelation, authority, religion . . .)." Part of the source of knowledge is declared inaccessible in advance, which means that free research is not free, and the openness is selective. The historical reaction against ecclesiastical dominance flips over in the other extreme; "We do not want anything to do with religion, Bible or faith." A choice has been made in advance that answers will not be found in the direction of 'God'.

This is even more wrong because Jesus is one of the greatest teachers of all time. The latter may seem a purely subjective statement, yet it is based on undeniable objective arguments. The words of Jesus (the Bible) are part of the most sold and translated book all times (with a big lead on the second), and his movement is the largest ever in history. After two thousand years, he still has 2.2 billion followers, a number that is still growing; good reasons to investigate his words very seriously! In this context, it is even irresponsible for any seriously seeking and open-minded person to not read his words! How can you, in advance, shove one of the world's leading teachers aside? This is not about humanists having to accept His statements as authoritative. Still, reading and researching them and allowing inspiration from them does not happen either.

Someone who is completely sincere and open in his quest for truth is willing to seek everywhere, in secular as well as religious sources. The big questions of life are much too important; this is about the sense or nonsense of everything, about life or death, about life fulfillment or nihilism. Someone who is roaming around in the desert, dehydrated and desperate enough will receive water from anyone, friend or enemy; it is a matter of survival.

2.8.6 Human dignity

Of all humanistic principles or values mentioned, this is the most substantive: humanity is central, and man's dignity is a criterion for all morality. Contrary to the previous principles, humanism and Christianity come very close (or totally) together here. It is also undeniable that humanism has derived this value from Christianity. Nevertheless, we must also make a number of fundamental observations here, both theoretically and practically.

According to the Christian vision, each and every person has an infinite value, (1) because he is created in God's image, his origin is divine, pure, and noble. And (2) he is a unique, original being; there is nobody else like himself. Everything that is unique (think, for example, of exceptional artwork) has an inestimable value. Humanism wants to take over the same image of man, but without this divine origin, but is that really possible? What is then the human, 'scientific', earthly origin? According to evolution theory, man is a coincidental product of a blind, meaningless process, the result of millions of times of wrongly copied genes, an accidentally evolved monkey. There is nothing deliberate about man, no planned beauty, no trace of 'noblesse'.

And if you look at man from a purely physical-chemical perspective, it is even worse; he is then just a coincidental temporary conglomerate of molecules, which has no more dignity than a clump of clay. On what then is this dignity of man based? The value of something or somebody is determined in part by the intrinsic value and in part by the value that others assign (the law of supply and demand). The intrinsic (objective) value is totally lacking in the humanistic perspective, and the assigned value is purely subjective; it depends on what one person wants to 'offer' for the other (according to Hitler, for example, Jews were only rats that were better eradicated). In other words, the foundation under human dignity is completely undermined. Humanism is like a bank that issues paper money that is not covered by a real gold value.

A second major problem is that in practice the human dignity argument is handled very selectively and arbitrarily. In the abortion debate, for example, the dignity and autonomy of the mother are regarded as absolute, but those of the unborn baby swept conveniently under the carpet for a moment. The plea for euthanasia is supported by the argument for 'human dignity' (because they do not want degrading human suffering). But the opponents just say, "It is precisely because of human dignity that you cannot give an injection; there is nothing unworthy in fighting till the end, on the contrary, it shows the will to live."

Humanists like to talk about human dignity, but how many people throw away their own dignity like dirt on the streets? There is nothing as sad as a drunken man, an addict, someone who bursts out in unrestrained rage or a scolding rant, sexual splurges, and blatant selfishness. God has a high plan for humanity, but man degrades himself to the level of animals and lower.

2.8.7 Brotherhood / solidarity

The focus of humanism is man, the individual, but of course it does not plead for unlimited individualism and egocentrism. The social dimension, commitment to others and for a better world, engagement and involvement, these are high values. 'Brotherhood' is the third value of the French Revolution: all people are equal (in opposition to the feudal system of classes) and are to be like brothers for each other, connected in solidarity in the same fate. This value is sometimes translated as 'universalism' or 'cosmopolitan thinking'. All people from all countries, classes and races, ages and gender are equal. Whoever wants to claim the right of human dignity for oneself, must also give it to others. Other values that are often mentioned and relate to this are 'good citizenship' and 'responsibility', which go in the same direction as 'solidarity'. Auguste Comte used the word 'altruism' (a secular word for 'love for all'). Also, in this moral value humanism and Christianity find each other. There are, however, differences in foundation, implementation, and elaboration.

Humanism very strongly advocates the autonomy of man, as if it were banging its fist on the table, but how can it then still accurately arrive at true solidarity? In putting self-realization first, fellow men automatically get second place. The question is, "How much energy remains for our fellow men?" If I get the lead, there is only a minor role for the other and I determine how big or small this is.

The difference is that Jesus radically puts the commandment of love at the top. Love thinks of the other first, placing fellow man above oneself. This, of course is much more difficult, and goes against our natural tendencies. It is as if Jesus says, "The stubborn self-centeredness of man must be overcome in step one"; otherwise he will always be limited and determined by self-interest ("What is in it for me?"). It is the same discussion as the one about rights or duties. Whosoever puts his rights in first place, does not get to the rights of the other. However, if everyone were to put his duties first, nobody would have to fight for his rights. It is this primary focus on oneself or on the other that makes all the difference! The Christian approach is much more logical; it is the only consistent and lasting road to real brotherhood.

We must therefore be realistic and also look at how it works out in the raw reality. Our fellow human being is not always a nice 'brother' and companion; sometimes he is a 'pain in the ass', an annoyance, an enemy, dangerous, unreliable, a profiteer, a bloodsucker, a predator. At such times, all idealistic brotherhood gets lost in the 'survival of the fittest', the jungle, a war of all against all. Then it is 'either him or me'. At that time, you must already have a very strong determination (or divine power) to refrain from falling into the foundational human attitude of 'me first'.

All attempts by humanists to substantiate or shape 'brotherhood' remain stuck in good intentions and non-committal informality. How can humanism, that first imprisons man on his own little island, escape from ultimate individualism, a world of seven billion little islands? How can it still make a real connection with others? That is the reason why Christianity, through its commandment of love, radically places fellow man first.

2.8.8 Conclusion: humanism and morality?

2.8.8.1 The 'humanistic' values?

Humanism thinks of itself as having brought tolerance and humaneness into the world, that it is a more humane version of Christianity. It did this though only on the basis of Christian virtues—which is logical because all Enlightenment thinkers were Christian. It reminded the Church of its own values and did not introduce new values. Later, secular humanism went even further in this direction by cutting these values off from any reference to God, and even positioning them in contrast to any 'religious intolerance'.

52. Humanism has not discovered or introduced a single new virtue: its virtues are derived from Christianity but stripped of any reference to God and deliberately weakened. 'Tolerance', for example, is a very diluted version of the radical, strong 'love' preached by Jesus. Humanism primarily fought for the freedom to *not* have to live the high Christian standards.

Humanism supposes that this 'cutting off' does not make a difference, as if you could saw a tree loose from its roots and it will still continue to live. Christian morality, however, is essentially rooted in a strong image of God and a specific image of man which are inseparably connected. Jesus allows no doubt about where His source of inspiration is. When these values are cut off from their breeding ground, they can, just like a cut flower, stay beautiful for a while, but it is just a matter of time before they go brown and die.

Sadly, we also see this in practice; moral values are—at times deliberately—weakened. All abovementioned values (autonomy, self-development, freedom, critical sense) are not or hardly moral values; they do not give moral direction. Those that are moral (tolerance, brotherhood, human dignity) are diluted Christian values, a conscious erosion! Enlightenment and the French Revolution brought more freedom, but what did this mean morally? It was mostly handled as the freedom that people can afford to not keep moral laws!

> 53. Taking certain Christian values and separating them from their source of inspiration (God) is like cutting beautiful flowers and putting them in a vase: they will look very pretty and bloom for a while, or even grow, but it is only a matter of time before they wilt and die. Christian principles detached from God Himself are only abstract rules and general wisdom and do not produce life.

2.8.8.2 Do absolute moral standards exist?

This is a crucial question where Christianity and humanism are diametrically opposed. Are there actually absolute, immutable moral standards laid down by God, or does man autonomously determine his values? A professor once illustrated this by asking his audience, "Who of you already invented a moral value?" Everyone giggled uncomfortably because they understood the foolishness of the question. Man is not to create the right rules, but discover them, just as Newton discovered the formula of gravity (and didn't determine it!). Moral laws are similar to natural laws: also, physical laws (e.g. gravity) or logical and mathematical laws (e.g. $1 + 1 = 2$) exist independently from us. Does this not apply as much for laws such as honesty and justice? Or can a person design an 'alternative moral system' with e.g. dishonesty as a value, or even with 'You must be at least 50% honest?' Can you even build a society without elemental honesty? Man must not only discover that moral laws exist but also that they are there to be obeyed. The consequences of not-obeying can be very painful or even fatal (conflict, fights, imprisonment, war, murder . . .). The guiding principle in seeking truth and wisdom must not be what we like, but what is logically correct (consistent and lasting) and what works in reality.

Accepting that man determines moral values himself inevitably leads to relativism and puts all morality on shaky ground. In practice, this becomes opportunism, because man chooses what best suits him in a given situation (pragmatism). In other words, moral standards and values become like a 'build-it-yourself'-kit for the DIY. The hard core of humanistic values can never be more than a greatest common denominator of all human values and so a minimalistic package. If you must then also share this package with billions of other people, what remains is as good as zero.

The infinitely high moral standard of Christianity can scare or discourage people, seem impossible or frustrate, and above all, produce guilt, and something to which modern man is highly allergic. The temptation then to dismiss them as impossible and undesirable is very big. But you can just as well reverse this; high standards can also challenge us greatly! Athletes who aim for a world championship, mountaineers who want to climb the highest summit, the urge of people to break world records . . . 'Turning the other cheek', for example, is the pinnacle of moral superiority, a sign of immense inner strength and freedom, but also extremely difficult and rare! However, 'moral world championships' are extremely unpopular in our culture. This also has to do with that enormous imbalance of body-soul-spirit. We would rather train our physical muscles than our moral abilities.

> "Universalist egalitarianism from which the ideals of freedom, collective life in solidarity, individual morals such as conscience and democracy came forth, is the direct inheritance of Jewish ethics of justice, and Christian ethics of love. Up until today there is no alternative, everything else is just postmodern bragging."
> —Jürgen Habermas, philosopher and atheist

For a Christian, God is not the 'bogeyman' of morality, a 'moral stick behind the door', as if his moral motivation is just external. God is his coach, who brings out the best in him, stimulates and encourages him, wants to raise him up above his mediocrity, and therefore, sometimes 'puts the whip to it'. That moral standards are associated with His person, makes all the difference. The world is not saved by rules and laws, not even by better rules and laws. The human motivation to comply to these is thoroughly spoiled, and there is need for a cure.

The Humanistic Vision

Formerly, the Church was generally recognized as the moral authority, but since it was expelled from that position, no substitute has yet been appointed. The moral throne is empty, and if it depends on humanism, the function is also declared non-vacant. There are thus seven billion substitutes, and that is also how they want it. Anyone raising a moral voice is labeled a 'moral knight' and silenced. Humanism declares many areas to be 'amoral', but this is only a short step away from 'immoral'!

> 54. Humanism rejects every existing moral authority and does not put any other in its place: any moral authority is discredited and muzzled as a matter of course. The statement 'each person determines their own values' is like saying: 'There are no common values'. There will be no tolerance for those who elevate their own moral values above those of another. Norms and values have become the great taboo of our time, a 'moral knight' is the biggest insult you can throw at anyone. But the slogan, 'you must not judge me' is also a moral judgment.

2.8.8.3 Humane or humanistic?

Humanism did not only separate Christian values from God, it even turned these against Christianity, thus presenting itself as *the* bearer and guarantee of humaneness against an 'intolerant God'. This is only possible through a fundamental distortion of the Christian God-image. However, the God of the Bible is infinitely more man-loving than all Christians together, and infinitely more humane than the noblest humanist. He is the inventor of man and of humaneness.

In a society where man determines the laws and values, we now complain bitterly about the 'blurring of moral standards', the 'vulgarization of morals', and the hardening of the people. Meanwhile, the list of 'victims' of our free society ever increases. The whole social sector and the aid relief sector are non-stop busy with cleaning up the 'mess' others (who set 'their own standards and values'!) cause. Thousands of broken youngsters in special youth care, for example, pay the price for the unrestrained freedom their parents claimed for themselves. But nobody has the courage to link this to the absolute freedom that is preached by humanism.

2.9 Atheism

Atheism is the conviction that God does not exist, nor any gods or supernatural beings; heaven is empty, there is nothing after death. It's one step further than agnosticism ('I do not know'). It claims to 'know' with certainty that there is nothing 'higher' and often relies on science for this. Of course, humanism is not equal to atheism because there are also Christian or religious humanists (see 3.3). There is, however, a straight line from one to the other; if man is placed at the very center, which role remains then for God? Many of the remarks in this chapter therefore, also apply to secular humanism.

2.9.1 Religion: abuse, violence, and wars

Atheism usually finds its ground for existence in the observation of many negative consequences of religions. We must fully admit that, when we look at the countless religions in the world, there are many foolish and dangerous aspects. Some beliefs are plainly irrational, obscurantist, and arguably

incorrect. Some practices are fanatic, dangerous, unjust, and immoral. Some habits and rituals are barbaric, mutilating and discriminatory. The number of deaths for (immediate) religious reasons runs in the millions; human sacrifices and child victims occurred in almost all ancient religions (with the Aztec, up to 80,000 in one day). We cannot, therefore, absolutely say, 'Religion is good, atheism is bad'. As soon as people start interfering with God, it almost inevitably goes wrong. When they try to speak in the name of 'the gods', religious principles and human interests always get mixed up. In all religions and in all churches, you can find examples of abuse of power, spiritual oppression (even terror), fraud and manipulation, self-service and self-enrichment.

Some atheists, however, take the step from there to (1) 'all religions are the same', (2) 'religion is essentially connected to intolerance and violence'[15],

---

15. In the above-mentioned brochure *Freethinking and humanism in Europe*, p. 9–10, Richard Dawkins unequivocally mentions religion as the greatest cause of all wars and

and (3) 'therefore, God does not exist'. But if we investigate these three statements rationally and critically (!), they prove to be full of logical and historical mistakes. In most of these 'religious wars', reliion was not the direct cause of the conflict. It was about political interests, economic power, racial and cultural differences, old feuds, insulted national pride . . ., mixed with religious legitimization. Without God or religion, these wars would have been carried out nonetheless. But 'God' was added for the 'pep talk'. Blaming religion for all the violence that has occurred in its name is just as unjust as blaming 'science' for all the destruction of nature, the war industry or the dehumanization that flowed from it. Thus, the abuse says more about the dullness of humanity than about the essence of religion. To arrive at the conclusion that, because of the many unjust religious practices, 'all religions are false', is yet again a reasoning error that goes against elementary logic. It is not because false money is in circulation, that real money does not exist. Even the opposite is true; it would make no sense whatsoever to make false money if there were no real money!

> 55. Humanism/atheism considers all religions as potentially dangerous. But this 'danger' is the flip side of something very positive. Since God deserves the first place in a believer's life, since faith can have such a strong appeal – it can flare up the highest passions, can cause people to rise above themselves — hence, its abuse is also so very destructive. Faith is very personal and intimate (like sexuality), and consequently its abuse is also very devastating (as is the case with sexual abuse)! But who advocates abolishing all sexuality?

When atheists use all the abuse of religion as an argument to not believe in God, believers can turn the reasoning around. It is precisely proof that we cannot believe in man because he messes up everything, even the most beautiful and holiest that exists. When, for example, a terrorist mows down people with his Kalashnikov 'in the name of God', it is not God holding the Kalashnikov! That the blame lies with man is not difficult to prove; everything is abused by man: money, power, knowledge, relationships . . . even the things that are the most beautiful, intimate, and holiest, such as sex and art.

If humanity would perfectly master all other 'neutral' earthly things and only religion would lead to bloodshed, then we would 'know with

---

conflicts: "It is not an exaggeration to say that religion is the most inflammatory enemy-labelling device in history."

scientific certainty' that it is religion that is to blame! But the facts show the opposite! Just imagine if all religions were to be removed from the world, would war disappear? This representation of things is so naive that it is no longer honest; people make war anyway, with or without God. Modern wars are about money, oil or power; where is the 'progress'? The risk that violence in a non-religious society would completely get out of control is even very real because the restraint of moral authority (e.g. the Old Testament ban on bloodshed) is no longer there.

2.9.2 Atheism, science, and (un)belief

Atheism constantly refers to science and reason. However, we must state clearly here that it is impossible for reason to be a deciding factor in favor of a world explanation without God! Believing that no God exist whatsoever is as much a belief as theism and is not more rational or provable than its opposite. Whoever does indeed assert this, is intellectually dishonest. The great certainty and firmness with which some atheists herald their (un)belief should amaze us because it is based on nothing rational. Agnosticism is more honest in this respect. You can never directly draw a philosophical conclusion from a physical observation. Confusion of understanding arises because the domains of science and worldview are continually mixed up. The Big Bang theory and the evolution theory are constantly cited by atheists as a satisfactory alternative to belief in creation, but this is not what they really are. They are on a different level and give answers to different questions. They can explain—in cases where scientifically proven—how things came into being, but not why. They can offer a technical answer, but not a spiritual one. It is like answering the existential question, "Why am I here in this world?" on a physical level, "Because your father's seed cell accidentally came together with your mother's egg-cell." This leaves the one asking the question with a huge emptiness.

56. Humanism/atheism often creates (or upholds) the false perception that 'believing in God' is religion and 'not believing in God' is scientific. Hopefully it is clear to everyone that both parts of this idea are equally impossible to prove: they are an ideological proposition that science itself cannot make any meaningful statement about.

Atheism clashes continually with its greatest weakness: you cannot explain everything from nothing. This not only goes against 'spiritual laws' but also against all scientific or philosophical logic. This is not just a little beauty flaw, but a fundamental insoluble contradiction. Atheism would be 100% right in all her criticisms of religions if (!!!) indeed there would be no God. This is, however, her weakest point: there is no reasonable or scientific argument to verify this. Purely rationally, you have to conclude: there is (at least) 50% chance that there is a God. There are however, seriously reasonable arguments for embracing an intelligent Creator; the incredible rationality in nature, the mathematical relationships between natural forces, the immaterial character of the laws of nature or mathematical laws, the incredible complexity of living bodies, the superior intelligence in our own brain and every living cell . . . are all very strong indications of an 'Intelligent Design'. Einstein once said, 'The only incomprehensible thing about the universe is that it is understandable'; that is, its rationality must have an explanation! You can repeat 1000X that everything 'just' originated like that, until you believe it yourself, yet it remains absurd.

> "Some scientists devote their entire lives to seeking intelligent life on other planets, God is still looking for intelligent life on earth."

> "Science without religion is lame, religion without science is blind."
> —Albert Einstein

In the debate between atheism and Christianity, rational arguments are actually never the decisive factor because purely rationally there is (at least) 50% chance that God exists. There are always other, deeper, non-rational motivations. When atheists, for example, accuse believers of believing out of weakness or cowardice, we can also turn the question around. Is the underlying reason for unbelievers perhaps laziness or comfort so they can, for example, stay in their warm bed on Sunday and do whatever they like? Even leading atheist Prof. Etienne Vermeersch admits, "Most people who become unbelieving in the West do not do so for intellectual reasons, but mainly under the influence of the consumer society; people have so much of everything." Their atheism is in fact 'apatheism'; it is not a result of persuasion but of indifference.

> "You do not become an atheist because God does not exist, but because He hinders you."
> —Rik Torfs, former rector of the Catholic University of Louvain and ex-senator

Atheism gets a very loud voice in the media nowadays, which makes it look as if it is very strong. In the context of the whole of the world, however, convinced atheists remain a very small group. Most people, even those who left church long ago, recoil from the no-God-hypothesis. The sense that 'there must be something' is very strong in people. Secondly, atheism is only a very recent phenomenon in world history. It was only in the 18th century that some dared to claim this out loud. Thirdly, atheism as an ideology, is hardly organized. Atheists are, as one of them told me himself, very individualistic and are, just like cats, very hard to gather together. This does not make it easy to know their 'official position', or to dialogue and negotiate with them. There are also major differences amongst them and opposing currents that fight each other.

> "Richard Dawkins assumes that religion is an error of reasoning that will disappear with more education . . . But religion has an imperishable value for many people, it will not disappear through a bit of education. The US is still as religious as one hundred years ago. The new atheists (like Dawkins) suffer from a kind of moral panic. Since the 1960s it was predicted that religion would disappear, and this clearly does not happen."
> —John Gray,
> British thinker and atheist

Atheism regards all religion as potentially dangerous; when it gets out of hand, it is impossible to stop it rationally and it can become terribly destructive. This, understandably, frightens people. This frightening power, however, is the flipside of something extremely positive. Faith can have a superhuman appeal, kindle the highest passions, and generate unprecedented forces. Because God deserves the first place and can claim all rights, He can raise man above himself; draw the very best out of him, giving him 'wings'. Perversion of the very best becomes the very worst! The parallel between religion and sex is again in place here. Faith is very personal and intimate, and therefore its abuse also so devastating and extra painful (just like with sex)! But whoever therefore wants to abolish all sex, would also remove her positive sides, the fiery passion and unifying power!

2.10 Secularity and neutrality

2.10.1 Secularization and secularism

Since the 1950s, the phenomenon of de-Christianization and secularization in European countries skyrocketed: the numbers of church visits have declined year after year. As the Christian majority and its social influence decreased, protests against the dominance of one worldview in society increased. It was then demanded for public spaces to become 'neutral': all Christian symbols had to be removed. But it went far beyond the physical removal of crucifixes. The mentality also changed, and in other public domains (the legal system, economics, politics, science, media . . .) every reference to God was deleted, including verbally. It was seen as 'inappropriate', or 'not done', to speak out God's name on the streets or on television; it became 'politically incorrect'. Even though the vast majority of the population was still Christian, faith was pushed back to the private sphere and the Church. Religion became a 'private hobby' and culture had to be 'godless'.

The discussion is not about—including for Christians—whether we should go back to medieval theocracy or a Christian monopoly. It is about what the place of religion can be in a pluralistic society and about the delicate balance concerning the role of government in this. Here again, Christianity and humanism collide head-on. The 'separation of Church and state' is namely extended—wrongly—by many to the 'separation of God and politics', as if the word 'God' is no longer allowed in politics. A pragmatic, political separation between two institutions is transferred to the whole of culture in all its domains. There is namely a fundamental difference between secularization and secularism (similar to that of pluralistic and pluralism: see 2.7.4). The first is a social fact which is 'measurable' by sociologists. The second makes an ideology out of this that considers secularity ('laïcité') as 'the' best, and the only correct solution.

In other words, there is a worldview behind secularism which is based on the (historically incorrect) view that God and religion are the greatest threat to human society. Religion leads, in this view, always to abuse, as if its

---

57. Humanism advocates an open pluralistic society, but actually suffocates the debate concerning worldviews by simultaneously striving for a secular, godless society: any discussion about 'the higher things of life' is seen as irrelevant and unimportant and so is pushed aside. As people almost never talk about their (lack of) faith, this leads to spiritual illiteracy and impoverishment: our spiritual vocabulary is noticeably regressing, and our spiritual antennas are not being utilized or refined.

pure application is impossible. According to this, therefore, society must be secular and pluralistic, as the best of any guarantee for freedom and tolerance. Secularism builds a 'barbed wire fence' around religion and Church. There can only be true religious freedom if a society is free from religion. This however, is a projection of the typical French situation, where the relationship between Church and State is very tense and hostile (as opposed to, for example, the Anglo-Saxon and Scandinavian countries). Secularists want to export this (French) false contradiction as the model.

Secularism creates an unhealthy taboo atmosphere because it reacts from a frantic fear. Just as it used to be 'offensive' and inappropriate to talk in public about sex, it is now so about faith. Old taboos are replaced by new ones! And so, in practice, the debate concerning worldviews is smothered and dismissed (also by the materialistic spirit of this age) as irrelevant and vague. This is the scantiest interpretation of 'tolerance' and 'pluralism'; we do not talk about our differences in order to not get in a fight, so we do not talk at all. And as people talk less and less about their faith (or lack of it, or about life questions), this leads to spiritual illiteracy and impoverishment. The spiritual vocabulary regresses and their spiritual antennae die off.

In the Middle Ages the Church stood undisputed above the State, and religion above politics. Today it is the opposite: The State determines which place and role religion and the Church can have in society. It has to determine the criteria for religious rules! In this way, however, the State is almost inevitably forced to take over some of the functions of religion, something for which it has no instruments. Again, humanism creates here (or amplifies) a false contradiction, namely between state and religion, as if the State should be constantly on its guard concerning religion and the Church. On the other hand, however, a government that is positive towards churches, can maximize to its own advantage, their social power, network, and social fabric.

Separating religion from public life is a humanistic dogma which goes right against the Christian faith. For a Christian, his faith and his life are inseparable. The relevance of the gospel becomes evident when not only it is applied to the life of the individual, but also on the level of society. The Church cannot help but interfere in society, otherwise she would be guilty of indifference and unworldliness.

The Humanistic Vision

2.10.2 Neutrality: politically, morally, and ideologically?

The humanistic principle of neutrality is a result of the demand of secular society. Namely, the State must be neutral in terms of religion, worldviews, and morality. It may not interfere with these and may not favor any one above the others. Since the official separation of Church and State, and the fact of a pluralistic society, the role of the State is of course essentially different from before. But what then does 'being neutral' mean? Is that even possible?

The requirement of neutrality is not a neutral requirement. It is the model of one world view for society, and then a very small one! When neutrality is defined as a ban of all religious expressions, then this is a victory for non-believers. Believers must then hide their symbols, yet a non-believer has nothing to hide (no symbols). Atheists sometimes argue that religious symbols offend or insult them, but this is a very questionable argument. If a Christian comes into a Muslim country and sees a half-moon in public buildings, is he then offended? Atheists cannot claim a 'right' to not see all religious symbolism at all cost. This principle results in oppressive, intolerant neutrality; it is not a-religious but anti-religious.

There are also very different (and opposite) ways to concretely handle what neutrality means. Does the government, for example give equal space to all religions, or does it not give any room to any? Who determines which religions are officially recognized and which ones are not? Almost inevitably different standards are being used here, depending on the personal preference (or aversion) of the one in authority.

A neutral society is soulless. Compare this with an apartment building where 10 families live together who want to decide which plants to put in the common hall. What happens when they do not agree? Neutrality opts for, 'No plants at all then'! Because another person's taste is not granted, nobody gets his way; the hall remains bare, boring, and dead. Pluralism would opt for, 'We put ten different plants in the hall'. Neutralism is a minimalistic notion, one that makes nobody happy. 'Neutral' has no soul, just like Esperanto, which receives no heartfelt response.

In this context, people sometimes talk about 'the morally neutral state', which then pertains to moral issues. The government cannot interfere with the private moral of its citizens. But is this not an illusion? Legislation constantly makes moral choices, such as, for example, from what age may young people buy alcohol or have sex! If it would not do this, it would create a moral vacuum, and be guilty of negligence.

> 58. Humanism often presents itself, consciously or subconsciously, as a neutral point of view. In the 19th century—and even still today—it regularly used the so-called 'neutral' state structure as a weapon against the power of the Church. But in the ideological sphere there is no neutrality: you cannot be impartial between good and evil, God and the devil. Whoever does not clearly choose against evil actually gives it free rein.

In a secular environment, a believer who honestly admits to his faith is regarded as non-neutral and partial, whereas a non-believer who admits to having no faith is seen as neutral, objective or unbiased. A non-believer will usually be chosen as a moderator in a debate or as a mediator. This perception is tenacious, but fundamentally unjust and often leads to practical discrimination against believers. In the humanistic spirit of this age, believers are held suspect in advance.

We must ask ourselves this question in a much more profound way: is neutrality even possible in the area of worldviews? Imagine a father who says, "I do not want to impose any religion on my son, but will leave him completely free, and when he is eighteen years, he can choose." This father does not want to exercise any influence, maybe with the best of intentions, and communicates nothing for or against this or that worldview. This causes two problems. Communication theories teach us that it is impossible to communicate neutrally. Even silence is significant, and your non-verbal communication often screams it out! This naive father also communicates to his son that religion is not important, and that you can live perfectly well without it. In front of his son he lives out that God is totally irrelevant. Neutrality does not exist when it comes to life or death, good or evil, God or the devil! A 'religiously neutral education' is an illusion; 'god-free'[16] education is in fact godless education. The same principle, when extended, applies

---

16. In this book, I want to distinguish between 'ungodly' and 'godless'. With 'godless' I just mean 'without God' which does not necessarily lead to 'ungodliness' in the sense of 'moral depravity, wickedness, debauchery'. A godless person can be morally high standing. Equalizing these two suggests that atheists can only be immoral people, which is certainly unjustified.

to a whole society and government. A culture that holds up 'neutrality of worldviews' as a high value creates (de facto?) a God-poor society, and a 'climate of structural unbelief'.

3

Humanism in Practice

An ideology must first be judged in its pure, 'ideal' form. So far, we examined the fundamental convictions, values, and worldview of humanism, and the reader can judge how original, rational, and consistent these are. But we must also consider the consequences of the beliefs for people and society in everyday life. What is the fruit? If a theory sounds good, but does not work in reality, then it is useless at best, but can also be harmful or dangerous. If humanism presents itself as a fully-fledged alternative to religion or the Church, then it must be judged as strictly as it judges the Church. Over the centuries, the Church has been systematically attacked, especially because she failed substantially to put her own theory into practice. All accusations of irrationality in doctrine, rigid dogmas or inconsistencies held against Christianity should also be held up as a mirror before humanism. All the hypocrisy it reproaches the churches for, all human failures, all gross scandals discovered about Christian leaders should also serve as a measure for its own judgment. All abuse of power or intolerance of an 'inert and fossilized institution' should also be investigated with atheist regimes or leaders.

> 59. If humanism wants to put itself on a par with Christianity as an equal (or better) alternative, it should be assessed with the same rigorous standards. Then we would most probably see humanism making all the same mistakes which it criticizes the Church for, simply because those mistakes are caused by people.

HUMANISM IN PRACTICE

3.1 The battle for worldviews

3.1.1 Organized freethinking

When comparing humanism and the Church with each other in this way, we immediately run into a major difficulty. Because of their DNA and organizational form, they are hardly comparable.

Humanism does (1) not have a credo that is fixed and recognized by everyone. Nobody has the right to determine principles and values for others, and everyone has the right to disagree with something. Even leading humanistic philosophers or writers do not have more authority than Joe Bloggs. Foundational convictions can be reinterpreted by everyone in all directions, which also happens in practice[1]. 'Free thinking' changes and shifts constantly, adapting to the spirit of time, and does not let itself be pinned down to anything. Humanism is constantly reinventing itself and is actually in a continual identity crisis[2]. This flexibility (or fluidity) is sometimes represented as a strength but is clearly a huge weakness as well. Flexibility is of course a nice feature, but what if nothing is fixed? What then is the difference between it and an amoeba?

This applies not only to the doctrinal level but also on the organizational level; humanism has (2) no central authority, no official body, no recognized spokesman[3]. There are organizations and umbrella alliances, but many humanists cannot identify themselves within these and prefer to remain independent; in fact, they are even principally opposed to such alliances because again, these want to force their members into a straightjacket and exert pressure. Humanism bumps into a fundamental inner contradiction here; it cannot and does not want to impose standards or obligations, but when it organizes itself, it inevitably does this! A 'real humanist'

---

1. The Dutch freethinkers' organization 'De Dagoraad' ('The Dawn') e.g. (founded in 1856, renamed in 1958 'De Vrije Gedachte'—'The Free Thought' -), changed its statutes seven times between 1856 and 1978!

2. The Dutch-Belgian philosopher Jaap Kruithof (1929–2009), prof. at the University of Ghent, strongly criticized 'classical humanism' with its unlimited individualism and relativism, and wanted to transcend the anthropocentrism with ecocentrism, 'Mother Earth' being a kind of new highest value.

3. We must of course note that this is not so clear for 'the Church' either. 'The Church' is not a monolithic block, but in reality, there are many churches and many currents within these churches. But there is a fundamental difference between them and humanism. All Christians recognize that there is an authority, one truth, and one standard. If not in a human (church) institution, then in God, in Jesus Christ, and in the Bible.

opposes this like a free bird who does not want to be caged. This, of course, also means that humanism can never be called to be accountable; no one takes responsibility for the consequences of its principles (such as the many derailments of absolute freedom and self-determination).

In humanism, (3) membership is also very unclear. You do not need to 'take a step', convert yourself officially, make a public confession or get baptized. You can of course become a member of an organization, but no rule can require commitment. There are no weekly meetings or (mandatory) financial contributions. It is like a free trump card. When you would ask about the number of members in humanism you would therefore hear very varied figures. Some would like to include all the un-churched and non-believers and then claim 20-30% of the population. But if you were to count the strict number of members, those convinced and committed, you would reach about 1%[4]. You could also ask yourself how many members of a humanist organization would remain if they would require/expect a weekly commitment and ask for a financial contribution (like the churches)? The degree of commitment shows the seriousness of the members' motivation, the strength of their beliefs and their weight in society. In other words, a committed and active member of one worldview 'weighs' ten times heavier than a passive member of another.

All this has consequences. When a Christian or Christian leader commits a big mistake (e.g. a pastor shoots an abortion doctor), the world expects all Christian churches to openly condemn and distance themselves—and rightly so! But this does not count for humanism; they proclaim tolerance and respect, but when a non-believer publicly mocks the Christian faith or the church—think, for example, of the French satirical magazine Charlie Hebdo—then nowhere do we hear an official humanistic condemnation of this. When a Bishop commits an offence such as pedophilia, this is a reason for thousands to leave the church. But when a prominent atheist does the same, thousands do not convert to Christianity. Is it not strange how the perception is very unbalanced?

There is another imbalance in the battle between humanism and Christianity. When a Christian leader falls into moral sin, this is seen as an

---

4. Some figures from the Belgian research by Elchardus and Dobbelaere, *Verloren zekerheid* ('Lost security') (2000): 63% of Belgians consider themselves as members of an organized religion, 1.1% are members of a freethinker's organization. If you ask them about worldview 7,4% (of those outside the Christian stream) call themselves 'freethinkers' in a broad sense, 3.2% 'believing but in a different way', 5.9% indifferent, 8.8% unbelieving, 9.7% 'compose their own faith'. . .

Humanism in Practice

accusation against Christianity. "You see, those Christians are no good and the Church is no better than anything else?" The perpetrator is perceived as a representative of his faith or his church. But the same does not apply in the other direction. Whenever an unbeliever does something horrible, no one has the reaction to condemn or leave atheism, and to become a member of a church. In this case, the abomination is seen as a private act. The Church is heavily brought down, but humanism as a worldview or ideology is almost never judged.

Humanism is against all forms of imposed authority, but when it organizes itself (because of political influence and public funding), it has all the characteristics that it accused the Church of: abuse of power, oppression, lack of freedom, imperialism, rigid dogmas, condescending rules, inner quarrels, and divisions . . . In short, all the mistakes it accused the Church of as an institution, it also commits, simply because these mistakes are caused by humans.

Humanism has another weakness: it mainly thrives with a small intellectual elite who are highly educated and economically strong. It therefore fits well with people living in a privileged luxury situation, but it does not catch on with people living in poverty, war, and oppression. How can they believe in the goodness of man if they only see the opposite around them? Humanism is not a people's movement, not because the people are 'stupid' but because it is, in itself, alienated and unsustainable; it does not stand the test of hard reality.

The more humanism organizes itself as a fully compatible alternative to the churches, the more it resembles the churches it fights. It organizes alternative festivals (e.g. spring feast), alternative ceremonies (initiations or de-baptisms), alternative saints (role models) and martyrs[5] . . . It creates 'secular gods' such as 'the earth', nature, the planet[6], humanity, science . . . without realizing how 'mystically' they speak about these.

---

5. In front of the 'Université Libre de Bruxelles' ('Free University Brussels'), is a statue of Francisco Ferrer (Spanish pedagogue and libertarian, anarchist thinker, shot on 13-10-1909) as a 'martyr of freedom of conscience'.

6. Especially in the current ecological movement, that wants to 'save' (a religious word!) the earth and humanity, 'the planet' becomes a purpose in itself, a semi-religious being spoken about in semi-personal terms.

3.1.2 Freemasonry and free thinking

Freemasonry is certainly not identical to free thinking and humanism, yet their history is inseparably connected. The masonic lodges of the 18th century were undoubtedly the breeding grounds for the Enlightenment ideas. In the regular lodges (especially in Anglo-Saxon countries), this leaned much more towards Christian ideas (theistic or deistic). In the irregular lodges (especially in France) this evolved in anti-clerical or atheistic direction. In the beginning, however, Freemasonry (The Grand Lodge, 1717)

had in no way an anti-Christian or even anti-ecclesiastical character. James Anderson, the writer of its main Constitution (1723), was himself a Presbyterian minister. Regular lodges, by the way, describe the irregular masonry as a monstrosity, something that goes completely against the original spirit of the founders.

The formation of Freemasonry clearly answered a need. The 'masonic lodge' offered more than free friendship clubs or famous 'salons'; they were a kind of shielded space where uncensored (without interference by the Church!) new ideas could be exchanged, where free thinking, rationality, and openness of discussion were central. Yet, there clearly is also a spiritual, semi-religious dimension; the many rituals and oaths, symbols and myths consciously create a mystical atmosphere around it. The 'success formula' of the lodge is that it offers a cocktail of mystery and friendship, spirituality and openness, mysticism and charity, moral ideals and philosophical wisdom.

However, big critical questions must be asked about the character and social role of the lodge.

(1) It is suggested that membership of a lodge is perfectly compatible with that of a church: the 'G' standing for a kind of universal god, Supreme Being

of the universe, defined as vaguely as possible, acceptable to all religions as well as to atheists. But this is jumping to conclusions because this 'god image' clashes inevitably with the biblical image (see also 3.3.1).

(2) The fact that you cannot just walk into a lodge and the membership fee is very high creates—consciously!—a character of exclusivity and increases the sense of 'importance'. A very attractive reason for someone to become a member is to have the opportunity to meet 'important people' who can definitely improve your promotion opportunities in society.

(3) It is not possible to explain how the requirement of secrecy (under terrible oaths of self-cursing and punishment by death!) can be part of an organization that supposedly intends brotherhood, spirituality, and charity. This hidden character is totally contradictory to the Enlightenment ideas[7]; the fiercely contested 'darkness of the Church' was replaced by another. Certainly, if what freemasons do is only good, there is no reason for secrecy; on the contrary!

(4) Although Freemasonry by no means wants to be a church, it places itself in a position where it competes with the Church. It provided a kind of alternative circuit, separate from any tutelage. Freemasonry claims things that the Church also claims such as bringing universal brotherhood, world peace, humanity, morality, self-perfection . . . It makes claims that Jesus made first, e.g., leading people to 'the light'. Thus, they claim (implicitly, unconsciously?) to do this better than Jesus—and this while everything in a lodge happens in secret, in a space without windows! They come together in a temple (again a religious word!), full of religious symbols, borrowed from all kinds of religions (emphasizing its universal character, suggesting a broader, more enlightened religion). Through its ceremonies and rituals, it consciously creates a sacred atmosphere and thus becomes a kind of ersatz church, a 'light' religion.

---

7. Freemasonry justifies its secrecy with the argument that it could otherwise be persecuted (as happened during Nazism). This is, however, a very weak argument; secrecy was already in the statutes in the 18th century when there was no persecution at all. And Nazi persecution was over seventy years ago; there is currently no threat of persecution. Also, this is a reversal of reasoning; the suspicion of a world plot by Freemasonry was precisely fed by the secrecy (not vice versa!).

(5) In a lodge one must swear costly (often bombastic) oaths, which raises the question about where one's first loyalty lies; will, for example, a Catholic freemason, if he must choose in a moral dilemma, be faithful to the Church or to the lodge? At the lodge, he swears very heavy oaths, not at church . . .[8] The suspect atmosphere surrounding Freemasonry ('friendship politics') actually has a reason, just by its own constitution. If, for example, a freemason is a judge and a 'brother' gets accused, where then will his first loyalty be? The suspicions are not purely fabricated gossip from the outside but are primarily derived from its own nature and structure.

Some go as far as to call Freemasonry a sect. This because of its (semi-)religious character, the very closed structure, the tight hierarchy, promise of obedience, and code of silence. Its charity is, in their eyes, just a cover-up (just as one reproaches this in some sects). In its worst form, Freemasonry can turn into a kind of mafia (also called 'brotherhood') which becomes a kind of parallel political system[9]. Some anti-clerics, for example, reproach the Catholic 'Opus Dei' of consciously and hiddenly infiltrating the highest political circles, but what does the lodge do? Everyone is free to set up clubs as he wants, but the lack of transparency is the big sting here. Therefore, it is a reasonable (!) requirement, for example for high political nominations, to explicitly ask freemasons to make

---

60. Freemasonry has in many ways been the hidden force behind humanism but is inconsistent with its own principles: it works in concealment, uses irrational myths, makes (selective) use of the Bible, and exerts strict control over its members (by the costly oaths they must swear). Freemasonry pretends in one of her rituals to lead people to the light but does everything in the greatest secrecy and in a room without windows! Everything that is hidden is, by definition, in darkness.

---

8. For a Christian, the first point of faith is that Jesus Christ is the 'revelation of God', and he asks exclusivity from his followers: "You cannot serve two masters" (Matt 6:24), "Whoever is not for me, is against me" (Matt 12:30), "Whoever loves (something or someone) more than me, is not worthy of me "(Matt 10:37). Jesus actually commanded to "not make oaths at all"(Matt 5:34)! It can in no way be explained how a Christian can make a covenant with an organization that positions itself so exclusively and semi-religiously. Secrecy is also absolutely incompatible with basic Christian values. "Everything you have spoken in the dark will be heard in the light and what you whispered in the ear in the inner room will be preached from the roofs" (Luke 12:3).

9. I certainly do not maintain this is always the case, but that it is sometimes the case is also admitted by some freemasons. In the 19th century, for example, the mayor of Brussels was chosen already, before the official elections, in the hallways of the lodges.

themselves known (certainly within a Christian church)! By the way, some prominent free thinkers are principally not a member of the lodge and are even opposed to it for these same reasons. And there are also prominent freemasons who are in favor of abolishing this secrecy.

Freemasonry proclaims beautiful ideals of unity and brotherhood, but how does it work in practice? There we see endless divisions, painful schisms, and fierce mutual controversies. And despite the fact that it is very internationally branched, no case is known where lodge brothers across the borders could stop or prevent a war.

3.1.3 The war for power and perception

In theory, the discussion about worldviews should be a very serene, pure, and noble dialogue; everybody sincerely seeks the truth, or not? Do not all people struggle with the same big life questions and existential pain like suffering and death, love and hate, sense and nonsense . . .? Reality, however, is very different; instead of an open dialogue we see more often a (trench) war in which both 'legitimate' and 'dirty' weapons are used. Typically, humans have a blind spot regarding their own mistakes. Undoubtedly, the Church has used improper weapons to proclaim the faith (all forms of coercion or pressure, physically, psychologically, mentally, politically, economically, culturally . . .). In this chapter, we also want to highlight the other side (which is almost never mentioned). The way in which the Church and Christianity were (and are!) attacked is not averse to disinformation and caricatures.

The 'war for souls' is actually a war for perception, and it seems that whoever shouts the loudest appears to be right. If you repeat a lie (or a half-truth) long enough, people start to adopt it as true. Whoever can bend the perception to his side, wins the war; whether you name those that are fighting 'rebels and terrorists' or 'freedom fighters and heroes' makes all the difference for their chances of victory. The choice of words is sometimes very subtle, yet strongly suggestive. Christian education is called

61. The errors of the Church (and these should not be minimized) are systematically and disproportionately highlighted by her opponents to muzzle her. The allergic response of some atheistic humanists to God, Church, and religion is irrational and out of proportion. And in this 'ideological war', the perception is often more important than the content.

'indoctrination' (as if an atheist education is not!). Evangelization ('bringing good news') is translated as 'imposing your faith'. Being critical, suddenly is called 'hate speech' (but only for one party!). 'Proselytism' is a swear word. The democratic rights of the Church are called outdated privileges. The mistakes of the past are systematically repeated, spread out broadly and magnified so as to silence Christians. The horror of the inquisition, the burning of witches and heretics, and religious wars are continually brought up, even though they are completely past tense for at least three to four hundred years. Recent church scandals (such as pedophilia) get endless media attention. The Church is pushed invariably into the conservative corner, even though it has often been the engine behind change, this while it is suggested that 'conservative' is bad at all times and 'progressive' by definition is good. Just as the media can make or break politicians, they can also do this with organizations and movements.

It is certainly not my intention to depict the media as 'the great evildoer'. There is also much honest reporting, balanced information, and liberating criticism. But the colored role of the media in this area is largely due to its own character. By definition, the media brings a distorted view of reality; only what is new, exceptional, dramatic, sensational, bizarre, and abnormal... gets attention. Especially when the media is commercialized, the cycle of sensationalism dominates almost everything. When we apply this for a moment to the secular media coverage regarding spirituality we see that religion is hushed up 'because it is religion'. This actually means that the secularist voice dominates, and pluralism is crushed.

Furthermore, if there is still spiritual news, it usually refers to alternative or exotic groups (e.g. oriental religions), or the deviant and extreme (sectarian excesses, scandals). Everything that is different is interesting; 'old Christianity' is assumed to be 'too-well-known' (while most Westerners have hardly any knowledge of faith anymore). It has a so called 'no news value' and is thus completely swept under the carpet.

Our society praises 'being critical', but this is particularly true in one direction. Whenever Christians are critical of modern 'acquisitions' such as

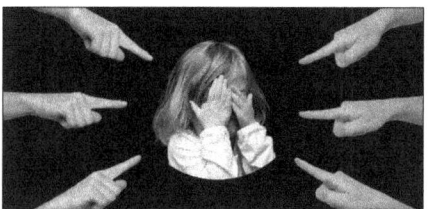

abortion, euthanasia, or gay marriage, they are reviled as 'intolerant'. Expressing your opinion about this is not even tolerated by the counter-party—an intolerance that is far greater than that of the other side! It is portrayed as a backyard fight, and any openness of debate is immediately shut down. In the abortion and euthanasia debate, for example, many human arguments exist that are against (relationally, socially, morally, philosophically, psychologically, demographically, legally, politically . . .), arguments that have only the good of man in mind and remain in the horizontal dimension. However, as they come from a believing corner, these arguments are rejected as religious ('You are against, just because of your faith') and thus all other rational elements are also swept from the table as if they were 'not' relevant. They are not even taken seriously but immediately classified.

Theoretically, humanism has much respect for other opinions, but in practice we often see contempt and mockery, even disgust; the arguments hit below the belt or play on the person. Some militant atheists/humanists, for example, openly call religion 'a mental disorder'. Certainly, not all do this but the 'more moderate' group does not correct the first and does not distance itself from their disrespect or intolerance. Does this silence mean they consent?

This battle for souls does not only happen in the media but also in politics, and here too a mixture of legitimate and illegitimate means are used. The struggle for power, influence, and public funding is always fierce and does not draw the best out of a man: power games, lobbying, political horse-trading, pressure and threat, the war for voters, the urge to profile oneself . . . Humanism has often accused the (majority) Church of doing this in a dirty way but does the same[10].

Another sociological mechanism plays a major role here. It is a well-known phenomenon that the political elite become alienated from the people, their voters. They live in a subculture, a 'bubble', and 'forget' their origins. Being in the circles of power does something to them. That is why they sometimes make completely different laws than what their electorate chose them for. Even when polls show that the majority of the people are against something, those laws are still voted for in parliament. We see the same in the area of belief systems. We already noted that humanism is

---

10. I could give many concrete examples of this media war and political struggle, but the space is unfortunately missing in this book. Only one: before abortion was allowed in Belgium (1990), atheistic doctors practiced it for years clandestinely (e.g. Dr. Willy Peers). This was consciously brought into the media as a kind of provocation and a strategy of accomplished facts: "And who dares to punish me for this?" These illegal actions were a way to force legislation; Willy Peers (who at least performed three hundred abortions) was never convicted.

rather the 'spirituality' of a small intellectual elite, especially in Freemasonry, and that it is good manners to be 'modern' there. Many humanistic laws pass through parliament, while they would have been rejected in a referendum. A large majority of Europe is still Christian in their views (even though they never or hardly ever attend church), but the elite clearly steers another spiritual course. As the latter also control the media, these can also be cleverly used to 'play' on the mentality. When a democratic majority is in their way, there are always ways to reach the goal . . .

Political influence has much to do with numerical strength of a movement. But in the area of worldview, this is not always easy to measure. What are objective figures? Who do you count as Christian, half-Christian, un-churched, atheistic . . . and what about the many subgroups and blends? When it comes to public funding, everybody is included, and as widely as possible. Catholics sometimes count all baptized members (even when they later turn away). But humanists sometimes also claim all the un-churched (agnostics, those that are indifferent or undecided, have an alternative faith, those who believe in 'something'. . .) to embellish their numbers for subsidies or social power. Although they are a very small group in society[11] (especially regarding its 'strict' membership), they manage to gain a disproportionately large social position, power, and influence, e.g. in the cultural and social sectors, and especially in education[12], the ideal channel to influence the spirits of young people.

> 62. The hard core of humanists comprises a very small group (± 1%). They have, however, managed to acquire a disproportionately high level of social prominence, power, and influence. In these 'modern' times, not believing is purported to be the 'standard' in public space, because it presents itself—falsely—as 'neutral'.

---

11. In Belgium, for example, the 'Humanistisch-Vrijzinnige Vereniging' ('Humanistic-Freethinkers Association') claims 'more than ten thousand members': this is even less than the Jehovah's Witnesses (24,000). According to Dobbelaere and Elchardus, *Verloren Zekerheid*, 1.1% of the population is member of a freethinker's association versus 59% Christian. According to Botterman, Hooghe and Bekkers, *Levensbeschouwing en maatschappelijke participatie,* ('Wolrd Views and Social Participation'), 7.7% call themselves freethinkers, versus 72% Catholic or Christian. If we base ourselves on the first numbers, there is one humanist for sixty Christians, the second count one to ten.

12. For centuries the Catholic Church in Belgium was, before 1830, the only one to organize education, which was at the same time an efficient channel to form the spirits of the youth. Therefore, since the 19th century, education in Belgium was one of the great battlefields between Catholics and Liberals who fought for public (and neutral)

Humanism in Practice

In Western culture a spiritual war rages about concepts and definitions, frameworks and reference points; conceptual boundaries are shifting significantly. Both camps fence with terms such as 'freedom' and 'human dignity', but the content is sometimes the opposite. Old people are given a life-ending injection, and this is called 'an act of love'. And whoever is against euthanasia is depicted as 'cruel' and inhuman. Choosing for euthanasia is presented as being 'brave', which simultaneously suggests that fighting until the end is 'cowardly'. Medicine has always been there to protect and save life, but now the killing of unborn life is called 'social assistance'. Abortion used to be a crime, now it is almost a right. The term 'marriage' is being defined fundamentally differently. While for thousands of years it was clear to everyone that it was about one man and one woman, the word is now stretched to something that it was never meant to be. 'Discipline' and 'sacrifice' used to be virtues, today they are regarded as harmful psychological self-torment, etc. In modern society, humanism has certainly won this war; the meaning of words stands on shaky ground.

The Christian church has been successfully pushed out of its monopoly position. In many respects, humanism is now the 'new State religion', the (so-called neutral) approach to life used by the government as a mode of operation. It remains amazing how fast this all happened, in just a few decades. This humanism was introduced in the west following 'salami politics'. The new ideas (which directly oppose 1800 years of Christian culture) were pushed through in very small steps, so people did not even notice. Humanistic thinking is so obvious and pervasive in our culture and the spirit of this age that it almost seems a crime to question it. Criticizing it is hardly tolerated in the secular and so-called pluralistic media. Because what is 'politically correct' is

> 63. Humanism has become the new 'State religion' in secular society: the vacuum created by removing the Church as an authority from the public sphere has been filled by a radical self-determination. There was (and is) a spiritual 'war' about concepts and definitions, frameworks, and reference points, and, as is often the case, those who shout the loudest impose their views and push through with them. Under the umbrella of a 'neutral government', humanism has managed to determine the new rules and to (re)define the parameters.

education. So, freethinkers used the (neutral!) state structure as a means and a weapon against the Church, as a competitive structure against the Catholic influence (Marc Reynebeau, *De Geschiedenis van België in woord en beeld*, ('The History of Belgium in Word and Image'), p. 78. Public education has long been known as a bastion for Freemasonry.

now clearly defined by the humanist spirit of today! Is the Christian voice too threatening here? Is it maybe too critical? Does it question the (humanistic) status quo? Does it ask too much from the openness and broadmindedness one can expect from a human being? Where does this anxiety come from? Maybe from the fear that there could be no alternative? The—irrational!—fear for a return to the (so-called 'dark') Middle Ages is greater than the love for truth! This also is a result of the war for perception; hardly any Christian today wants to go back to the Middle Ages or to the Church having dominance in every area of life. This fearful image, however, is constantly depicted so as to keep the war going (just as the picture of the enemy image was heavily exaggerated and constantly fed during the Cold War).

3.1.4 Excesses of humanism

Humanism wants to put man at the center instead of God for the main reason that in the past, religions were too often the reason for inhumane wars and bloodshed. Placing man at the center seemed a perfect remedy to prevent all this in the future. Well, we are now living some centuries later and we are 'fortunate' to see where this has led. The facts (!) are extremely painful and shameful; non-religious, atheist regimes have shed much more

blood than ages of religious wars caused, and this in just a few decades[13]. The 'Black Book of Communism'[14] comes to a total of 94,000,000 victims. Not only are the numbers staggering, but also how it all happened: Stalin's cruelty, ruthless executions (also of

---

13. Timothy Snyder, *Bloodlands* (2011), states that Hitler and Stalin together, in thirteen years (1932 to 1945), consciously murdered 14,000,000 people (next to the millions of 'ordinary victims' of war, fallen civilians and soldiers!) by organized starvation, executions, and gasification ... Hitler was of course not an atheist, but he was non-religious. He also, in his way, put man at the center, namely the Arian man. Stalin, however, was many times worse than Hitler; he killed more people in peacetime than in wartime.

14. Stéphane Courtois and Robert Laffont, *Le Livre noir du communisme: Crimes, terreur, répression* ('The Black Book of Communism', 1997), sums up: 65,000,000 in the People's Republic of China (Mao), 20,000,000 in the former Soviet Union (Lenin and Stalin), 2,000,000 in Cambodia (Pol Pot), 2,000,000 in North Korea, 1,700,000 in Africa, 1,500,000 in Afghanistan, 1,000,000 in communist states in Eastern Europe (Ceaucescu, Honecker, Hoxha), 1,000,000 in Vietnam ...

Humanism in Practice

his own relatives and almost all of his close associates), calculated mass massacres, organized starvation (3,000,000!), pitiless deportations, extermination camps . . .; the de-humanization broke all records! In these communist regimes, human beings were counted as nothing; one million more or less made no difference.[15] The unscrupulousness with which this happened was phenomenal; any higher moral power that could have possibly kept this cruelty in check was pushed aside. Atheist regimes are head and shoulders above any competition (even fascism); they are the most murderous regimes ever.

The tragedy is that communism began as a beautiful utopia of an ideal society of equality and prosperity for all! The Biblical belief of paradise was rejected, and man would now realize his own paradise, in a scientific manner, without God. The dream however turned into a nightmare! When man takes over and is going to realize God's plan on his own . . .! Here we see what happens when God's inhibitory influence against violence and inhumanity falls away.

> "When they ask me why 60,000,000 of my countrymen were sacrificed, the answer is, we forgot God."
> —Alexander Solzhenitsyn, Nobel Prize winner literature (1970)

Now, humanists will probably respond, "But this is not real humanism, only an excess and derailment." Of course, this is so, but why then do they write off Christianity on the basis of religious wars, crusades, inquisitions or some corrupt and warlike popes? Humanism does not, of course, promote dictatorial regimes and Stalinist practices, but they cannot as easily pretend they have nothing to do with it. A society where man only determines the laws without any God can evolve in that direction as well! May this be a serious exercise to reflect on what an anthropocentric ideology can lead to! There is no guarantee that this cannot repeat itself; we know well enough that man does not learn from history! The constantly repeated accusation

> 64. Humanism constantly presents religions as the source of all wars and bloodshed, but conveniently ignores the fact that this view is no longer consistent with reality: the god-less (atheistic) dictatorships of the last century (e.g. Russia, China, Cambodia, North Korea . . .) made far more victims than all religious wars put together.

---

15. When Mao implemented agricultural reforms in China between 1959 and 1963, 20,000,000 to 40,000,000 people died of hunger. At the start of this plan, Mao even took into account a potential for 50,000,000 deaths!

that religions are the main cause of wars and cruelties should once and for all be eradicated; (historical) science and the facts speak clearly enough.

3.2 The 'fruit' of humanism

3.2.1 Medical ethics

Humanism strives for a more humane society and believes this is more possible without God than with God. Here too, we need to critically review where this leads to, particularly in the area of medical ethics. This is one of the biggest battlefields between Christianity and humanism as it pertains to the beginning and end of life. Humanism claims as some of its 'great victories', for example, the right to abortion and euthanasia. But the stakes of this fight are very ambiguous, are they not? Can anyone seriously call this 'progress'? There is nobody who finds abortion something great that needs to be promoted as much as possible ("The more, the better!"). Of course not! In other words, humanists as well recognize abortion as a necessary evil! From there then it should follow that abortion is strictly limited to real emergencies and is not opened up to 'abortion on demand'. This is not only against the Christian norm, but also against the humanistic principle of the dignity of every person. This is however, in any case denied for the unborn person; his 'right to live' (the first of the 'Human Rights'!) is not granted. If the unwanted fetus disturbs the mother in her personal self-development, it is described, for convenience, as a 'thing' and thus de-humanized. The trivialization of life advances step by step. In the meanwhile, the number of abortions around the world is horrible: 56,000,000 fetuses are aborted annually (Guttmacher Institute, for the period 2010–14). This is more than during the whole

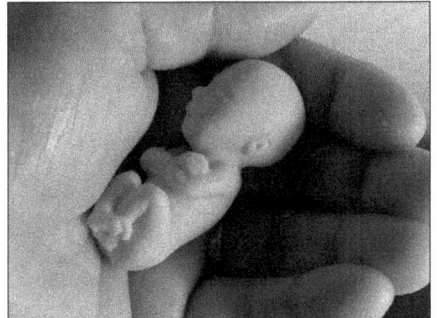

---
65. Humanism suggests that it is more humane than Christianity but in its 'fruits' we see the reverse: degradation and devaluation of man. In the application of its positions (abortion, euthanasia . . .) the value of human life is systematically decreased instead of increased.

---

of World War II. What does this say about the level of humaneness in our society? Is this not a horrible blemish on our blazon?!

Also, if abortion is called 'social assistance', then it is bad social assistance. It only thinks in the short term, not in the long term. It only takes away the urgent 'physical problem' without taking the emotional, psychological, and spiritual context into account. In the humanistic discourse about abortion, the moral dimension is completely swept under the table. It is reduced to a technical issue and therefore an a-moral choice. When it really comes down to it, high-sounding moral principles are mostly relative for a humanist. The concept 'quality of life' is used as an argument, and the term 'degrading suffering' is (often too quickly and unjustly) brought in. But who determines when a life is worthwhile? And on the grounds of which (necessarily arbitrary) criteria? Man is here simultaneously the one concerned, the judge, and the executor.

These humanistic 'acquisitions' have in fact contributed nothing to the respect for life; on the contrary, they made death more accessible and brought it closer. What is so profoundly wrong with our 'modern, enlightened' society (with more prosperity than ever) that more and more people want to leave it prematurely? And how can someone sell this as 'progress'? The Christian passion against abortion is based on a much deeper passion, one in favor of life! Every human being is unique and irreplaceable. Even though reality can be very complex and at times painful and raw, and people do get confronted with moral dilemmas that tear them apart, life is worth fighting for, always!

3.2.2 Marriage, family, and relationships

In the area of marriage, family, and relationships, we see similar processes and mechanisms as in the previous section. The Christian ideal of monogamous marriage, which has been the model for eighteen hundred years, has been undermined slowly but surely by humanism. They fought for the right to divorce and for the right to other forms of cohabitation and were successful. Again, we must ask, did this truly bring progress and improvement? Has a (higher, better) standard been truly set? Or was it actually more about claiming the 'freedom' to not have to stick to norms which everyone must admit, are good? The undermining of the social basis of marriage has caused an avalanche, an epidemic of divorces, which seriously disrupts the entire social fabric of society! The statistics[16] are mind-boggling and painful, and each 'number' in the charts is again a tragic personal drama or trauma, a dagger in someone's heart.

Humanism, of course, does not promote divorce as an ideal, nor does humanism advocate infidelity and lack of commitment. Yet, this is a result of its values, and here also, a great inner contradiction is evident. Putting autonomy of the individual at the top undermines the (subordinate) value of solidarity. 'The other' becomes too easily an obstacle to my self-development! Humanism does not plead for divorce and flirtation, but because it does not plead for marriage and unconditional faithfulness, it enables them to in fact fall apart. All the 'alternative models' that are experimented with (cohabiting, LAT relationships . . .) never offer a true alternative ideal. It is just because people 'do not believe anymore in true love' that they try out these forms, as 'plan B'.

The price we pay all together for our autonomy is invaluably high. Relationship breakdown, loneliness, being emotionally ripped up, constant inner insecurity, low self-esteem, depression, family dramas . . . We sacrifice a huge amount of our 'gross national happiness' on the altar of our holy freedom! Then there is also the price paid by others; many young people pay the bill for the 'unlimited freedom' of their parents who sacrifice their own children on the altar of their 'being right', their insulted pride or stubbornness. The deep need of each child to belong somewhere, to be 'safely attached' is so fundamental that it is not permissible to experiment with this or 'play games'; people are not guinea pigs!

66. The humanistic value of autonomy inevitably leads to individualism: it clashes head-on and fundamentally with our deepest human need for a loving and committed relationship. It should not surprise us that marriages and relationships today are dramatically falling apart: the emotional price we pay for our sacred self-determination is immeasurable.

In the Christian view of life, marriage—just as life—is sacred, beautiful, and extremely valuable. The love between a man and a woman is one of the most precious things on earth, rich in mystery and divine dimensions. It is delightful and reaches into the depths of body, soul, and spirit. It is exactly the exclusivity of that relationship that makes it irreplaceable and

---

16. In 1960, one in fifteen marriages in Belgium ended in a divorce, in 2013 one in two.

gives it an inestimable value. The satisfaction and fulfillment this gives is more than worth transcending our own self-development and our short-sighted self-interest!

3.2.3 Sexuality, pornography, prostitution

Strongly connected to the previous chapter is the view on sexuality. The humanistic plea for freedom and self-determination led to the sexual revolution in the 1960s. The latter was presented as a major liberation from old-fashioned yokes, one big emancipation. 'Sex only within marriage' was depicted as a rigid, oppressive catholic dogma, and breaking down all inhibitions would lead to much more happiness. That the pendulum swung completely to the other side, cannot be denied, also not by humanists. Nowadays, our society is 'oversexed', nudity is indiscriminately used everywhere and commercially exploited to the maximum. The standards are shifted, often reversed: free sex is exalted, 'you're only a real man if you do it with many', masturbation is 'normalized', porn depicted as 'art' or as 'good for your sex life', prostitution as a 'social service' . . . The Christian moral standard has been replaced by the Hollywood-norm, thus purely commercially determined, and its image of sex and marriage is abominably low. Women are downgraded to lust objects, and men to predators.

The consequences are undeniable; this battlefield may be even bigger than that of relationships. People have more sexual problems than ever before: impotence is on the rise everywhere, sex and porn addictions are epidemic, ever more in front of the screen, less and less in bed. Sexologists have their hands full with work and pull the alarm

---

67. Humanism has radically changed the perception of sexuality and has brought so-called 'freedom' from the 'suffocating, narrow-minded' ethic of Christian marriage. But today, the pendulum has completely swung the other way; the current sexual freedom is more destructive than the earlier sexual taboos were. Faithfulness in marriage is sacrificed on the altar of individual autonomy, and the children are sacrificed on the altar of the absolute self-determination of the two parents.

---

bell against the pornification of society! Ultimately, this (excess of) freedom destroys sex itself!

The biggest problem is people wanting 'loose' sex: separate from relationship, love, responsibility and commitment. The spirit of the time reduces sex to something physical; the physical comes first (the orgasm kick), the psychological second (pleasure and fun), but the moral dimension (faithfulness and dedication) is completely ignored, and certainly the spiritual dimension (love that is aimed at the other). The taboo on sex and nudity can certainly be excessively heavy in some cultures but is not negative in itself. A taboo is actually a protection that is built around something that is valuable or delicate.

Christian morality puts the standard for sexual purity unreachably high. Jesus says without batting an eye that a man who looks lustfully at a woman, already committed adultery with her in his heart (free after Matt 5:28). Not only the act but even the thought, the fantasy is already 'dirty'. However, even if not one man could claim that he can handle this and even if most do this daily, can we then argue that this norm is wrong? Looking with lust—and what is porn then?—produces a distorted image of women as well as a distorted sex life.

In the social (political) debate about prostitution, we see a similar evolution. After decades of a process of habituation and de-blaming, some launch campaigns to consider and legalize it as 'a profession like any other'. They do not realize the absurdity of their own words. What normal sixteen-seventeen-year-old girl can say with a smile and pride, "I want to become a sex worker later?" And which parent would say, "Fine, we totally support you. We are proud of you?"

In the Christian view, sexuality is so beautiful, a gift of God, intimate, delicate, and vulnerable. Therefore, it needs much protection; an unconditional promise of faithfulness (marriage) and the greatest tenderness (love) are the only things that are good enough here. The strength of the framework is proportional to the value of what needs to be protected. Even though the area of sexuality has previously been too inhibited and narrow, our current society has tipped the balance in the other direction much more. The present sexual freedom is much more destructive than the former sexual taboos.

Humanism in Practice

3.2.4 Postmodernism, relativism, and nihilism

In this chapter, we look at the concept of 'truth'. Is there something like 'objective truth', 'one absolute truth', or is this a relative concept, a man-made construction, an illusion? Humanism actually breathes the atmosphere of 'modernism'. However, when critical thinking also directed its weapons against this stream of thoughts, all 'great stories' (the classical ideologies) were pulled apart and dismantled. Thus, postmodernism (± 1950) came on the scene. "All major stories have been deconstructed! Truth is an illusion. Everyone has his own truth." There is no longer one unifying religion or ideology in society; everything is dispersed, fragmented. No teaching can or may claim the truth; whoever attempts to claim the truth wants to dominate others with it. Thus, if someone in the philosophical or ideological area speaks of 'truth', he is 'pretentious', arrogant, intolerant, narrow-minded, outdated, and medieval. The truth-claim itself is already suspect.

Philosophical relativism states that everything is relative. It is of course true that every person has his own perspective on 'the facts', colored glasses, a partial view of 'the reality'. But to say, 'because I do not know the truth, I declare that it does not exist', is obviously a logical error. Our cognition is relative, and therefore not the truth. Relativism relativizes (destroys) itself in particular, because this is only the truth of this one person, and therefore does not apply to me!

One step further than relativism is nihilism: "There is just no truth, goodness, ideal, moral ... everything is suspect, untruthful." This is actually philosophical cynicism. On the one hand, this nihilism is very understandable, even a 'logical' step. It is the expression of a postmodern sense of life, of disappointment after the high promises of an ideal society made-by-people. You can call it a 'philosophical civilization disease':

---

68. In this era of so-called 'postmodernism', it is considered 'politically incorrect' to claim to believe in 'the one truth'. However, in fields of mathematics and science this is regarded as evident; in courts and politics it is sought after. Yet anyone who dares to refer to this with reference to their world view, is called pretentious, narrow-minded, and medieval. Even the question of truth itself is perceived as suspicious. It is contradictory, however, to think that 'the truth' exists at lower levels and not at higher ones. The statement "Everyone has their own truth." is a cheap 'feel good' slogan and is at the very least contradictory with itself.

critical thinking turning against itself, becoming self-destructive. It actually translates as a sense of 'god-forsakenness'. This expression contains something profoundly sad, something tragic, because if even God left this place, how bad must it be? If there are no big stories anymore, there are no big goals anymore either! Nihilism has everything to do with aimlessness, but what is worse for a human being than meaninglessness and emptiness? When someone takes a train, it is obvious the person has a purpose and a destination, but when it comes to 'life' this is laughed away! This is of course the culmination of cynicism. We end up in 'a culture that throws itself out', that 'shits on itself': a kind of spiritual masochism.

Humanism will always disapprove of nihilism but finds it hard to see  that it is precisely a branch of its tree, a fruit of what it initiated, a conclusion from its own premise. It has abolished the great story of Christianity, and according to the same principles, others will break it down ... until everything is broken down.

3.2.5 Spiritual emptiness and new idols

Postmodernism can evolve in two possible directions; either into indifference and emptiness, or into filling up this emptiness through all kinds of alternatives. It is shocking in this age, how few people talk with each other about 'the meaning of life', the 'purpose of why we are doing all of this anyway'! The ultimate why-questions give us an uncomfortable feeling and so we prefer to ignore them. They are the elephant in the room that everyone is demurely quiet about. When God is hushed to death, it creates a deafening silence. In our secular society, unbelief ('only trust in what you see') is the 'default setting', and faith must prove or justify itself.

But if people do not (cannot) talk about deep things, only the superficial remains. The emptiness that arose after the church abandonment is eagerly filled in by the media, where the tyranny of the viewing figures-and-profits increasingly dominates. The viewer is flooded with an overdose of superficiality! There is an addiction to amusement—the word 'a-musement' comes from 'no muze': inspiration-less. People watch the screen many hours a day to kill 'the time', but if television actually kills time, it is the greatest mass murderer of all time. Why do millions of people seek to escape time, one of the most precious things God gives us on earth? The emptiness and spiritual boredom in people's lives is often terrifying.

The other track is the one of alternative spiritualities: the market of life-and-world-views is declared open to everyone, and there are no more rules! There is total freedom to proclaim everything as well as its opposite; everyone gets a stand in the big 'life-and-world-views' fair. When God is thrown out the back door, idols come in through the front door. Alternative and exotic religions are lining up, promising spiritual experiences, healing, and rest (all this Christianity offered as well, of course). As much as people are critical and distrustful towards the 'former faith', they are eager and greedy to drink in all the 'new'. As long as it is different, it is good. This also means there is a green light for religious charlatans and market vendors, spiritual gurus and sect leaders, manipulators and profiteers. The paranormal fairs attract them by the thousands. The spiritual 'flea market' runs at full speed; people shop to their heart's content and the cash registers ring cheerfully under all the naivety. And if modern man is so rational, where then does that strange interest come from for horror and creepiness, zombies and vampires—the more hideous, the better? It is spiritual junk food of the lowest kind.

> 69. In secular society, the whole spiritual dimension of man is simply hushed to death, ignored, suffocated. It is no coincidence that there is an upsurge in nihilism, emptiness, and boredom. Humanism claims to create a better, freer, and more open society, but the growing discontent in the Western world shows a different picture: escalating suicide rates, a rise in psychological and psychiatric problems (especially young people), anxiety, increasing loneliness, outbursts of senseless violence, etc.

Today, the dimension of spirituality is dealt with the same way as with clothes. "What is in fashion today?" People want variation nowadays; why not try on a different one every few years? In fact, in this way, people choose a life or world view 'that fits them' (such as Buddhism or Zen). But how absurd is this attitude? "As long as it feels good!" The decision center lies 100% in man; "If I decide there is no God, there is no God! Or if I prefer He is this way, then, He is this way." Another expression of this spiritual poverty is the enormous rise of those who belief in 'something', sometimes called 'the fastest growing religion in the world'. People indicate that they do believe in 'something'. It does not matter what, it does not have to be logical, it is a vague feeling and that is enough. The truth question is completely irrelevant.

For the less spiritually-seeking person there is, besides semi-religious idols, also a wide range of secular ones. The media creates idols and stars as if it is a conveyer-belt, often from the world of sport, culture, film, art, music . . . Other 'new religions' arise around nutrition and health, sport and body culture, art and culture, which get attention of an almost sacred character. For many, 'the planet' is—in the context of global warming—the secular 'highest good', which leads to a kind of 'eco-religion'. The way one speaks about 'mother earth' is semi-religious. Man can in principle make an idol out of anything; a god to fit everyone's size. 'Where you cling to in life, that's actually your god', Luther said.

Other examples are found in the most important two feasts in our culture which have a Christian origin, Christmas and Easter. The replacement of Jesus by Santa and the Easter bunny is an eloquent illustration of what happens when a society secularizes. A very profound, multidimensional story must make way for superficial, meaningless stories devoid of content, which are created by business and do not have any added moral or spiritual value. That people nowadays replace Jesus with Santa says much about themselves! Old, valuable, crafted oak cabinets are discarded and placed in the rubbish dump, and replaced by fibre cabinets.

70. For non-believers, faith is like a bubble, like a fantasized, unreal, make-believe world. For believers, it is exactly the opposite: it is this current, earthly life (without God) that has little realism and authenticity, but a great deal of pretense, deceit, illusion, and camouflage. According to believers, faith in God can set people free from tenuous, earthly, false securities and bring them to the eternal, sustainable sources of life.

When spiritual authority is gone, commerce almost automatically takes over, and this means: mammon rules. It dishes out to people what they want to hear! The popular culture (in literature, music, movies, TV shows . . .) goes in like sweet cake, like lemonade and sweets. It does not require any effort and appeases us collectively into a spiritual sleep.

In short, the indifference for spiritual matters is abnormal in our culture, and actually extremely worrying! In politics, there are great concerns about climate change and the destruction of the planet, but hardly anyone dares to say this is linked to an overall spiritual malaise, a disposable culture, an addiction to consumption, a spiritual dullness because all higher ideals and values have been taken down. The planet is crashing because human beings are running crazy!

3.3 Christian humanism and humanist Christianity

3.3.1 A reasonable, modern, adjusted belief?

Since the Renaissance and the Enlightenment, there has been a significant shift in Western culture in how God and religion are viewed. Before that time, 'That is what the Bible says', or 'This is what the Church teaches' were sufficient arguments. However, as man moved increasingly to the center, he also wanted to have his 'say'; reason demanded a voice in the debate. First a small and modest voice, but later increasingly demanding and arrogant, and ultimately dominant. In any case, faith had to 'evolve' with time and adapt to the 'new (scientific) insights'. In fact, it was even indispensable for faith to adjust to the changing times. 'New wine must be put in new wineskins', said Jesus (Matt 9:17). Concerning the forms, rituals, and styles of worship there is much room for creativity, renewal, and variety, but also when it comes to the DNA itself of faith?

Over the course of the centuries, we saw this adjustment also occur regarding the content of faith, sometimes to unprecedented lows. Even when the intentions are good, for example in order to make religion relevant again or bring it 'to the people', when this is done in an improper manner, it causes more harm than good. The Christian faith had to and would become 'modern', but 'subordinate to our judgment'. From now on, man would himself determine what was acceptable and what was not; science and reason provided a higher and decisive criterion. The Bible was 'polished', 'improved'; all unscientific matters (such as miracles) had to go. Once 'the brakes were loose', this evolution continued more and more. In later centuries the image of God was adapted to 'how modern man prefers it': an abstract, philosophical, intellectualistic God ('The Being'); a soft God who caresses my head gently (a kind of Granddad with a long-beard); an anti-authoritarian God ('my best mate'); a universalistic God who is present in every religion or a 'scientific' God (the primeval Energy). Flexibility and broadmindedness are no doubt beautiful features, but how 'stretchy' can you be before you completely lose your identity? How low do you make the threshold? Until God has become an impersonal primeval Power, a common denominator acceptable to everyone, a 'G' as in the freemasonry? The expression 'humane Christianity' is in itself already erroneous; as if there were a different direction within Christianity that consciously chooses to be 'inhumane!'

> 71. Humanistic thinking has been infiltrating Christian churches for centuries. Each well-intentioned attempt by 'modern' churches to make the gospel more acceptable to contemporary man, to lower the threshold, and to take away whatever is offensive, creates more problems in the long run: less credibility and less appeal, more leveling out and watering down of the faith. In short, it results in a kind of emasculated Christianity.

Some apparently would want the Church to adapt to every new social trend, fashion, and hype, as a chameleon does. The tendency to make the gospel more acceptable is very human, and each of us is susceptible to it, but it is based on a fundamentally wrong premise. Man does not determine the criteria for how God should, can or has to be; it is God who determines the rules. Otherwise He is not God. God *has* to be different; He will always offend, confronting us from time to time with our natural laziness. Jesus offended much, and intentionally; he had to wake people up out of their spiritual sleep. God does not have to 'match me' but vice versa!

However, this adjustment strategy is so widely spread in our current culture, so tough and ingrained, so 'evident'! The intention was likely to make the Church relevant again, but in the long run, it led to irrelevance. Due to its new 'camouflage colors', the gospel was no longer different and lost its appeal. Every politician who adjusts too much to the people starts to just talk along, like a weathercock, meaningless, and this applies even more to the Church. The problems the Church wanted to solve were getting bigger; there was less clarity, less sharpness, less credibility, and even less reason to choose this path consciously.

3.3.2 Academic theology

The humanistic mindset has also largely and deeply infiltrated into Christian theology, and from there sown in the highest ranks of the Church! The thinkers and intellectuals, philosophers and theologians

Humanism in Practice

lingered of course in the same circles, and the rationalistic paradigm has thoroughly spread there. Somehow the idea that theology should also be 'scientific' crept in, according to the standards of other sciences. It wanted to prove itself and be taken seriously by its colleagues. But this led to serious inner conflicts because theology deals with a very different 'object': God. How can someone study God 'objectively and academically', as if a created being could observe its Creator through a microscope or telescope as a neutral, impartial outsider! Yet again, human reason stands central in this approach, and as the absolute judge over everything; reason can analyze everything and analyze it until it falls to pieces.

The Cartesian spirit of science (a Greek, dualistic thinking) brought death into the pot of Western theology and church: the separation between theory and practice, words and deeds, truth and love, knowledge about God and relationship with God . . . If theology wants to be academic, it must remain at a distance, it cannot get personally involved and thus has to remain only on the periphery. Regarding the external conditions, science can indeed be useful in this area and must be 'professional'; text criticism and manuscripts, historical context and archeology can and must be studied as openly and honestly as possible. But what happens when it pertains to the content itself? If theology is called 'knowledge of God', then the main purpose must be 'to know God'[17], or not? But God is not a thing or a formula, but a Person, and absolutely unique. What can science provide here? It always seeks the common, the regular, the universal, and filters away all that is particular. Whoever wants to study Jesus scientifically, for example, can only look at those things where He resembles other religious founders. The absolute uniqueness of Jesus cannot be seen through these glasses and annihilated. The problem therefore lies in the approach. Can you get to know God better if you stay far from Him, or only if you come very close to

> 72. Much of academic theology is permeated with humanistic thinking: wanting to cut out theology according to the same pattern as other sciences is a fundamental mistake and leads to bad theology and bad science. Academic theology carries the DNA defects of the spirit of this age and infects the whole Church with them. 'God' is not an object of study in the way stones or plants are, and true 'God-knowledge' requires a completely different, spiritual approach.

---

17. Jesus describes eternal life (the highest good!) as the 'knowing of God'. In other words, this means having a relationship with Him as with a Father and Creator, and being one with Him (John. 17: 3).

Him? If a journalist wants to write a biography about a famous person, it will always be better if he meets the man in real life and 'tastes, smells, feels' what the person is really like.

Why then do theological studies so often result in students losing their faith? Is there something thoroughly wrong with the structure, the curriculum, and approach of theological faculties? If studies in theology do not lead to more faith, hope, and love, then they are more a distraction, an obstacle to knowing God Himself[18]. Who has the right to call himself a theologian: he who knows much about God, or he who knows God? He who spends many hours a day studying highly intellectual theories, or he who prays many hours a day? Why does theological education contain an exam in Greek, Hebrew, and dogmatics, but not an exam in holiness, prayer, and charity? Why are students only tested for knowledge and intellect, a very small, one-sided, and relatively insignificant part of a believer's life? The words of Jesus give us much thought when He said, *"I thank you, Father, because you have hidden these things from the wise and prudent and revealed them to infants."* (Matt 11:25). What does this say about theologians and a rational approach to faith? Knowledge can kill, faith and love bring life.

3.3.3 Humanism in the churches

This man-centered, rationalistic thinking probably seeped from theology into the rest of the Church. And, the law of spiritual gravity also plays a major role here; the tendency to lower down 'from heaven to earth' is constantly present, with all people and believers, in all churches and Christian institutions. It is very subtle and unnoticeable when the border is crossed. As we, in this book, hold the humanist view of life to the light, as Christians we must also search first and foremost our own lives, our own churches, our own speech and patterns . . . Some examples:

(1) What plays a role is that in these modern times the complaint was often heard that the Church is focused too much heavenwards and too little towards earth—which could still be true; some believers, church leaders or groups can be too 'highbrow', over-spiritual, mystical, and therefore

---

18. This can sound very hard, but Jesus says something similar about the theologians of his time: "Woe to you, scribes and Pharisees, hypocrites, because you close the kingdom of heaven to the people. You are not going to enter it yourself, and those who want to enter it you don't allow to enter." (Matt 23:13).

unworldly and 'antisocial'. The Church from then on had to be judged more by its social utility, its 'measurable' results[19]. However, a false opposition was created in this way between 'being directed toward God' or 'being directed toward man'. It is namely God Himself who sends the praying person back to earth with the commands to 'love your neighbor', 'give food to the hungry . . .' (Matt 25:35). Whoever truly focuses first on God will then be able to focus much more on man. Those who want to have more love for man must not have less love for God, on the contrary[20]. In any case, the pendulum swung to the other side; the Church wanted to be 'modern', sympathetic, proving herself relevant to the world and therefore went along with it, and often placed the horizontal dimension above the vertical. This is an expression of humanist disposition, and the Church became an ennobled social institution. For millions, the shortest summary of faith became 'Love for your fellow human being'. Yet the first commandment is, 'to love God' (Matt 22: 37–39), and 'loving your neighbor' is, though directly linked to the first, indeed, the second. Charity is a result of God's love, not the other way around!

(2) Humanistic thinking is also found in theology when it thinks that it needs to make biblical words and stories into a 'doctrine'. The underlying thought is often: "Oh, the Bible is written by simple fishermen and therefore quite chaotic and with a primitive worldview. We intellectuals will thoroughly improve and organize it and make it rational." Theology can easily become somewhat arrogant, as if it would bring great pleasure to God to have His words 'upgraded'. One step further is when a church says, 'You must not read the Bible any more, but read our catechism' (for it is clearer, more logical, better). They consider their own formulations and credos superior but overlook that 'the kingdom of God does not consist of words but of power' (1 Cor 4:20). Beautifully formulated formulas do not necessarily bring life. Rationalist theology brings spiritual death into the Church.

---

19. In 1783, the enlightened Austrian Emperor Joseph II, for example, closed all contemplative monasteries since they were regarded as 'useless'.

20. A beautiful example of this is Mother Teresa; although she did impressive and gigantic social work among the poorest, the priority for all the sisters was to pray first. When the bell rang for prayer, the sisters immediately left their work with the sick and the suffering. It was necessary for them in order to be able to fulfill this exhausting love work in the long run.

(3) Also in church structures we see a similar evolution or danger. Of course, the young church, which was a sparkling movement, had to get organized and structure itself after a while. But after all these centuries, so much formal structure and rigid organization has grown around the core of the church: hierarchies, procedures, committees, constitutions, dogma, confessions, church law, and church courts ... At a certain moment the Church looked back with a feeling of superiority to the primitive first church which was 'an amateuristic mess ...' 'Look how much more professional we've made it'. But what was the reality? All of this led to inert, stiffened institutions where all life was squeezed out, and this while the first Church was full of life, sparkling, fresh in the Holy Spirit, and growing unstoppable because she was full of God's life! The source of spiritual life is from above, not from below. Even in a church, someone can 'idolize' his own work, and put it above God when, for example, the 'holy tradition' and liturgy are so tight and untouchable that even God may not disturb them. The fear of 'chaos' and unpredictability is sometimes so great that 'order' is a sacred cow in God's house. Can God at all times sovereignly intervene in a church and throw everything upside down when it pleases Him? That would be a sign that He is the Boss! We have to admit, this is very threatening to 'our' (!) order, to our need for human security! In the first church, however, this happened continually; a bit of chaos is really not the worst problem, being spiritually dead is.

> 73. When a church becomes stuck in formal rituals and unchangeable traditions, this is also a form of humanism: it prefers to trust in man-made rules and constitutions rather than on God's living presence. It wants to keep everything under its own control and 'play it safe' leaving no room for the Holy Spirit. Any Christian community which would perceive God's sovereign intervention would be 'disruptive' shows that it trusts primarily on human endeavors, and actually denies its own reason for existing.

(4) In the Western world, the vast majority still calls itself (traditionally) Christian, but what do they actually believe? In practice, they pick and choose what they find 'good' from the Bible and faith. Just as there are 'freethinkers', there are also masses of 'free believers'; they allow themselves complete freedom to disagree with anything. They 'shop' from the Bible like the modern consumer in the supermarket. The vast majority of traditional churches are full of them; you can call them 'modern' or 'liberal'

believers, 'progressive' or 'illuminated . . .' They usually use the argument, 'You should not take the Bible literally', and this is true to some extent. Many texts in the Bible are to be understood spiritually. This expression, however, is used far too easily as a maneuver, an excuse for explaining away everything that we do not like or that does not fit in our box. Deep down, 'liberal believers' are humanists with a thin Christian varnish. They have, above all, an unwavering confidence in their own ability to distinguish between right and wrong. Even though they go to church, and regularly quote Biblical verses, on other points, they consider themselves to 'know it better than Jesus'. Strictly speaking, this is not even religion ('serving God'); man 'safely' remains his own boss.

> 74. Humanism is not always fundamentally opposed to religion and claims to have respect for 'reasonable' religion, a practice of religion which fits within humanly acceptable frameworks. But it fails to grasp the essence of true religion: the conviction that, if there is a God, He determines the rules and frameworks, not mankind. Any attempt to create or define a 'reasonable religion' (think of deism, or positivism of the French Revolution) turns out to be an uninspiring flop. It is humanism with a thin Christian veneer.

(5) The same is true of how these 'free' Christians behave outside of church, in their daily lives. Their 'believing' makes hardly any difference in practice. These are the so-called 'Sunday Christians'. Faith does not have any influence on their daily decisions (e.g. "What do I watch on TV; how do I spend my money?"), and certainly not on their big life choices (study, partner, job). 99.9% of their energy and attention goes to earthly things, and maybe, if there is time left, a 'small left-over' goes to church; it is at the bottom of their list of priorities. They are not theoretical atheists but 'practical atheists'; they actually live as if God does not exist. That is why you sometimes hear about believing (or even practicing) Christians who do terrible things; in their lifestyle they do the very opposite of what Jesus teaches and, in this way, they destroy His image and reputation! Paul says with tears in his eyes, "Many (and he means Christians!) walk like enemies of Christ." (Phil 3:18). In practice, God is not Lord over their lives because at any given time they determine in what areas God may enter.

(6) But it goes still a step further; also with a motivated and sincere believer, there is a stubborn 'natural reflex' to try to solve his problems first himself,

trusting in his 'own ability'. And when he has tried seven human solutions and it gets worse, he will then cry out to God: God as the 'last lifeboat', the

'last aid in case of emergencies'! A spiritually correct attitude however involves God in the plans from the very beginning, as well as in every step of the execution. At a church board meeting, for example, ten 'professional' plans can be made and then, at the end, God is asked to 'bless our plans'. Or at the start of the meeting, God can be asked to 'show His plans'. The difference is subtle but decisive. A Christian who does not pray (or prays very little in practice) actually professes a kind of humanism, namely that he can (to a very large extent) actually manage by himself. It is no coincidence that Jesus' famous Sermon on the Mount begins with "Blessed are the poor in spirit" (Matt 5:3). He hereby places a bomb under our human complacency. A prayerless church is spiritually dead. The big and difficult question that cuts deep into our soul is: does God get a 'role' in our life (a small one, or even a big one), or is He the director? Every honest believer must cry out, "Help, there's a humanist in me!" The tendency to trust in ourselves is more tenacious than we can eradicate by ourselves.

75. In opening his world-famous Sermon on the Mount with the words 'Blessed are the poor of spirit', Jesus put an extremely powerful bomb under all our humanism, our flagrant self-confidence, our complacency. There is, after all, a humanist in each of us. Whoever wants to fight humanism will first need to remove the persistent self-centeredness from their own heart and from the church.

We have to notice here of course that 'humanism in the churches' is not an ideology or theoretical viewpoint, but a practical attitude and focus of life: the 'habit' of going out from oneself, of taking oneself as criterion. This mindset hangs as a 'cloud' in the air and rules over the whole culture. It seeps into the thought system of the modern Christian without that he is even aware of it: he considers himself a believer but actually does not even know what this truly means in practice.

Medieval (not always very humane) Christianity was first adapted to a 'humane Christianity'. This then evolved unnoticed into a 'humanist

Christianity', but when this quietly became 'Christian humanism', it had turned into something totally different, or actually, into the opposite of itself. 'Christian humanism' is something like 'heliocentric geocentrism' or 'idealistic materialism', two concepts with a fundamentally opposite principle, that do not match, just as 'watery fire' or 'a square circle'.

3.3.4 A clash of god images!

Underlying this battle, about 'whether-or-not' humanistic Christianity, lies a fierce clash between God images. It is 'in' and postmodern to say, 'Everyone has his own way of believing'. From a human point of view (psychologically) this is certainly true, and every believer is indeed unique in his approach and experience, but seen from above, this is not at all correct. Jesus Christ alone has the right to define 'Christianity'!

> The gospel came to Greece and became a philosophy, it came to Rome and became a legal system, it came to Europe and became a culture, it came to America and became a business.

Modern man cannot, in essence, redefine it and still call it Christianity. You can compare this to the economic world: an inventor of a product gets a patent, and certain brand names are protected. E.g. only the true, original Coca-Cola may bear that name; marzipan may only be called 'marzipan' when there are at least 50% almonds in it; 'champagne' can only be labeled as such when it comes out of the Champagne region, etc. This is logical because there are always hijackers who want to counterfeit, bring cheaper versions to the market and distort competition.

In the market of worldviews, this battle is even fiercer and uglier. No one can impose unequivocal rules or even less, enforce these. But even if no one can prevent another from falsifying, the moral principle remains. No one has the right to make his own version of Jesus: no catholic or protestant, no conservative, progressive or fundamentalist and not even a modern, humanistic or liberal. Jesus was not a 'hippie avant-la-lettre', no 'super-psychic', not a communist or a socialist, and certainly not a capitalist, a republican or a royalist either. You cannot reduce Him to a teacher, a miracle-worker, a social worker, a political activist or a revolutionary, at your own preference. To 'improve' or 'adjust' Jesus, always decreases, diminishes, evens Him according to our own image and likeness, our private preference or need. Whoever gets to know Him as He is, only has the desire to make Him bigger. Those who were closest to Him and knew Him best (John and Paul) could only describe Him in the strongest superlatives[21]. The great prophet John the Baptist said, 'He must increase, but I must decrease' (John 3:30). Precisely these people saw themselves, in His Light, as the humblest, 'I am not worthy to stoop down and untie the straps of his shoes' (Mark 1:7) or 'I am the worst of all sinners' (1 Tim. 1:15).

Humanistic Christianity is a genetic engineering of the DNA of Christianity. Perhaps this is well-intentioned and can seem beneficial in the short term, but in the long run it brings irreparable damage and spiritual death. You cannot seriously call yourself a 'Christian' if you do it 'your own way'. Religion means the serving of God; to serve a self-made God is self-service. God is by definition, the first in one's life; whoever gives Him third place 'in

---

76. No-one has the right to make their own version of Jesus: whether a catholic or protestant version, whether an old-fashioned, conservative, or even a 'modern', 'humanistic' or 'liberal' version. A Christian has no right to 'water down' or 'dilute' Jesus' radical and exclusive words. Creating a customized version of Jesus is like buying the 'Lamb of God' painting by the Van Eyck brothers, taking it home and getting out a paintbrush to 'improve' or 'modernize' it.

---

77. When a church or theological view has the pretension to 'improve' the gospel, then this is indicative of a very misplaced arrogance and it leads to the reverse. People who consider themselves part of the 'humanistic movement within Christianity' will have to make a clear choice who they put at the center, which Lord they serve: God or man? Do we adapt (downgrade) the Bible to contemporary views, or do we adjust (upgrade) our minds to the God of the Bible?

---

21. Jesus, 'as He truly is', is only revealed in the visions of John and in the letters of Paul (who also had visions). He is calles "the image of the invisible God and the firstborn of all creation. For by Him all things were created that are in heaven and on earth" (Col. 1:15–20); "The King of Kings and Lord of Lords" (Rev. 19:16); "The First and the Last" (Rev. 1:17), He who has 'all power in heaven and on earth' (Matt 28:18) etc. For those who look with eyes of faith, Jesus can never be too big.

great generosity' does not understand anything. The spiritual battle in the thought life of a believer is, 'Who is on the throne, Him or I? Who determines the rules?'

Jesus does not leave us any doubt here: "He who loves father or mother more than Me . . . even does not lose his own life, is not worthy of Me (or cannot be My disciple)." (Matt 10:37, 39 & Luke 14:26–27, 33). If God is not allowed to ask everything of us, He is not God in our lives.

3.3.5 Water or wine?

Western Christianity today is very secularized and in a major identity crisis. Large parts of the church have gone bad from the inside out and are maybe beyond saving. For decades sociologists have predicted the end of Christianity in Europe (a tendency that is, however, counteracted by other phenomena). Still, the abandonment of churches and the spiritual emptiness is dramatic. It is even incomprehensible how rapidly this has happened, how a centuries-old heritage has been thrown down in only a few decades. There are of course many external factors, but we want to focus here on the substance. Christianity began with extraordinary power that endured terrible persecutions and even conquered the Roman Empire. Erasmus already said it, in the midst of the great crisis of his time: we must go back to the source, where the water is pure.

Jesus turned water into wine—even the best wine of the party (John 2:10). Every humanistic adaptation, however, turns it back into a watered-down version, or at best, alcohol-free wine. The churches have, by presenting a diluted gospel, made the people detest it because of its weak taste. To illustrate this with a medical parallel we can say they produced a serum of the gospel and

> "The Christian ideal has not been tried and found wanting. It has been found difficult; and left untried."
> —G.K. Chesterton (1874–1936), English writer, poet, philosopher, journalist, and art critic

in this way Western man has become immune to the gospel. After all, many people today think, 'We know Christianity. We tried it, but it did not work'. The truth is, however, that they have not tried it, certainly not in full.

Whoever wants to make Christianity modern or reasonable produces a moralistic infusion, a superior moral doctrine. Christianity is, however, not in essence a moral teaching, but a message of salvation. It clearly states that morality cannot save man, or better said, man cannot save himself by doing his moral best. Man needs salvation from the outside, salvation from his addiction; the message of the cross is the core of the gospel, the crossroad where the roads break up, where 'the spirits separate themselves'. This message is 'bloody' and 'inhuman', and crashes into all rationality but is part of it because our rationality is infected and corrupted. Therefore, it is the only medicine that can truly help, the only antidote against our incurable self-centeredness. The patient is so sick that only a total blood transfusion can save him. If someone amputates the message of the cross from the Christian message, it collapses like an under-baked pudding.

---

78. Jesus brought the kingdom of God in a powerful way in both word and deed: signs and wonders, healing and casting out of demons are normal elements of the kingdom. If a church leaves no room for the supernatural, it must examine itself carefully as to whether it is seeking God's kingdom or whether maybe, under the influence of the humanistic spirit of this age, it has swept an essential part of the gospel under the carpet.

We must urgently search for 'Christianity-à-la-Jesus', not 'à la carte', 'à la modernism', 'à la rationality . . .'. Jesus preached the kingdom of God with power (Matt 12:28, 10:7–8). He did not only tell beautiful stories, He proved that it was reality. He did not only talk about a dreamy, far-away kingdom, but brought it to earth and drove away the darkness. Signs and wonders, deliverance from demons, and healings were an integral part of His mission on earth. He never stated this should change, on the contrary, He explicitly instructed His disciples to do the same: 'Heal the sick, cleanse the lepers, raise the dead, and cast out demons' (Matt 10:8). These are normal to His kingdom; if they do not happen in a particular church, they must thoroughly question themselves whether they are dealing with the kingdom or not. If it is not supernatural, can you still call it 'Service to God'?

'Modern church' has a bad habit of following the trends of the

---

79. The so-called 'modern' movements within churches resulted in a humanistic Christianity: they tried to run after the world and follow the trends instead of being prophetic forerunners. "Jesus performed a miracle by turning water into wine; modern theology performed a new miracle and turned it into water again!" This tasteless Christianity was—understandably—spat out in disdain by many. The dramatic decline of the European churches demonstrates that God was not given first place!

world instead of changing them. The calling of the Church is prophetic; it should not, like a thermometer, indicate the temperature of the world, but determine the temperature of the world. The Church is clearly in the opposition at this time, but this is not bad for anyone who has a 'prophetic mission': countercurrent keeps you sharp. It is then better to wrestle through the whole cure of opposition which can only be purifying. It is better to let go of quantity, of the desire to be a 'people's church' and keep a crowd at all cost, and rather go for quality. The Church often 'excused' herself for Jesus' hard words in order to make him more acceptable. Thus, she made her own 'core product' fuzzy. And whoever is uncertain about their identity communicates vaguely and automatically loses 'market value'.

'Jesus' is a strong brand, a market leader, and trendsetter. He is a moral authority whom you cannot get around; He has set the standard! There is a 'before Christ' and an 'after Christ'. No one—no humanist either—can seriously talk about 'moral values' without referring to Him. The value of his 'product' we also see in the price that Jesus suggested; he demanded of his followers—without any embarrassment!—the highest sacrifice, 200% dedication. Never did he give in to the temptation to make it cheaper! He did nothing to draw more followers, on the contrary, he discouraged them almost by telling how high the price was: 'no place to lay your head' (Matt 8:20). He first went for (heavenly) quality, fully confident that quantity would follow. The cure for the abandonment of the Church is not 'more of man and less of God', but simply 'more of God and less of man'!

4

Conclusion: humanism[1] vs. Christianity

4.1 Historically: history falsification

Humanism can only be properly understood from the background from which it originated and against which it reacted. That this background is Christianity is clear to all. And that the Church made mistakes in the Middle Ages, even fundamental and structural ones is hardly denied by any believer. Just as is said about sects, humanism, freemasonry or atheism also present the unpaid bills of the Church; there where the Church left a 'hole' and did not fulfill her role, a vacuum was created that was filled by others.

In order to introduce themselves as the 'light', the Enlightenment had to present the Middle Ages darker than they were (and antiquity 'lighter' than it was). Up until today, this presentation is very distorted, and injustice is done to history. By distancing itself from its own past, Western civilization denies its origin, condemns its own ancestors, and cuts itself off from its legacy.

---

1. At the beginning of this book, we tried to define what we mean here with 'humanism', namely 'man as the starting point'. At the end of this book, we more clearly distinguish between three kinds of humanism in this approach. (1) Erasmus' humanism was actually a more humane version of Christianity; Erasmus rightly understood that God's will by definition is good for mankind, and therefore does not include cruelty and intolerance. (2) Secular humanism took the element of 'man' from this, extended it, and cut it off from its religious roots: man at the center of everything instead of God. Though organized freethinking comprises only a very small group, these thoughts have strongly influenced the spirit of this age, and Western culture is very secularized. (3) Humanism in a broad sense includes this anthropocentric spirit that permeates all culture, including large parts of the Church.

Conclusion: humanism vs. Christianity

Furthermore, humanism arose from an incorrect observation and diagnosis: the problem of religious abuse of power was not with God, religion or the Church as such, but with people who practiced their religion in a wrong way and abused spiritual power for their own purposes. Its criticisms focus mainly on outward rigidity and irrational traditions, rarely on the core itself. They reacted most often against caricatures, often with little discernment. Humanism thus builds on a questionable foundation, inevitably making the same mistakes for which it criticizes the Church.

Moreover, secular humanism denies that the entirety of Renaissance humanism and all the Enlightenment were still thoroughly Christian. The founders of original humanism never meant it to be an all-around-worldview-without-God. They would fight today's anthropocentrism and militant atheism as an absurdity! When contemporary humanism lays hold of champions such as Erasmus as its forefathers, it seriously distorts history. Freethinking does not have the right to pull 16th century humanism into her camp and claim it! Secular humanism is a kind of Christianity-minus-God; it is not a worldview with its own roots, but a parasite (like mistletoe) that smites its roots in another tree and feeds on it. Its strength has its source in the weaknesses of the other.

Humanism has, in other words, a Christian mother and a Greek father; it is like a child out of wedlock, with a strong portion of pagan influences. But even then it behaves like a child who wants to get rid of 100% of its maternal side. Humanism derives all its values and principles from Christianity (for example, the infinite value and dignity of man) without acknowledging this and without saying 'thank you'. On the contrary, it fiercely fights its mother, and silences Jesus to death in its philosophical or moral discourse. It refuses to acknowledge or pay 'copyrights'. This is not only ungrateful, but also dishonest; this is called plagiarism, using spiritual heritage without permission, and pretending to have invented it.

> 80. Humanism and laity are a by-product of Christianity, an offshoot, or an illegitimate child, conceived by a 'different father'. The Christian notion of freedom, for example, has become detached from its religious breeding ground, separated from God, who is essentially a Liberator, and even turned against the Church. When such values or '-isms' start to lead a life of their own, they become life-threatening.

And what's more, the Christian concepts got seriously distorted; the living heart itself ('God') was cut out, in the naive assumption that all the rest would remain the same. It would be like someone taking the famous 'Ghent Altarpiece'—the 15th century painting by the brothers Van Eyck -, scratching away all the religious references, and thinking that after that it would be just as beautiful. For example, the Bible creates room for the free development of the mind (unlike other cultures), but then, this is precisely turned against Christianity! When its high values and principles (e.g. freedom!) are loosened from their religious breeding ground and roots, they become potential weapons in the hands of those wanting to abuse them, even for destruction.

The greatest merit of humanism is that it reminded the Church of its own mission of humaneness; the alternative it put into place however is something very different.

4.2 Theoretically: inconsistent

Humanism pretends to offer a rational view of life, but when we apply this criterion to itself, it appears to fail its own standard. Humanists like to see themselves as 'critical', but from a Christian point of view, humanists are not critical enough, certainly not toward their own concept of man and thought system! Just as many believers are very ignorant of their own faith and understand only a fraction, this also applies to humanists. They are poorly informed of the fundamentals of their beliefs and the inner contradictions.

The principle of self-determination makes man the highest criterion, as if his judgment is infallible. But firstly, we all know that each person can be wrong in any area. Also, this would mean that there are seven billion 'highest criteria'. It is therefore doubly untenable.

> 81. Humanism advocates 'never submitting to dogmas.' To believe however that 'only others do this and we don't' shows a lack of self-knowledge or of understanding of the human condition. Humanism has dozens of other unprovable propositions, generally accepted views that are not (allowed to) be called into question or critically examined in depth. It is not even consistent with its own principle of rationalism.

The punch line of humanism is its concept of man: 'believing in man' is the central dogma. But this also wavers in all directions; we know with scientific certainty that humanity is perfectly capable of destroying the world (and is actually working on this right now)!

Humanists say, Christians have a blind belief in something they do not

Conclusion: humanism vs. Christianity

see and cannot prove exists. But worse is: humanists have a blind belief in something they can see does not exist, and which one can prove every day as not true. How can man save the world if he cannot even save himself? How can he solve all problems, if he is the cause of them? 'I believe in man' is undoubtedly a beautiful, sympathetic sentence, but has no more 'rational substance' than an advertising slogan or a populist electoral promise. Humanism can exist in a militant, intolerant, anti-theistic form or in an open, mild, broadminded version, but, the principle remains the same. Man as the ultimate criterion is untenable; the 'mild version' applies this less consistently, but its theoretical framework is the same.

What makes this debate about belief systems far more difficult is that there are several thinking-errors in humanism; much conceptual confusion, false oppositions, and blending of categories. It transfers, for example, methods and instruments that work well in the field of material and inanimate objects to living and spiritual subjects. Different levels of knowledge are mixed up, invalid conclusions drawn, and unproven premises put forward as axioms. In a serene philosophical debate, some humanists can admit that their philosophy of life is not more scientific than the religious one, but outside of this, the false presentations are constantly repeated that 'at least we are critical, rational, and scientific': the dishonesty in communication is stubborn—by which I am not maintaining at all that the other side is always honest: it will be due to 'man', I am sure!?

It is hard to establish humanism's own core of belief, because the decisive principle is, 'without God'[2]. It is mainly a negative self-determination, and what this is replaced with in the positive ('man') does not stand. Therefore, humanism itself is in constant crisis, and must constantly redefine its identity.

By removing 'God', humanism does no longer have a central point that keeps everything together. Its principles (freedom, autonomy, separation of Church and state . . .)

> 82. The philosophy of humanism is like the man in Jesus' parable who built his house on the sand. Ultimately, self-created and gathered values have no holding-capacity as a foundation for life. When storms and crises come, it slips away under one's feet like quicksand. When too much pressure is exerted, it leads to total disintegration. The essence of humanism is 'loose sand', without a bonding agent or a fixed identity.

---

2. Prof. Richard Norman, member of the Humanist Philosopher's Group (British Humanist Society), honestly states: "Humanists agree on rejecting religious beliefs, but have much more difficulties with their own humanistic values" (*Freedom and Humanism in Europe*, p. 17).

are good without doubt and have their value, but whoever turns them into absolutes undoubtedly gets into trouble. The partial truths are correct, but the sequence and interrelationships are disturbed. Man always tends to turn an intermediate goal into a final goal, thus creating '-isms'; one-sided, forced systems that in reality become idolatry in practice and, because they are out of balance, can even become dangerous.

Jesus finished his famous Sermon on the Mount with the parable of the house on the rock or on the sand (Matt 7:24–27). But what is the difference between rock and sand? They consist of the same material; sand is 'shattered rock'; the right cohesion or connectedness is gone, and therefore also the substance and stability. Humanistic principles are unsuitable as a foundation because they are 'out of context', disintegrated. There is not a more unstable being than man; how much rain or how many storms (pressure or crisis) are needed before his steadfastness is washed away?

A great merit of humanism is that it created freedom for science and rationality, but this does not mean that it is suitable as an overall view for the interpretation of life and the world.

4.3 Spirituality: meagerness

Humanity must be compared with Christianity in terms of philosophical content because it originates from it and reacts against it. If we indeed put these two views next to each other, we see an enormous reduction. Rich Christian spirituality is narrowed down to a vision that tries to explain the world in a purely horizontal, human, worldly manner. It goes from three dimensions (body-soul-spirit) to two. The whole supernatural, spiritual world—above and below, left and right, front and back—is completely 'cut away': origin and destiny, every transcendence and divine plan, the closeness of a Creator-Father, the ultimate hope of goodness, beauty and righteousness; everything that is eternal and lasting and transcends the earthly ... is pushed aside as a fairy tale. There is no paradise and no heaven; how poor, meagre, and limited life then becomes!? A humanist prefers to live without hope or perspective, without higher values

Conclusion: humanism vs. Christianity

or goals, without direction. He chooses tunnel vision over a wide mountain landscape.

The 'humanistic credo' is some kind of the greatest common denominator of values and meaning. It came about in a so-said 'democratic manner', so that everyone could find themselves in it, and therefore it is vague and general. In essence, you can summarize it as follows: "Where does man come from? Coincidence! Where does man go? Nowhere! What's after death? Nothing! What is the purpose of life? You tell me! How should man live? Decide for yourself!" To fathom the centuries-old Christian heritage you need ten lives; humanism can be explained in ten minutes. It is a minimalist package, a spiritual hunger ration. The spiritual needs of a human being for meaning and purpose, his hunger for justice and truth, are smothered.

> 83. The hard core of humanistic values can never be more than a lowest common denominator of all human values, a compromise, a minimalist package about which everyone agrees—in fact virtually nothing, an empty box. A secular alternative to every organized religion is like alcohol-free beer.

The decision center is shifted from God to man. We decide on values, norms, and laws, and, if a God is allowed, then we also decide how He must be. The logical consequence is that we choose a god that suits us, just like choosing clothes in a supermarket as an extension of ourselves. This, of course, is putting the spiritual world upside-down. That man naturally perceives and thinks from his own viewpoint and that he places himself at the center may be clear to all, but to make this into an ideological approach to life, a commendable value system, is very strange. Self-centeredness is a natural tendency that we must fight or transcend, and this is why education teaches small children to think of others. It is precisely the cause of almost all conflicts in this world, and when an adult does not learn this, it is a sign of immaturity.

When you make man the center of everything, it all becomes utterly meaningless; there is nothing that holds things together anymore, no absolute truths, no ultimate

> 84. Putting man at the center of the universe is not a philosophy that needs to be promoted, but a natural tendency to self-centeredness that one should learn to overcome. For a baby, toddler or child, this is a 'normal' approach to life, and all education is targeted precisely at helping children to rise above that. But for a mature adult to exhibit such self-centeredness is a sign of immaturity, a pathetic impertinence which is the very source of all misery on earth.

authority. To declare that man is his 'own boss' can give a short-term 'good feeling' of unlimited power and freedom, but what does it mean? If man is a little god, and each man is a god, this does not give any real power or status, just like when everyone is king. It flatters us but gives a false sense of power or importance. That feeling of 'limitless' freedom is also one big illusion; it is bound on all sides by physical conditions and by seven billion surrounding others.

Something made by humans can never inspire to something higher. Only what comes from above can inspire to 'do more than the ordinary' (Matt 5:47), more than the human and average, to transcend above oneself, to give oneself for something or someone. It is instructive to observe that a man-made religion never works (e.g. the rational religion of Auguste Comte). It is like Esperanto; in itself creating a 'universal' and reasonable language is very smart, very practical, and efficient, yet . . . it does not fascinate or charm, it has no 'soul'. Humanism is like a religious Esperanto; it does not appeal or challenge, has no inspiration or depth, no poetry or riches: it is a theoretical construction that does not produce life.

Humanism speaks of giving meaning, but at the same time it saws off the legs from under it. It supposedly offers a framework of meaning but the frame is completely empty! Many of the humanistic 'deeper' speculations about meaning and life goals stay stuck in generalities: they are nice, noble ideas but the words have no longer any covering. They are well-intentioned but meaningless, without power or credibility. The 'link' to the reality they refer to has been disconnected. Or worse, it is also not always honest: sometimes it is rather a smoke screen, intended to clothe itself in an appearance of philosophical profundity! It is full of sham arguments in order to 'get away with it' and get on with one's life undisturbed by God! For a believer, all the humanistic discourse about life's meaning remains only talk 'in the box', and does not touch on the real, essential issues. It is like soccer players who seriously discuss the rules of the game or the color of the jerseys on the field, but never go out of the field and wonder, 'Why do we actually play soccer?'

Humanism imprisons man in his own tiny framework and world. You can compare it to a scene in the film 'American Beauty' (1999) where a married man (actor Kevin Spacey) lays in bed next to his (beautiful) wife yet satisfies himself. He may have a relational problem with her but prefers the easiest and fastest way to fulfill his sexual needs. Satisfying yourself with erotic fantasies is much 'cheaper' than a complex relationship with a living person who is different and, in fact, has his or her own will. But contrary to what the

Conclusion: Humanism vs. Christianity

word suggests, self-satisfaction does not really satisfy. The physical need may be gone for a while, but afterwards, only emptiness and shame remain. And it prevents him from addressing the core of the problem: the relational disorder with his (beautiful!) wife. To have a relationship with God is really not that easy; every believer regularly and seriously clashes with his Creator. But does this make it 'better' to choose for ideological self-satisfaction . . .?

To stay in the same atmosphere: Humanism is like spiritual inbreeding. Nothing is allowed in 'from the outside', so everything has to be 'arranged amongst us': we just inseminate each other constantly with our own ideas, because we 'find ourselves so wonderful'. The word 'inspiration' however, comes from 'in-spiritus', which means that from somewhere outside, from higher-up, the Spirit plants an amazing, original idea in us: 'we could not have thought of this ourselves, it was suddenly there'. Inbreeding, on the other hand, always leads to shrinkage, impoverishment, and abnormalities.

In photography, one speaks about bird or frog perspective. In his approach to life, the humanist resolutely chooses the last one; walking around in the maze of the earthly jungle, he denies himself the opportunity to view things from above. You cannot blame a frog for looking at things from below, but should man do this!? Man has the ability to rise above things and look at the maze of life from a higher viewpoint, but if he chooses obstinately to look at everything from below, he fails grossly in his calling as a spiritual being. This is precisely what is liberating

> "The tragedy of modern man is not that he is increasingly less aware of the meaning of his own life. The tragedy is simply that this meaning interests him less and less."
> — Vaclav Havel, writer and former President of the Czech Republic

and enriching in Christianity: to think 'outside the box'. By looking from the outside and from above at this world, we see the bigger goal, and find our way out of the maze. We also discover that God intends endlessly more for us than we have already received. Jesus' statement 'For those who believe, everything is possible' gives wings!

Humanism is also a kind of spiritual myopia: it only has an eye for what is nearby, the here-and-now and the materialistic reality. It is like football players who only see the field and not the stadium around it. There are twenty-two players remaining on a bare field without an audience and supporters, without applause and without medals, and without a (world) football federation who determines and sanctions the rules. The game becomes ultimately futile and boring.

95 Theses on Humanism

> 85. To humanists, as to all people, Jesus' words apply, 'According to your faith will it be done to you'. Those who do not believe in miracles will not see miracles. Those who do not believe in high moral standards, values, and ideals will always see standards slip and the quality of life diminish. Those who do not believe in 'true love' will not encounter it in their life. Those who do not believe in truth will not find it. What a man sows, he shall reap.

For a believer who has tasted a higher contentment and divine joy, it is impossible to be 'completely fulfilled' by what is under the sun. It seems to him to be so poor and empty when people put all their hope in this. It is not only sad, but even tragic, that people are satisfied with this, while just around the corner, such a rich offer has been prepared, and even for free! Even more tragic is that this offer is being made to look suspect in all possible ways; people prefer to live without answers while there are such soul-uplifting and hope-filled answers! Because of their distrust, cynicism, and pride they condemn themselves to spiritual famine.

Jesus, on the other hand, promises an 'abundant life' (John 10:10), 'exceedingly abundantly beyond all that we ask or imagine' (Ephesians 3:20), richer and more fulfilling than we can fathom. A Christian can say with utmost confidence, God is 1000% for humans! He is love and therefore totally and selflessly focused on our good. Man can only become better with God. Separate from God, however, man can throw himself (and others) completely down to the ground. Without God, the earth is a life-threatening place! Humanism is a kind of spiritual anorexia; the spiritual food lies before him on the table, but for some non-rational reason he prefers to go hungry. He chooses not to eat, and also finds arguments to suggest that this is better.

Humanism wants to offer a fully-fledged alternative to Christianity, and replace faith in God with something horizontal, but the substitutes are of a different order altogether. Like when someone seeks love and gets sex offered. Or like a man who throws out his wife and takes a cleaning lady instead. Or like someone who wants to help his friend out of a deep depression by telling him a 'good joke'. Humanism gives

"Dominus illuminatio mea" ("The Lord is my enlightenment"): text above the entrance of the Examination College in Oxford, UK.

paramount importance to science, but science has nothing to offer at this level. You cannot fight cynicism and despair about the futility of life with a pill. Science certainly brings progress, but not in a moral sense or the area of an all-around approach to life. 'Believing in man' can never be a substitute for 'believing in God'. These two can stand brotherly next to each other but are not on the same level!

An important observation in the debate between humanism and Christianity is that Christianity came first and humanism afterwards. Humanism would therefore be legitimate if it would offer more, and bring a spiritual upgrade and strengthening, a substantive deepening and widening. But . . . we only see a reduction and a thinning, a lowering of moral standards and of human dignity. Humanism did not invent any new values, or enrich the world; it only deleted, weakened, and diluted. When a teabag (the gospel) is used for a second (or third . . .) time, you get very weak tea; strong faith has become vague hope, love has become tolerance. Christianity promises the highest happiness, the most amazing afterlife, the deepest peace, the purest love, ultimate hope, and the restoration of all things. Humanism however undermines all these essentials and critically questions everything. It tears down the Church, but it does not put a new building in place; it leaves its people spiritually homeless.

Humanism is playing with fire when it thinks it can amputate the Christian heritage of Europe just like an (unnecessary) appendix. It is generally recognized that our civilization rests on three pillars: Greek, Roman, and Hebrew. But meanwhile, the third one, the Judeo-Christian, is being sawn away from underneath! A stool resting on three legs is stable but on two legs . . .? And that just this pillar is being removed and not the other two speaks strongly.

Humanism certainly created openness to other worldviews but provided no substantive spiritual contribution whatsoever. It—naively—assumes that methods and solutions on the level of technical problems (better living conditions, medical progress . . .) can be automatically transferred to the level of life views and spirituality!

4.4 Morally: 'long live anarchy'!

Since humanism does not believe in divine commandments, (self-made) morals are very important for her. Practically, however, it blows hot and cold when it comes to moral values. A lot of value is supposedly contributed to them, but when it really comes to it, they are swept aside without a problem (e.g. 'abortion is not a moral issue'). There is a kind of love-hate relationship with moral standards. A humanist can equally be a convinced libertine.

86. Humanism as an ideology is an 'easy solution': 'If we lower the moral standards, then at least we can keep them'. But even these (lower) morals cannot be attained, and so in the next phase they are lowered even further, and the downward spiral becomes unstoppable. Humanism lacks the inner strength to realize its own project.

When there are no absolute moral rules, and everyone determines their own values, this inevitably leads to opportunism and situational ethics. The norms are 'adapted' to what is desirable, achievable, opportune, whatever seems best in a given situation. The noblest moral standards of humanist moral philosophers are not more valuable than the flattest materialism and hedonism of Joe Bloggs. Not only in the spiritual domain does humanism present its life-approach as a 'self-built package', (create your own religion) but also morally, as if it were a board game where you can make up your own rules!

87. Humanism does not have the spiritual and moral strength to hold a society together or to inspire it. Values that have been invented or laid down by a fellow human are never superior to us and cannot be imposed upon us. They can never call people to a higher level or challenge them to go beyond themselves.

Humanism not only has no official authority to set even one rule (no one can impose rules on someone else) but also no stimuli, no 'incentives' to challenge people to transcend their natural selfishness. It is like a plane that has no pilot and no flight plan, but also no 'power' in the engine. Humanism has no guidelines to lead an entire society, nor any moral strength to enforce any norm. It has no moral backbone and no stick behind the door. It lacks the power to realize its own project, no matter how low the goals are set. It stays stuck in absolute lack of commitment. Its call for humaneness, solidarity, and commitment to others lacks any persuasive power. Its scope does not reach much further than 'well-calculated self-interest'.

The power of a philosophy of life can be measured by its power to mobilize people, to inspire them to higher things. Jesus teaches that following him is worth leaving everything behind, bringing the highest sacrifices, even your own life. Humanism, however, does not ask for sacrifices, no

Conclusion: humanism vs. Christianity

total surrender, no mission, and no self-sacrifice. The value of something is what it may cost you.

Humanism is not directly responsible for the moral anarchy of this time in the sense that it does not advocate 'as much immorality' as possible. But it can also not deny its responsibility for this as if it has nothing to do with it. The current normlessness is undeniably the consequence of its vision, its concept of man and its values of freedom and self-determination. In this sense, humanism (philosophically and morally) is organized chaos! A politician who expels an 'old dictator' and then declares 'absolute freedom' in the country, whereby everything gets out of control, destroys the country. Even if he does this with good intentions, he is guilty without a doubt and has blood on his hands!

Humanism preaches more moral freedom—sometimes rightly!—but does not add anything in terms of moral values. On the contrary, it seems to believe naively that it can detach Christian values from their religious roots without this having any effect.

4.5 Practically: derailment

Secularization is now well advanced in Europe and we are 'lucky' enough to judge the first fruits in practice. So, what do we see? Theoretically the principles of humanism were already incorrect, but also practically its results do not bring improvement: it is not true and it does not work. Since man has been sitting on the throne, society has become less humane. Since God, the interconnecting point, has gone, everything—logically—falls apart and disintegrates; a child could have predicted this.

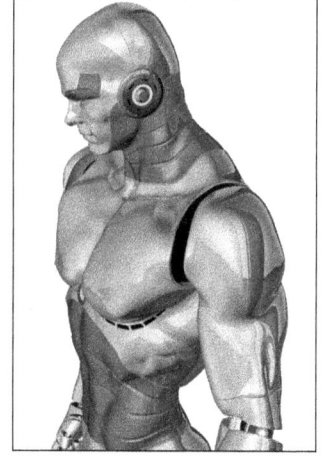

Values and standards are up for sale, on private as well as public levels: the economy is out of control, mammon makes our society run wild, democracy is crippling itself, and all major institutions are in crisis. Psychological pressure is unbearable for more and more people; stress, irritability, and mental illnesses are on the increase, the waiting lists for special youth care are off track; we live in 'border line times' (psychiatrist Dirk De Wachter). Moral consciousness seems to get blunted or anesthetized, we see less tolerance, more outbursts of irrational, meaningless violence, unbridled ego-tripping, even a 'psychopathization' of society (the Belgian top lawyer Jef Vermassen). Because of the increased freedom in our society and the increasing abuse thereof (because man cannot handle it!), the government must make more laws and rules to seal the gaps and cracks until man is suffocated under the rules, bureaucracy, and greed for control. Increasing lack of freedom and lack of privacy are the result. Social media make us increasingly asocial and superficial, individualism and loneliness increase painfully. More sexual freedom should have brought more happiness, but we see a battlefield in the sphere of marriages and families, a mess of broken relationships, a relational massacre. The scant positive benefits have been overcome by the negative effects since a long time. Humanism does not give an answer to the crises of this world, but only aggravates them.

There is a profound crisis in European civilization: a general discomfort, a malaise. The more culture and technology we have, the less we feel at home in our own, self-made world. Young people can go to the best schools but are tired of school. For the elderly, there is the best health care, but they are weary of life. The democracies are among the best in the world, but the whole political system is 'tired'. The high prosperity brings masses of physical and psychological 'welfare' diseases! The removal of God from society should have brought an end to religious wars and bring peace, and what do we see? The 20th century with its godless regimes saw multitudes of victims of war and human cruelty. Europe is often proudly presented as an enlightened continent, but there is no continent in so much bondage, so unfree. The demons we thought were chased away, have returned sevenfold, but are now so much better disguised and refined. Europe is like an old, sick, cynical man. The political, economic, and financial world can completely collapse in the next big crisis; the experts know this but prefer to keep silent. The world is still functioning (fortunately), but this is because in practice, people do not implement humanistic principles, and the centuries old Christian heritage has still its effect.

In our modern day, people are looking for authenticity and sustainability, but what does this mean practically? It is like with clothes or handbags; they like an original, exclusive, decent handbag, but are not

> "The average European humanist thinks it is a good thing that we have been delivered from Christianity, but he does not realize that this Christianity was at the heart of our identity. As soon as faith is gone, man is nothing more than a consumer. We do not want to bring any sacrifices anymore for our values and ideals."
> —Roger Scruton (° 1944), British philosopher, professor, and writer

willing to pay the price for it, so they buy a fake brand (which looks very similar but is much cheaper). In the moral domain, people crave authenticity, but do not want to pay the high price Jesus sets. They really want gold for the price of tin. When, however, will they be so disappointed with all the cheap counterfeits that they turn their backs on it? But by then, maybe they will be so 'morally spoiled' that no resistance is left anymore and they are too weakened to turn back . . . Our age does not want to pay the price for a life according to God's norm but has not yet calculated the price of a life without God. It is of course cheaper (in the short term!), but not sustainable, and in the long run, the 'final invoice' will be a multiple of the original cost sheet.

> *"I have been raised with Christian values that are now being set aside as worthless. I think it is the great flaw of our civilization, even though I'm atheist."*
> —Wim van Rooy (° 1947), Belgian philosopher and publicist, atheist and freemason

A tree is judged by its fruit, according to Jesus (Matt 7:16–17). In any case, the freedom and happiness, peace and tolerance promised by humanism, continue to be absent. If a humanistic society were to be judged on the basis of its own standards, it would have to condemn itself as guilty; it is not even able to consistently and practically apply them. It is very distressing to see how our society is derailing, but nobody dares to put the finger on the hurt: nobody is allowed to make the link with the secular spirit of this age, a godless society!

4.6 Subconsciously: irrational allergies and fears

A full review of an ideology cannot only remain on a rational level. Man is so much more than that! The real reasons why someone chooses for or against a religion are ultimately not rational! When atheists assume or seek impure motivations behind the believers' faith (escapism, childishness, weakness, fear, social pressure, dependence . . .), you can,

> 88. Humanism fundamentally arose out of fear of abuse of religion—which is understandable—but that should mean that humanists ought to be very happy with a pure expression of religion. In practice, however, humanism fails to overcome this anti-attitude, and to many, this has become an irrational aversion, a phobia for every 'trace' of religion. If the objection is raised that the deepest motivations for faith are irrational, then the deeper reasons for unbelief are no less so. Fear is, by definition, a bad counsellor.

with every right, lay the same measuring rod to the unbelievers' unbelief. Which irrational mechanisms, hidden motives, secret agendas are the real driving force?

Did humanism not originate as a counter-reaction against the dominance and intolerance of the Church? The excessively strong emphasis on autonomy and individual freedom point to this at least. But when fear of abuse of power and dominance become the driving force for rejecting any authority, then this counter-reaction is completely out of balance and irrational. Rebellion against every form of authority is an immature, adolescent reaction. Whoever cannot submit to any superior has a problem; it is (hopefully temporarily) a phase of willfulness, and untenable in real life (where inevitably we are under many forms of authority). Not everyone who asks critical questions about authority has a 'rebellious spirit', but some do, and then it becomes unhealthy. It is a kind of allergy to authority, a hypersensitivity, and a consequence of an injury from the past that was never healed. Slavish obedience is regarded in psychology as childish; being against everything is juvenile behavior, but mustn't there be something like adulthood?

Faith can indeed arise from weakness, but unbelief too; an atheist who frantically denies that he needs God, resembles a man who frantically denies that he needs a woman. Due to some negative experience, he has concluded that 'all women are dangerous' and for fear of hurt and loss of self-determination, he has built high walls around himself. But perhaps the cause was due to his own immaturity and he is not willing to take on board the consequences of a real relationship. Is it not much more honest, brave, and relaxed when a man just admits he needs a woman? And what is so shameful about saying that we need God? When a man allows a woman in his life and gives her the right to make decisions together, does his life gets worse because of this?

We can ask ourselves the same about God! The franticness with which some people try to remove

> "We feel so incredibly emancipated that we are all convinced that we can all manage by ourselves, that we do not need others to make the best choices in our own lives, that no one knows better than ourselves what is best for us, that we and we alone are the best gauge of our own emotional life, that nobody else should decide what we should and should not do. Authority and dominion are seen as remains of a stone age."
> —Dirk De Wachter
> Borderline Times, p.27.

Conclusion: Humanism vs. Christianity

God from their world resembles an irrational trauma. Why does our age suffer so much from philosophical bonding anxiety or spiritual attachment disorders? And how can it be that so many people are afraid of a God who is described as pure goodness? Modern man is displaced, alienated from himself, and suffers from an ontological 'lack of basic trust'.

Humanism and atheism also have something haughty: the pride to do it alone. A certain degree of pride and self-reliance is of course beautiful and good, but when this flips into stubbornness, it becomes offensive arrogance. Willfully putting oneself in the center of the universe and believing that your own opinion is superior to everyone else's shows a lack of realistic self-assessment, of elementary modesty, and thus, of outrageous arrogance! Not being able to ask for help is something very irrational. In the case of technical problems, we have no problem asking for help, but why not then for the most important areas of life? Does our reputation get a dent, or our image of 'I need no one else'; does it give us a sense of failure? Or do self-assertion and self-justification play along? Are we fearful of giving away control over our own life? High-sounding intellectual words can sometimes be a way to camouflage baser motives. Is boasting in 'I do not need anybody', not simply a lot of acting tough and spiritual macho behavior? A macho is a man who denies his feminine side. He thinks and communicates, 'I'm die-hard, I stand above this'. Either he does not know himself or he is afraid to show his weaknesses. Deep on the inside he is starving for affection, but he prefers to remain hungry rather than to lose the hard bolster of his image. It would be very liberating for himself and for his environment if he could be just honest with himself. Arrogance is very irritating for the surrounding people and this 'being puffed-up' must and will be punctured at some point in time, perhaps with a loud bang.

It is also a sign of immaturity to push away responsibility for our own actions and mistakes. A person who points the finger at God (or the Church) as the cause of all world problems does not prove to be very responsible at all. The cause of wars, torture, and rape is man, not God. Criticizing others is often the easiest way not to investigate oneself. And, criticizing God is usually a form of projection. But also, these are usually unconscious, non-rational processes. Similar immature mechanisms in people are 'postponement behavior' and 'ostrich politics': pushing away what we do not like or find easy. It is actually childish, but every adult is guilty of it, also in the spiritual area. Believers may do it daily—from weakness and lack of faith—unbelievers do it structurally and systematically.

In any case, we must not overestimate human rationality and honesty in the field of belief. If a non-believer, with his own eyes, would see a dead person raised, would he believe? Even facts (miracles) do not convince—in Jesus' time it was no different. Man's prejudice is startling in this area. The many childish images of God contemptuously rejected by atheists also illustrate this. We see the irrational aspect of humanism clearly emerging when it rejects the Christian God as primitive, but then returns to Greek and Roman polytheism, ancient pagan gods and idols, or creates many new secular gods. Where is the thin boundary between 'I cannot believe in God' and 'I will not believe in God'? The pre-rational decisions are subsequently substantiated with rationalizing arguments.

Atheists sometimes say that Christians, because of their imaginary faith, have lost contact with reality, but believers say, "Humanists who still believe in the goodness and improvability of man have lost contact with reality." Or even stronger, this whole world has lost contact with The Reality!

4.7 And the future? A dreadful vision

Christian prophets do not really need to cry out anymore that the world is going downhill and its end is near; the secular prophets (intellectuals, philosophers, and media watchers) do this enough already. This is not only about physical world problems (climate and nature) but also politically, economically, socially, morally, etc. Why are most culture philosophers pessimistic about our time and the future? Rationally speaking they are right because the facts offer little hope! The feeling that the world is dying and that this can no longer be stopped strongly dwells within large sections of the population. Science fiction films almost always show a future that is (much) worse than today; even a world designed and 100% controlled by people is terrifying! Although it may seem many times more efficient and rational, it is gruesomely unattractive, not to mention the pictures of total world domination by one world leader; we absolutely do not trust any human (!) or system for this. This says much about the general feeling toward how this planet will be when man takes it all over: many times worse than what religions ever produced.

Humanism can potentially grow into THE dominant world ideology, whereby 'belief in man' will be imposed. as the only religion This can lead to a world tyranny 'in the name of freedom, equality, and humanity'. Already now we see new taboos in our culture, new variations of (humanistic)

Conclusion: humanism vs. Christianity

fundamentalism, and unmistakable signs of intolerance. Secular society is already busy depicting Christians as the evil ones; those who stand up for life are suddenly the 'intolerant ones' and their plea for truth and values is suddenly considered 'hate speech'. When such tyranny does come about, it will be more to be 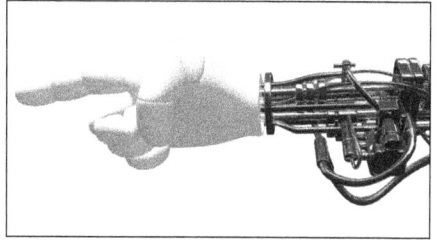 feared than Stalin's because the technological means to accomplish this have in the meantime been progressing dozens of times more than in his time.

In the long run, humanism will inevitably lead to its own collapse because of its internal contradictions and the disintegration to which it leads. As society further evolves to 'Everyone determines his own values', it will bring such insoluble problems that it will become unlivable and absolutely 'unpayable' for society. The machine will run out of oil and get overheated, block irrecoverably, and finally stall. It will be like a democracy that collapses, causing people to call for a dictator! These are not cries of overheated prophets; secular thinkers are also saying this. And they make it even bleaker than Christians who still have faith in a God who has everything in His hand.

> "In times of universal deceit, telling the truth will be a revolutionary act."
> —George Orwell (1903–1950), British writer, journalist, essayist, and literary critic.

Humanism has no answer to the question, 'What about when man himself degenerates into an animal'? Humanism wanted to free us from every religious inhumanity but has no remedy against human inhumanity. The atheist-communist regimes have already shown this in detail. If, for thousands of years now, humanity has not been able to fix and correct itself, what real hope is there that this will suddenly happen tomorrow[3]? If it barely succeeds with the Christian God-of-Love, how can it succeed without this God?

> "Can the world afford a faith-meltdown in Europe any less than it can afford a financial meltdown?"
> —Jeff Fountain, founder of 'The Schuman Center'

---

3. "Let us humbly admit that humanism is a utopia", prof. Jean-Pierre Van den Branden, Honorary Conservator of the Erasmus House in Anderlecht, Brussels (*Freedom and Humanism in Europe*, p. 23).

95 Theses on Humanism

4.8 And nine more comparisons

Finally, we want to very briefly elaborate (or further elaborate) on some 'modern parables' to help visualize the relationship between humanism and Christianity.

4.8.1 The Titanic

The Titanic was in its time (1912) the largest and most solid ship ever made by people. It was regarded as 'indestructible' and people whispered, 'Even God cannot destroy this'. Therefore, it was not considered necessary to provide enough lifeboats. The captain steered this ship with such self-assurance that even when there were reports of icebergs, he hardly took them seriously. After the collision, when the ship was already sinking, the orchestra was ordered to continue playing so as to 'not to worry the passengers'. This disaster went through the world as a shock wave and unmasked the naive confidence in technological achievements as arrogance.

A more tragic parallel to modern society can hardly be found. Human haughtiness so often clashes with invisible forces we do not control, but how long will it take before we hit the fatal iceberg from which the ship can no longer recover? Politicians, economists, climatologists, philosophers, and all kinds of experts all know that this is perfectly possible within the foreseeable future. At the same time, the people remain over-actively busy arranging the chairs nicely on the deck around the pool and hanging up the paper lanterns: 'the show must go on'. Humanity plunges itself ever more exuberantly into entertainment and amusement, festivals and self-intoxication, but nobody cares for the essential questions, the course of the ship, the meaning and purpose of it all, and the sustainability of our modern way of life.

---

89. The financial crisis or banking crisis is a powerful parable for the present ideological crisis: when derivative financial products are no longer covered by real values, the system collapses. Just like the banking crisis was caused by too much investment with borrowed money and by trading with virtual money, so the whole 'ideological market' staggers. Humanism works purely with 'borrowed values'.

4.8.2 The banking crisis

In 2007–8 an unprecedented banking crisis raged from America all over Europe and the rest of the world. What happened in financial

Conclusion: Humanism vs. Christianity

terms is a quasi-perfect parallel to what is happening spiritually in our culture. The market collapsed because the banks created and sold very complex financial products, and no one knew any more what real economic value was behind them. This was only possible due to a few decades of deregulation (easing of the rules) by governments, and because rating agencies did not take any responsibility, control was virtually non-existent. In other words, a huge bubble had grown and needed to burst. The few professors and economists who warned against these practices were laughed away. Economic capitalism did not seem to have a mechanism to stop the derailment. The system was only saved with the utmost effort, and in the end, the ordinary citizens and taxpayers paid the full bill for this. The parallel to the 'spiritual bubble' is hallucinating; deregulation in the ideological market is complete, and humanistic values were piece by piece borrowed (!) from Christianity. Humanism is a kind of religion-without-God and Christianity-without-Christ, and its values are unsecured cheques because there is no 'gold value' behind them. How long will it take before this system completely collapses and ordinary people pay the bill?

4.8.3 The sorcerer's apprentice

Humanism is like the sorcerer's apprentice from the Walt Disney cartoon. The naive pupil wants to experiment with his magic powers and formulas, to make the broom clean by itself, and it succeeds. The problems start, however, when these forces derail, begin to lead their own lives and he cannot hold them back—until the master arrives and rescues the situation. Humanism has certainly initiated something (in itself positive): a movement of freedom, openness, empowerment, individualism, independence, self-development ... but the forces that were released cannot be constrained or limited. The humanistic culture derails because every '-ism' that is cut off from its source (God) can grow into a demonic power: it is a potential

> 90. Humanism is like the sorcerer's apprentice: it has started up a movement and has released certain forces (such as empowerment, individualism, independence, self-fulfillment ...) but is unable to restrain these unleashed forces. It is clearly running out of control, and is very dangerous, because these forces have grown into demonic powers. And humanism has no weapons to fight against demonic powers, because it denies their very existence.

4.8.4 The torch opposite the sun

The torch is the self-chosen symbol of humanism and is actually very telling: a self-lit light that is carried by one self. One of the symbols for Jesus, on the other hand, is the sun. A Christian wonders: how can anyone choose a torch when the sun is there? Humanism prefers, as it were, to close the shutters and light a lamp. The relationship between a torch and the sun is indeed an excellent illustration of the relationship between a human being and God.

In this context, the word 'Enlightenment' is actually very unjust and misleading. The word has been so normalized by now that no one asks the question what light it brings and into which areas? Yet in the thoroughly Christian culture of the 17th–18th century, which believed in Jesus as the 'Light of the World' (John 8:12), it seems strange that this word was chosen for a movement that promoted mainly science and knowledge; a spiritual concept was lowered to a cognitive concept.

Furthermore, we see the same with a word such as 'renaissance' which indicates a certain cultural (!) movement. The word 'rebirth', again, comes straight from the Bible, but indicates a truly new birth of an individual in the deepest of its

---

91. The torch is a very striking and eloquent symbol of humanism: a light, self-lit and carried by oneself. But who would prefer to keep the blinds and curtains closed and light a torch while the sun is shining outside?

92. Enlightenment claimed to bring 'light'—as humanism and freemasonry also claim—, but those who make such a pretentious assertion must prove that they can fulfil it. This claim is not without danger; just like someone who says he can heal someone using psychic abilities, but fails, may end up bringing death rather than healing! The 'light' that the Enlightenment brought only works at the level of science and technology, not at the level of meaning and moral values. Moreover, this pretension is stolen/copied from Jesus: it is a parody of his claim (to be the 'Light of the World'), a poor 'remake'.

Conclusion: humanism vs. Christianity

being. Only God can make a man be born again and give him a new spirit (John 3: 1–8). Applying this however to the rediscovery (in the 14th century) of classical antiquity gives this concept a much less weighty meaning than what Jesus meant. This is similar as when someone says after a good shower, 'I feel born again'.

Even the claim to 'bring light' is already dangerous and pretentious, just as when a charlatan claims to heal people! The charlatan will cause a seriously sick person to not go to the (true) doctor and perhaps die! Moreover, this pretense was stolen from Jesus, and is a parody, a bad 'remake'. This precious, rich, divine word was reduced to something that has absolutely nothing to do with it. When someone sits in a deep depression and desperately says, 'I am spiritually completely in the dark', then you do not arrive with a flashlight, do you!?

4.8.5 The sun and planets

For millennia, man thought the earth was the center of the universe and the sun turned around it, until Copernicus came and reversed the roles, or rather, put it right. Mankind was no longer at the center of everything. It was not pleasant (!) at all for humanity to hear this; it hurt our planetary ego to be pushed to the margins. In the spiritual area, however, exactly the opposite happened: some found it highly uncomfortable to think they turned around a Creator-God and decided not to do so. They declared man to be 'the creator of values and norms, meaning and purpose'! How absurd! As if a person can just decide this like that!

The parallel is so clear that it requires almost no further comment. After centuries of indoctrination it is, however, more necessary than ever to shed some light on the evidence of this. The earth derives its entire life and existence from the sun, its warmth and its light. Through a delicate interplay of balance between gravity and centrifugal force, the earth is at exactly the right distance from the sun for life to be possible here. If the earth would suddenly rebel against that 'authoritarian and intolerant' sun, choose self-determination and the freedom to 'disconnect itself' what would be the consequences!? If we were to turn the 'gravity button' off—even for a moment—the earth would completely 'derail', fly infinitely far from the sun and all life would definitively freeze. If we would only realize the absurd price we pay for our (overestimated) autonomy—and it does not even yield anything positive for us!

4.8.6 Conductor and orchestra

Humanism 'amputates' the cohesive factor (God) from Christian culture, as if you could do so just like that, and remain unpunished. Compare this with a symphonic orchestra where the musicians suddenly get irritated with the conductor who they then call 'dictatorial' and oppressive and start to rebel. Instead of searching for another, better conductor, they decide, "From now on, we'll do it without a conductor; nobody can be my boss any longer, everyone decides their own rules and is autonomous." What will the next rehearsal look like? Everyone plays his own score, each in their own pitch, rhythm, music key and style: in note C and note D, in ¾ time and 4/4 time, jazz and classic, heavy metal and Gregorian . . .! No-one can dictate the others what piece to play, no-one indicates the initial bar, no one can even sound the tuning fork to align the instruments because everyone thinks 'the others need to adapt to me'. Even though they can all be very good musicians, the result will be a cacophony! In the end nobody will come to the rehearsal anymore and they may even start to hate music itself . . .

> 93. Humanism thinks it can just cut God out of society and culture, without making a difference. As if you can sack the Conductor, and the orchestra will keep playing perfectly; as if traffic continues to flow smoothly when everyone drives by their own rules; as if all train passengers in each railway station could determine where the train will go next.

It is not difficult to transpose this to a whole society with seven billion people, which is even much more complex than an orchestra. Because the same rule applies to all areas of life: imagine an army without a general or a platoon without an officer, a company without a CEO, a boat without a captain or a bus without a driver, a government without a prime minister, a football team without a trainer and a football match without a referee, a banking world without a national bank, a world without calibrated measures . . .

Conclusion: humanism vs. Christianity

Imagine an army where one hundred thousand soldiers all have equal decision-making rights, a world where everyone has its own measure of length and volume size, an economy where each person determines its own currency and exchange rates, a train company where (in every station) all passengers decide 'democratically' where to travel, a country where everyone can freely choose how much tax they pay, a traffic rules that is only optional, a prison where the doors are always open (because no one can oppress another). Fortunately, there are few real humanists in this world, and certainly none who apply this consequently!

4.8.7 Diagnosis and medicine

Humanism wanted to solve the 'disease' of the late Middle Ages (religious wars and intolerance), but what was the diagnosis and what was the proposed remedy? Because a wrong diagnosis leads to wrong medication, and this can make the disease progress for the worse and even lead to death. As long as cancer is not diagnosed correctly, it continues to spread. Every doctor knows this very well and dreads it; he can be prosecuted due to a medical error and severely penalized for this. However, 'free' philosophers and 'innovative' thinkers take all the liberty of making nice-sounding analyses and enjoy breaking down all existing 'holy houses', without wondering what will come instead and what social havoc this may wreak. They also cannot be prosecuted for the disintegrating influence of their theories.

Secular humanism states unequivocally, 'God and religion are the problem, and man is the solution'. But this diagnosis is extremely superficial and undifferentiated; it is 'sloppy work' and does not even match the facts. The cause is much deeper than they hope or want to admit; man unquestionably caused the problem (and the believer can add to this, 'and God offers the solution'). You can compare it with AIDS, where the virus attacks the immune system itself. Man is infected in his system, in his operating program! By underestimating the problem, humanism prescribes a medicine that is way too light. In the meantime, the disease continues to spread, and even gets worse. By blaming 'religion and God' for centuries now, man has even been made resistant to the medicine! 'A soft doctor makes stinking wounds', says an old proverb, and this is very relevant here. He seems loving and kind to his patient but is actually unloving and a coward; he is more concerned with what the patient will like than with saving his life.

4.8.8 Genetically modified food

With the following 'parable' we stay a little in the medical arena. For several decades now, we have been experimenting with genetic engineering of food (cereals, plants . . .). This has been undertaken with the best intentions of making plants resistant to insects and diseases so as to increase productivity. There are, however, serious objections and protests against the safety of this: do we know the consequences in the long run? Maybe this has side 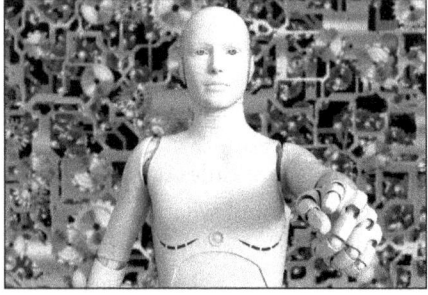 effects which we will only discover after ten years or in the next generation (think of the ten thousand 'Softenon babies', born with major abnormalities after the mother had taken the medicine Softenon)? Our culture however is very schizophrenic because when our physical food is threatened, we make a big fuss, but when it comes to our spiritual food, everyone continues to mess around cheerfully. Medical and pharmaceutical tests are strictly regulated, but when belief and worldview are genetically manipulated, when concepts of man, life and world views are unrestrictedly tinkered with, there is completely carelessness, as if total freedom will not have any effect! It is allowed to cut the very core (God) out of the DNA of our Christian heritage, and it is even thought that this will not make any difference! How frivolous and naive this is regarding the most essential areas of life! Any public health minister who would display such irresponsible carelessness would be branded as a criminal, but on the spiritual level, as many experiments as possible are encouraged, as if existential questions are just free play, a hobby for those who like it. We see spiritual 'softenon babies' all around us!

---

94. In the case of genetically modified foods, people are genuinely concerned about possible long-term adverse effects, even for the generations to come. But when it comes to genetically engineered ideologies, world views, and views of man, our society is absolutely unconcerned and thinks that total freedom will not have any consequences! It is in the most crucial areas that we are naive and irresponsible to the point of absurdity.

CONCLUSION: HUMANISM VS. CHRISTIANITY

4.8.9 The sustainability of the planet

The very highest authorities of this world are increasingly aware that the earth has a 'fever'; environmental pollution, depletion of land resources, and climate warming really jeopardize the planet's survival—if only the tide can still be turned! But in what kind of hypocritical and schizophrenic society do we live! We continually 'preach' about sustainability of the environment but promote unsustainability (volatility) for the rest of all human values. One pleads fiercely for the protection of species that are dying out, but some call even more fervently for the abolition of all religions. There is concern for endangered seals, but not for (unborn) human life. Action is taken against environmental degradation, but moral degeneration is applauded. What an idiotic society we live in where billions are spent on saving our natural resources, but human resources (love and relationships) is systematically squandered! The (emotional) price humanity pays for this, the loss of true joy in life, runs in the trillions! Even a child could see the connection between increasing moral normlessness and climate degradation, but only technological solutions can be provided. No one is even allowed to make the link with moral pollution because judging others or making them feel guilty is considered much worse. Spiritual poverty (materialism and individualism) leads to ecological damage, and this is the big blind spot of this age, the new taboo. Politicians decide on strict quotas for CO_2 emissions, but not for the emission of verbal or spiritual pollution. They close their eyes to the fact that the lack of 'spiritual sustainability' (lack of an overall perspective and spiritual long-term thinking) is precisely the cause of the greedy overconsumption of land resources and the short-sightedness of making a quick profit. God is thrown out, and the earth becomes a kind of new, secular god (think of the ecohumanism of Kruithof), but precisely this 'god' we are destroying ourselves.

> "The approach of humanism denies evil in man and seeks happiness only on earth. This leads to the worship of man and of the material. This in turn opens the door for the demonic."
> —Alexander Solzhenitsyn, 1918–2008

If humanity were spiritually fit, balanced, and morally healthy, then the worldwide problem of global warming would be resolved in a couple of meetings. It would then indeed only be a technical problem. But it is a spiritual problem, of unbridled selfishness and economic interests, short-term thinking and protectionism, pride and prestige, nationalism and international feuds, blindness and rigidity, inability and unwillingness. Spiritual powers are not tackled with official statements, subsidies, and diplomacy; they are irrational and play dirty. Unclean spirits only disappear through a stronger pure spirit. Hate only vanishes through stronger love, despair through greater hope, nihilism through a stronger faith. But humanism pulled the 'plug' out of faith, hope, and love, opened the 'valve' and let all the air ('spirit') out.

Warnings about the effects of 'global warming' were sounded long before today, but humanity is slow to hear this. It is difficult to believe because it seems such a high price to change our luxurious lifestyle. But the spiritual question is even much more urgent and dire: are people willing to pay the price for a true turnaround of the entire civilization? The planet does not need to be saved; man needs to be saved because he is the one destroying the planet! Man has a fever and has infected the earth with it. How much worse does it have to get? The future of our planet depends much more on our spiritual condition because with one click of a button it can already be destroyed. And be aware, man controls this button, not God! Whether or not somebody will push this button one day has everything to do with spiritual realities: to trust or to distrust, trusting in our own abilities or in God's ability; because 'trust' is synonymous with 'faith'. And this brings us to the very last chapter ...

4.9 Finally: anthropocentrism or theocentrism?

Western culture made an incredible and incomprehensible shift in a short period of time: in the Middle Ages, God was central and man was taboo, now man is central and God is taboo. Nobody denies that many things went wrong in the past in the area of religion and the Church, but this does not justify this total reversal in any way. Furthermore, placing man in the center is in no way a sustainable or valid alternative. Anthropocentrism can only work 'in my own head' (and even this is not consistent); it cannot function in the real world, in the interaction with billions of others.

God was thrown from the throne, but when man is put on the throne, how much chance is there that things go wrong? Let us just take a look at reality: what percentage of absolute monarchs abuse their power, 70-80-90%? But even if it were 60-50-40%, it is still an irresponsible

> Humanism made man big-headed, which ultimately will make mankind fall flat on its face.

Conclusion: humanism vs. Christianity

choice to give such an unreliable creature the ultimate decision-making power, 'all the power on earth'! Humanism presents man as a kind of *absolutum* while he is merely an extremely fragile, transient, and fallible being. It is so absurd and paradoxical that it is hard to imagine that intelligent people could believe in this. And if the error is in the system, even the best solution is still part of the problem!

If seven billion planets would declare themselves to be the center of the universe and decide to 'ignore' the sun—as if that could be possible!—everything would get out of balance and all relationships would be disturbed. In a similar way, people constantly get entangled with each other, and also with themselves and with nature. There is actually something essentially 'out of place' with all of mankind. Just as a shoulder can come 'out of its socket', man has gotten 'loosed from God', uprooted, on the drift. Not respecting the correct order, and cutting corners, ruins everything. Humanistic values and principles are all valuable in themselves, but if the order and cohesion are disturbed, they collide with each other and cause major damage. We also see this, for example, in the desperate quest of mankind for much sought after happiness; too much direct and strong focus on happiness makes us unhappy!

The argument that 'giving God the first place' inevitably opens the door for blind fanaticism, intolerance, and bloodshed, is actually a big lie. What man messes up, he cannot blame on God. The Middle Ages did not have 'too much God', but exactly 'too much of man'; there was too much of the flesh in the work of the Spirit!

Our Western culture needs a fundamental correction of perspective; God is not the evil-doer and scapegoat, but the Creator and Savior. The God of the Bible does not bring oppression but freedom and has created man for life-to-the-full. He is Righteousness itself, Light without shadow, Love without any hidden agenda. If anything or anyone can be an absolute and reliable cardinal point, He can. This is precisely the only valid definition of 'God'. If there is one absolute Ruler who is trustworthy, who else could that be? His tolerance exceeds thousands of times our human imagination! He is by far the most rational Being because who else placed rationality in nature and in the human brain? He is the only impartial Judge who can rise above all parties and who is at the same time for all parties. He is also the only one who can keep the right balance between justice and mercy. He is the Champion of humaneness, because He happens to also be its 'Inventor'; He has the patent on it. He is the Original, we only are the copy.

It is humanly impossible to get rid of our self-centeredness. Naturally, we inevitably think from ourselves and this is precisely what causes all the misery. Humanism proclaims freedom but does not provide liberation from this most subtle slavery, the tyranny of the 'I', our addiction to our self. Every person knows that it is a liberating experience when you put your  own little interests aside to serve another, and occasionally we even succeed in this. But God wants to do this structurally in us, and only a total focus on God can break our stubborn self-focus. A half-religion—a little bit of God, occasionally, in some areas of life, somewhere in the margin—is not a cure, and can even do more harm than good. Theocentrism[4] is the radical reversal of anthropocentrism and is therefore the only valid alternative. All approaches that do not radically deal with man-at-the-center remain weak and infected with the problem. The only true, lasting, comprehensive solution is God-at-the-center: principally, totally, always, systematically. This is a consistent, reasonable, logical solution, because all other humanistic principles (including science and rationality) will then find their right place in the whole, and justice will flourish.

In the eyes of secular man, religion is about the most boring thing he can imagine; he looks for his kicks in one hundred and one other things that give him the necessary adrenaline rushes, such as extreme sports, clubs and festivals, sex and alcohol, exclusive hobbies and vacations . . . But for a believer who has really met God, there is no more powerful kick experience than this! Whoever touches God, touches

---

95. Self-centeredness is so ingrained, so resilient, so matter-of-fact, and difficult to overcome that only God can liberate us, from the outside, of the tyranny of our ego, of our addiction to ourselves! Only a perfect, good, and holy God can be the central calibration point for norms and values, for purpose and meaning. Only He can be an impartial arbitrator between people and between groups and help us to survey the human maze of life from above.

---

4. This plea for theocentrism is not a plea to 'install' theocracy (like some streams in Islam want to do). It is impossible for people to just 'organize this' as this would also mean 'forcing it'. In my view, this is the biggest lesson we can draw from the Middle Ages: the kingdom of God cannot be realized by people, only by God Himself.

Conclusion: humanism vs. Christianity

as it were a nuclear power plant. Moses spoke with God face to face and radiated completely (Ex 34:29). King David said clearly that he loved God's presence above all the distractions of his palace (Psalm 27:4). He found the top experiences of his life in the presence of God! When Ezekiel had seen his hallucinating vision, he was turned topsy-turvy for seven days (Ezekiel 3:15). The priests in Solomon's temple could no longer stand on their feet when God's glory appeared (2 Chr. 7:2). John fell on the ground when he saw the glorified Jesus (Rev. 1:17). Thousands of other Christians can probably share similar experiences[5]. Even the angels in the innermost circle of God's throne throw themselves continually on the ground in the purest worship, when observing God's glory (Rev. 4:8–11). This is the purest heavenly theocentrism without any distraction! How could God (or Heaven) ever be boring?! For a person who has seen or experienced only a glimpse of God's glory, this is the greatest possible kick and all the earthly stuff is boring.

Theocentrism is also the best guarantee for humaneness! Placing the God of Love at the center makes all relationships between people fall in the 'right' place and allows their (blocked) love to flow again in all directions. When man is 'plugged in the right place' again, it works so much better, more harmonious, more peaceful, and smoother; there is oil again in the machine. God at the center creates the right conditions for human happiness to flourish abundantly. Making room for God or for man is a false contradiction; whoever gives God the first place automatically creates more space for man! God's interests do not compete with those of man. His supreme interest is for humanity to thrive! It is therefore absolutely not true that Christians do not believe in man, on the contrary: they cannot but believe in man because God does too! This is precisely His command, and He is the valid guarantee that this belief is not a dangerous wish or dream and will not turn into a nightmare.

> God is never a threat to man. On the contrary, He is the only guarantor for when man becomes a threat to himself and to his fellow human beings.

Placing God at the center does not mean either that man then passively waits and looks on with arms crossed. On the contrary, when we give Him the supremacy, then it is our turn to take our responsibilities and work

---

5. This is not the place to share details, but I also personally experienced the presence of Jesus on 10th of May 2014 and this with a 'nuclear intensity' that filled every cell of my being like a fireball. This was my strongest experience of Life ever,—I wouldn't have survived stronger than that.

hard, to use our talents (also our rationality) and seek solutions. He will not do it in our place because He gave man dominion over this planet (thus, a good deal of autonomy!) and refuses to treat us as toddlers. It is a matter of the right order: firstly, the architect must submit the plan and only then will the contractors build the cathedral. How much time will we need to put the reversed Copernican revolution right? Then, everything will get better. And man most of all!

Previous publications by Ignace Demaerel

'*Gebed, diepgeworteld en wijdvertakt. 40 groeischeuten voor gebed en voorbede*' ('Prayer, deeply-rooted and widely branched' - 40 growth shoots for prayer and intercession'), 2009, published by 'Face to Face', Mechelen, 176 p. (ISBN 978 907 4901000)

'*Jezus 2.0 Wat heeft hij ons vandaag nog te vertellen?*' ('Jesus 2.0 - What does he have to tell us today?'), 2015 published by Davidsfonds, Leuven, 120 p. (ISBN 978 905 9086487)

'*Wie Mij eet . . . Er zit meer in brood en wijn - Sleutels naar al onze rijkdommen in Jezus*' ('Whoever eats Me - There is more to bread and wine'), 2017, published by Boekscout, Soest (NL), 188 p. (ISBN: 978 940 2238082).

'*95 stellingen over het humanisme - Christendom en Verlichting, secularisme en vrijzinnigheid*' ('95 theses on Humanism - Christianity and Enlightenment, secularism and free thinking'), 2017, published by Boekscout, Soest (NL), 232 p. (ISBN 978 940 2239157)

Columns / articles at www.knack.be (website linked to the Flemish weekly magazine Knack) since December 2012

For more information, also about other articles and brochures, see: www.ignacedemaerel.be

Bibliography

Snyder, Timothy, *Bloodlands: Europe Between Hitler and Stalin*, Basic Books, 2011, 524 p.
De Wachter, Dirk, *Borderline Times*, Lannoo, 2011, 136 p.
Reynebeau, Marc, *De Geschiedenis van België in woord en beeld*, Lannoo, 2005, 320 p. (*'The History of Belgium in Word and Image'*)
Courtois, Stéphane, Werth, Nicolas et al., *Le Livre noir du communisme: Crimes, terreur, repression*, Editions Robert Laffont, 1997, 846 p. (*'The Black Book of Communism'*)
Botterman, Sarah, Hooghe, Marc and Bekkers René, *Levensbeschouwing en maatschappelijke participatie. Is levensbeschouwing nog steeds een motiverende factor? Studiedienst van de Vlaamse Regering*, *Vlaanderen gepeild*, 2009, p. 7–29 (*'World View and Social Participation. Is world view still a motivating factor?'*)
Humanistisch Verbond, *Humanisme vandaag*, EPO, 1987, 138 p. (*'Humanism Today'*)
Derkx, Peter, *Humanisme, zinvol leven en nooit meer ouder worden'*, VUB Press, 2011, 232 p. (*'Humanism, a Meaningful Life and Never Again Growing Old'*)
Dobbelaere, Karel and Elchardus, Mark, *Verloren zekerheid. De Belgen en hun waarden, overtuigingen en houdingen*, Lannoo, 2000, 272 p. (*'Lost security. The Belgians and their values, convictions, and attitudes'*)
Vrijzinnige Koepel and Humanistisch Verbond, Campinne, Marc ed., *Vrijzinnigheid en humanisme in Europa*, EPO, 52 p. (*'Freethinking and humanism in Europe'*)

Index

Abortion, 94, 112, 118–119, 121, 124–125, 156
Agnosticism, 100, 102, 120
Anthropocentrism/Anthropocentristic, 11, 29, 31, 111, 123, 146–147, 172, 174
Anti-theism/Anti-theistic, 149
Augustine, 19
Auschwitz, 43, 80
Autonomy/Autonomous, 9, 33, 39, 48, 50, 54, 63, 82–85, 87, 94–95, 97, 126–127, 149, 160, 168, 176

Boccaccio, Giovanni, 3
Bonaparte, Napoleon, 14
Bruni, Leonardo, 3

Calvin, Jean, 7, 16
Cicero, 3, 26
Collins, Anthony, 12
Communism /Communist, xv, 32, 122–123, 142, 163
Comte, Auguste, 95, 152
Copernicus / Copernican, 8, 28, 167, 176

Dawkins, Richard, 91, 100, 104
Deism /deistic, 12–13, 30, 61, 114, 139
Diderot, Denis, 13
Dualism /dualistic, 19, 39, 135

Ecocentrism, 111
Einstein, Albert, xii, xvii, 43, 103

Erasmus, Desiderius, 4–7, 29, 31, 143, 146–147, 163
Esperanto, 79, 107, 152
Euthanasia, 94, 118–119, 121, 124

Fascism, 43, 50, 79, 123
Freemasonry, 12, 30, 60, 114–117, 120–121, 134, 146, 159, 166
Freethinker/Freethinking, xvi, 2, 12, 30, 34, 60, 91–92, 100, 111–112, 114, 117, 120–121, 138, 146–147
Fundamentalism, 35, 141, 163

Galilei, Galileo, 8
Geocentrism, 9, 141
Heteronomy, 82, 84
Hitler, Adolf, 43, 79, 94, 122

Intelligent Design, 103

Jews/jewish, 6, 16, 92, 94, 98

Kant, Immanuel, 10–12
King, Martin Luther, 71, 76

Laïcité, 30, 105
Luther, Martin, xii–xiii, 7, 16, 65–66, 132

Marx, Karl, 32, 53
Mengele, Joseph, 80–81

Newton, Isaac, 9, 11, 59, 97

Index

Niethammer, Friedrich Immanuel, 29–30
Nietzsche, Friedrich, 26
Nihilism, 41, 45, 93, 129–131, 172

Opportunism, 98, 156

Pascal, Blaise, 64
Petrarca, Francesco, 3, 30–31
Poincaré, Henri, 67
Prometheus, 48
Protagoras, 3–4, 38

Reform Hinduism, 78

Relativism, 98, 111, 129

Solzhenitsyn, Alexander, 123, 171
Stalin, Joseph, 55, 122–123, 163
Syncretism, 78

Theocentrism/Theocentric, 7, 11, 29, 31, 172, 174–175
Theocracy/Theocratic, 7, 20, 74, 105, 174
Tindal, Matthew, 12
Toland, John, 12

Voltaire, 13

www.ingramcontent.com/pod-product-compliance
Lightning Source LLC
Chambersburg PA
CBHW071444150426
43191CB00008B/1228